D0333628

The Ashes
According to
Bumble

The Ashes According to Bumble

David Lloyd

HarperSport
An Imprint of HarperCollins*Publishers*

HarperSport
An imprint of HarperCollins*Publishers*
77–85 Fulham Palace Road,
Hammersmith, London W6 8JB

www.harpercollins.co.uk

First published by HarperCollins*Publishers* 2013

1 3 5 7 9 10 8 6 4 2

© David Lloyd 2013

David Lloyd asserts the moral right to
be identified as the author of this work

All photographs © Getty Images with the following exceptions: page 1 (right),
page 2 (top), page 5 (top right), page 6 (top) © Popperfoto/Getty Images;
page 3 (bottom right), page 4 (all), page 6 (bottom left) © Patrick Eagar via Getty
Images; page 7 (top left) © WireImage; page 7 (top right) © AFP/Getty Images;
page 8 © Gareth Copley, Getty Images

A catalogue record of this book
is available from the British Library

. ISBN 978-0-00-738285-9

Printed and bound in Great Britain by
Clays Ltd, St Ives plc

All rights reserved. No part of this publication may be
reproduced, stored in a retrieval system, or transmitted,
in any form or by any means, electronic, mechanical,
photocopying, recording or otherwise, without the prior
written permission of the publishers.

MIX
Paper from
responsible sources
FSC
www.fsc.org   FSC® C007454

FSC™ is a non-profit international organisation established to promote
the responsible management of the world's forests. Products carrying the
FSC label are independently certified to assure customers that they come
from forests that are managed to meet the social, economic and
ecological needs of present and future generations,
and other controlled sources.

Find out more about HarperCollins and the environment at
www.harpercollins.co.uk/green

CONTENTS

Acknowledgements   ix

Introduction   xi

1 Plans to Scon the Don   1

2 In the Line of Duty   28

3 The High Fliers   87

4 Preparing for Battle   93

5 Dogs of Waugh   141

6 Vipers   232

7 Black and White and Read all Over   250

8 Skinfolds at the Ready   258

9 My All-Time Ashes XI   274

RICHARD GIBSON, who worked with David Lloyd on the writing of this book, is a freelance sports writer who has covered international cricket home and abroad since the late 1990s. Trekking around the globe means he sees a heck of a lot of Bumble, and they naturally formed a special bond given that they hail from two of the United Kingdom's modern utopias – Accrington and Hull.

In addition to the *Sunday Times* bestseller *Start the Car: The World According to Bumble*, his other collaborations include the autobiographies of Graeme Swann and James Anderson, while he is a regular contributor on cricket in the *Sunday Mirror*, *Guardian* and *Daily Mail* newspapers.

ACKNOWLEDGEMENTS

Richard Gibson – if you don't like the book, it's his fault. I get enough hassle in the day job and from irate Indian supporters.

Gareth Copley – the lad needed a leg up, being from Huddersfield.

INTRODUCTION

One of the first things you notice as an England cricketer on an Ashes tour is the aggression shown towards you by the locals, even when they're trying to be nice.

'G'day,' they say, lips pursing into a smile, before rolling the rest of the sentence off the tongue like a lizard toying with a defenceless ant: 'Ya pommie bastard.'

Such uncouth language. Surely, everybody with a bit of culture about them knows that on first meetings it is the done thing to be as formal as possible. No shortening of words, and certainly no use of slang. 'Good morning, how do you do?' Now that would be a far better address to a visitor to one's country. It's what our good queen would approve of, and let's not forget that for all our historical sporting differences we are united by one thing at least. We have remained kind enough to share her good ladyship with that other rabble.

And anyway, if this pseudo-hostility from our Australian hosts was designed to intimidate they clearly chose the wrong bloke. Regular greetings like that were unlikely to break me psychologically; after all I'd suffered a lot worse during my upbringing in Accrington. Let's face it, when your mum dresses you in pink frocks, insists on growing your hair long and calling you Gwyneth, as mine did, who cares what you get called outside your front door? Mum had wanted a girl, you see, and for a time she was not prepared to let the fact I wasn't one get in the way of her dream.

You see, it's easy to lose your sense of perspective when it comes to the phoney war that develops before every England v Australia series. But while Dennis and Jeff could bruise my bones, names would never hurt me.

As it happened Dennis and Jeff did such a good job of hurting me, and limiting my runs to boot, that my Ashes playing experience was confined to just one series, the 1974–75 whopping down under. So to justify writing an entire book about it, you will notice in subsequent chapters that I have by-passed some of the most enthralling episodes of its great heritage to talk about my own involvement. You will recall me top-scoring in an England win on New Year's Day that winter; battling valiantly for six hours on the trampoline at Perth. You what? You've no recollection of your hero's bravery in the face of much provocation from those uncouth wombat worriers? Well, let me tell you in the most exaggerated terms possible exactly how I quelled the charge of these savages – softening them up sufficiently for others like Sir Ian Botham to ride in and finish them off in future battles.

I should also probably mention here that some of the names in this recollection of Ashes history have been changed – not, as in some books, to protect true identities but because, after

Introduction

50 years in the professional game, my recall can be a little hazy. What I can promise, however, is that after half-a-century my enthusiasm has not diminished and I remain as excited as a kid at Christmas when it comes to England v Australia clashes.

There is something so magical about tussling with the old enemy – the great rivalry between Celtic and Rangers, or indeed football internationals between England and Germany, the most comparable things I can think of among other sports – and I have been party to some real ding-dongs in my post-playing career, both as England coach and as a commentator with the BBC's *Test Match Special* and Sky Sports.

A series between England and Australia is like no other in cricket and resonates as much now as it did at the turn of the 20th century when news of the exploits of the likes of WG Grace, Ranjitsinhji and Sydney Barnes would be devoured by readers of newspapers like the *Manchester Guardian*. When you think of years gone by, the ones of 1948, 1956, 1981 and 2005 stand out. Those were years when this country was host to great Ashes series.

In this age of 24–7 media coverage our heroes are so much more familiar than those of the past, and reporting and analysis so much faster, that you can actually feel as though you are a part of what is taking place. You can follow the scores or even watch the action on the move; read about the latest session's play on your iPad or download a podcast to your iPhone. Don't worry, I'm getting there with technology too, and recently invested in an iRon for my good lady wife. Pleased to report it keeps her occupied when I get home to watch the highlights.

There is something so appealing about a duel with the Australians that it is hard to keep your eyes off it, or to restrain yourself from watching re-runs again and again. Generation upon generation of English cricketers would forego any of their other achievements in the game to be a part of a successful team, to be an Ashes winner. Me amongst them.

Our relationship with the Australians in general is interesting. They say that love and hate are pretty close together, don't they? And we sort of love them, and sort of hate them at the same time, don't we?

Australians tell us how much they adore being Australian, and of a devotion to their beautiful country; glad that they haven't had to grow up around whingeing Poms, who don't wash and drink warm beer. The lack of gratitude as they badmouth us always gets me here. Have they forgotten? It was us kind lot that sent them there in the first place.

The rivalry between the nations has always been best expressed through cricket, I believe, and on the field there is without doubt a begrudging admiration on both sides for the other. Yes, we've heard all the jokes before:

What do you call an Englishman with a hundred to his name? *A bowler*.

What would Glenn McGrath be called if he was English? *An all-rounder*.

What's the definition of optimism? *An England batsman who applies sunscreen*.

Of course, we give plenty back too, and I think most Australians understand that when the Barmy Army remind them of their ancestry – how Great Uncle Jack arrived kitted out in clads – it is done so in good spirit. Furthermore, despite their mercilessly cruel song about Mitchell Johnson – altogether now *'He bowls to the left, He bowls to the right, That Mitchell Johnson, His bowling is you-know-what'* – a good percentage of the throng will have admired his match-winning performance at Perth during the 2010–11 series. Because secretly we like them, and secretly they like us. It just doesn't pay to admit it too often.

In a work capacity I have spent a hell of a lot of time in the Sky Sports commentary box with Botham, and there is no greater verbal jouster than he when it comes to the Aussies. He is digging at them all the time – and that's just his friends. He cannot help but get stuck into them. I think he earnestly believes it is the primary duty he was put on this earth for. No wonder he used to treat them with such disdain as a player.

For Sir Beefykins – or His Royal Beefyness or Sir Osis (of the liver) to give him his other nicknames – getting stuck into the Aussies is the be all and end all. Some of his very best friends are Australians and he just damn right insults them the whole time he is in their company. His words are pretty choice towards them even when he is not. You should see some of the foul-fingered texts he sends to them. It's like his phone's got Tourette's. To give them their due, his pals don't hold back either. If you read some of these insults being batted this way and that you would think there was nothing but pure hatred between them. Yet dig beneath the expletives and you find there are keen friendships formed in his playing days that have stood the test of time. He is even in business with one of them, the winemaker Geoff Merrill, exporting bottles of Botham Merrill Willis Shiraz around the globe.

During the modern era of Ashes skirmishes, around the time I was England coach, there was some mischief hanging around regarding the value of the series in Cricket Australia's international scheduling. During two decades of Australian dominance, it was occasionally suggested that five matches against England was too many, that Ashes campaigns should be downgraded to three matches and that Australia would be better off playing four and five match series against other leading nations.

Not sure that would go down well with the public on either side these days, particularly given that the boot has been shifted firmly to the other foot. Prior to this double Ashes year of 2013, there is no doubt that England have been the dominant force over recent meetings between the countries, and Australia are now the ones trying to rebuild under a new chairman of selectors in John Inverarity and a new captain in Michael Clarke. They will have felt under pressure to get that little urn back, and the focus of their player management over the past few months will undoubtedly have been to get their best possible XI on the park for Trent Bridge in July.

It is a rather historic time for cricket's greatest competition, with 10 back-to-back Tests over six months split between home and away. These two series on the horizon could prove to be defining moments in the careers of many of the players involved. The challenge for England is to show that they are among the best if not the best Ashes team in history, that they can now be favourably compared to Australia from the late 1980s and 1990s.

Okay, this England team was defeated by South Africa, and relinquished their world number one status as a result, but this is the series that matters most to the fans, the one they demand is won. In the English cricket psyche it is okay to lose to almost anyone but not Australia. That's tradition for you. No matter where the two teams stand within world cricket's rankings, this is the big one, the one that means the most, and the passing of time has not diluted that.

For these England players, to win three Ashes series in a row would be something special – two generations of cricketers before them failed to win one, so imagine a treble on your CV. Without getting too far ahead of ourselves, an England side last won four series in a row in the 1880s.

What a challenge sits on the horizon. These players can go down in history as the most successful we've ever produced in Ashes terms. And as things stood, they entered the 2013 summer in good fettle. Sure, New Zealand provided an unexpected jolt or two and came close to winning the series, but overall the winter was positive. England had previously struggled in India, but having conquered the subcontinent at long last under Alastair Cook's leadership, I feel they are on the verge of something very special.

People talk about the demise of Test cricket around the world but you only need to see what is happening around this country's Test grounds in the summer of 2013, and how the Australian public will reciprocate that enthusiasm by turning out in their thousands over the winter, to show the appetite for the traditional form of the game is as healthy as it has ever been between the two most traditional foes. Recession or no recession, there will be a mass exodus from these shores to Australia in the 2013–14 winter, too.

We can only hope that this most ferociously contested cricket is played in the kind of spirit shown in the recent past. One Ashes moment that people will never forget is when Freddie Flintoff consoled Brett Lee, who was down on his haunches on the edge of the pitch in the immediate aftermath of the agonising 2005 defeat at Edgbaston. Fred obviously just felt it was the natural thing to do. Two great blokes, two great competitors, going at it hammer and tongs; it summed up the essence of England v Australia matches in a snapshot. You can call each other whatever you want, and within the spirit of the game do or say pretty much anything you like to your opponent between the hours of 11am and six o'clock in the evening, but this is a series that promotes unbelievable friend-ships and ultimate respect.

Chapter 1

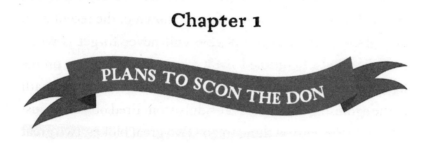

PLANS TO SCON THE DON

Can there be anything in sport so small that creates such a big fuss? After all, when you break it all down, us English and those Australians have spent one and a quarter centuries skirmishing over a six-inch terracotta urn. If it's in your possession – metaphorically speaking, of course, because it never leaves its safehouse at Lord's – then everything is fine and dandy in the world. But if the opposition have their mucky paws on it, then start drawing up the battle plans because we want it back.

It is the primary rivalry in cricket and dates back to 1882, when England's sorry chase of 85 to beat Australia at the Oval fell short, leaving star man WG Grace embarrassed and *The Sporting Times* bemoaning the death of English cricket in a mock obituary.

'In Affectionate Remembrance of English cricket, which died at the Oval on 29 August 1882, Deeply lamented by a large circle of sorrowing friends and acquaintances – R.I.P.

– N.B. The body will be cremated and the ashes taken to Australia,' wrote Reginald Shirley Brooks. I am unsure he can have imagined what his words would lead to.

Players from both countries have made their names on the back of performances in this greatest of series, and some of the attitudes of the greatest names have recurred in subsequent generations. Grace was quite a character of course, and one who used to inform opposition bowlers: 'They've come to watch me bat, not you bowl.' Sounds familiar, does that. I am sure there is some bespectacled bloke who played for Yorkshire for donkey's years who used to say exactly the same, who now believes folk turn on the radio rather than TV for similar reasons. I actually got him out a couple of times but the name escapes me.

Grace was a beauty. You had to uproot his stumps to get rid of him apparently, as a nick of the bails would simply result in him setting the timber up again and carrying on as if nothing had happened. No wonder he scored more than 50,000 first-class runs in his career. Sounds like it was three strikes and you're out in his rulebook. 'I'll have another go, if you don't mind. Oh, you do mind? Well, I'll be having another go, anyway.'

Then there was the godfather of bowlers Sydney Barnes, who, plucked from the Lancashire League, used to scowl and complain if asked to bowl from the 'wrong' end. He had a frightful temper, it was said, and aimed it at his own teammates as much as he did at opponents. 'There's only one captain of a side when I'm bowling,' he brashly once declared. 'Me!'

Technically, England were the first winners of the Ashes 130 years ago under the captaincy of the Hon. Ivo Bligh, who announced his intention to put Skippy on the hop upon arrival in Australia. 'We have come to beard the kangaroo in his den – and try to recover those Ashes,' he is said to have told an audience at an early dinner on the tour. He did just that, returning to Blighty with a commemorative urn full of ashes of some sort, which was then bequeathed to the Marylebone Cricket Club upon his death in 1927.

Bligh's victory began a period of dominance of eight England wins on the trot, a record sequence that the Australian teams that straddled the Millennium managed to equal but not surpass. Eight series victories in a row sounds as if it would dilute the intensity, but not a bit of it because in this duel you simply cannot get bored of coming out on top.

If there is one thing I really love about England v Australia clashes it is the win-at-all-costs mentality that prevails. I'll declare my hand here. I hate losing, always have done, always will do. Bunkum to the stiff-upper-lip brigade who believe it is all about the way the cricket is played rather than the result. For my mind, as long as you do not transgress into the territory of disrepute, as long as you behave as you would if your parents were stood at mid-on and mid-off, and as long as you are acting within the laws of the game it's all a fair do to me. In short, play as hard as possible.

Of course, there have been times when this ship's sailed a bit close to the wind, but the history of the Ashes is richer for its great conflicts. Growing up as a cricket fan, there were some legendary tales to take in. As series that outdate me go there are none more memorable than that of 1932–33. So memorable in fact that it took on a name of its own: Bodyline.

During its course, the Australian captain Bill Woodfull exclaimed: 'There are two teams out there on the oval. One is playing cricket, the other is not.'

Now that Douglas Jardine, the man in charge of the team alleged to be not playing cricket, sounds like an intriguing character. One who went around treating everyone else with utter disdain. Seems he didn't like the Australians much, and didn't have a great deal of time for his own lot either if they were 'players' rather than 'gentlemen'. England captain he may have been, but he was from the age of teams being split between the upper classes and those ditching hard labour for graft on a sporting field. But as an amateur, he had little time for those who sought to make cricket their profession.

His task was fairly simple: to stop Don Bradman's free-flowing bat in its tracks. His mind was devoted to curbing Bradman's almost god-given skill, and he was chastised for coming up with a solution that served his England team's purpose. One of the phrases I like in cricket is 'find a way'. It is after all a game of tactics and, in Jardine, an Indian-born public schoolboy, England had a master tactician who found a way to win.

I guess he was the first in a long list of uncompromising captains in what is undoubtedly the greatest rivalry in cricket. From both English and Australian perspectives it is *the* series that matters. The number one. Possibly the only one to some.

There is no point downplaying its appeal because here is a series that draws the biggest crowds, the largest television audiences and generates the most chat down the local. Others are simply incomparable. In political terms our historical arch enemy has been Germany. The sporting equivalent is Australia.

Sounds to me like Jardine treated the Ashes as a war. Or perhaps more accurately, he tried to turn it into one. In his mind, all Australians were 'uneducated' and together they made 'an unruly mob'. He lived up to this air of superiority by wearing a Harlequins cap to bat in. I guess that was the 1930s equivalent to go-faster stripes on your boots, peacock hair, diamond earrings and half-sleeve tattoos. I am not sure Jardine needed a look-at-me fashion statement, though, to draw attention to himself.

There was something more significant in Jardine's behaviour that put him ahead of his era, though, and that was his use of previous footage to prepare for that 1932–33 tour. He watched film of Bradman caressing the ball along the carpet to the boundary during the Australians' 1930 tour to England, and most probably grimaced. Bradman piled up 974 runs in Australia's 2–1 victory that summer. But, having reviewed the action, Jardine is said to have noticed something from the final Test at the Oval. Although he took evasive action, Bradman apparently looked uncomfortable at short-pitched stuff sent down by that most renowned of fast bowlers Harold Larwood. He did well to spot it amongst the flurry of fours, I guess – Bradman scored a double hundred – but he was prepared to test the theory that Bradman did not like it up him.

The planning stage took in a meeting in Piccadilly with Larwood and others in August 1932, and continued in September when the England team set off on their month-long voyage down under. You can just imagine Jardine on the deck of the ship, rubbing his hands together, scheming like a James Bond villain. The evil henchmen that would make Bodyline famous were the Nottinghamshire pair Bill Voce and Larwood, a barrel-chested left-armer and a lithe, fairly short paceman whose cricket career rescued him from the daily grind of the pit. It was said that Larwood's work as a miner gave him the extra strength to generate extreme pace. Just as now, pace has always been the ingredient that worries top batsmen most, and the one that made the Bodyline tactic successful.

The Ashes has had a habit of bringing out the dark arts and series like that have taken on almost mythical status. It seems like another world when you read about Mr Jardine but you can't help chuckle at his behaviour. It's like one of those 1930s talkies at the local cinema. This bloke turns up from down pit and is met by the villainous boss. 'Now this is what I want you to do for me, Larwood. Are you clear?'

'Certainly, sir, no problem. I'll knock their heads off, if that's what you want?'

These days a short one into the ribs is a shock weapon for a fast bowler but in Jardine's tactical notebook it was a stock delivery. They say that the potency of Bodyline was evident even in the final warm-up matches of the tour when Bradman began to lose his wicket in unusual ways. In attempting to duck one bouncer, he left the periscope up and was caught at mid-on. Another piece of evasive action had resulted in him being bowled middle-stump. Suddenly, Bradman's batting was no longer Bradman-esque.

Uncertainty does strange things to players and the photograph of Bradman's first ball of the series – he had missed the first Test defeat citing ill health – shows it can even infiltrate the very best. The great man is well outside off-stump as he bottom-edges a Voce long-hop to dislodge the bails and complete the very first and very last golden duck of his international career.

Australia actually levelled the series in that second match at Melbourne. But it was in the next Test at Adelaide, upon the liveliest of pitches, where it all kicked off. Big style. It was from the dressing room at the Adelaide Oval, where he was laid out recovering from a blow to his solar plexus administered by Larwood, that Woodfull's famous assertion that England had fallen short of the necessary spirit of the game made its way into the world.

To suggest the crowd were unhappy with the bombardment sent down to a leg-side trap would be like saying Marmite polarises opinion. In an age when the crowd reaction tended to be rounds of applause and hip hip hoorays, imagine how collective chants of 'get off you bar steward' or words to that effect would have sounded. From some pockets of the stands came the 10 count, as used in boxing, to suggest that the bouncer assault should be stopped.

Good old Jardine thrived on the confrontation, and could not give a hoot that the locals were sufficiently roused to tear down their own ground. An England captain in Australia has to have a thick skin. Luckily, Jardine's exterior was the human equivalent of a rhino's hide. Even his own tour manager, Pelham Warner, was uneasy about the conduct of the tourists in setting leg-side fields and aiming for the line of the body. It boiled over, of course, when Aussie wicketkeeper Bert Oldfield was felled by a top edge into his own skull, shaping to hook a Larwood bouncer. With blood on the pitch, no wonder Larwood and Co feared being lynched by the mob.

The best players through history adapt, yet when Bradman did in this particular series, eschewing conventional technique for shuffling this way or that as the bowler hit his delivery stride, he copped criticism. There were even calls for him to be dropped. This bloke, a flippin' genius whose career Test average of 99.94 put him as close to cricket immortality as anyone has got, finished the series as Australia's leading run-scorer. But there were still those questioning him, and whether he had the stomach for the fight against the fast stuff. The triumph of Larwood, who claimed 33 series wickets, over the boy from Bowral was key to England's 4–1 win.

I would suggest that Anglo-Antipodean relations were at an all-time low that winter, and the Australian board's wire back to the MCC claiming that the bodyline bowling had challenged the best interests of the game only added gasoline to the barbie. There is nothing like the use of the term 'unsportsmanlike' to ignite things. Unless the practice was stopped at once, it warned, the friendliness between the two countries was under threat. The MCC response was to insist no infringement of the laws, or indeed the spirit, of the game had taken place and that if the Australian board wished to propose a new law that was a different matter.

The MCC even volunteered culling the remainder of England's tour. But that would only have halted the best thea-tre Australia had to offer. Of course, when there is some niggle, when the cricket is at its most hostile or spectacular, out they come. Think of the crowds shoehorned in during 2005 and the incredible television viewing figures that went with that, or even those of the following series in Australia when Ricky Ponting's team sought and exacted their ultimate revenge. When the entertainment is box office, up go the attendances.

Some players like to stoke themselves up by engaging in chat with opponents, not necessarily with ball in hand but with bat, and Jardine was one for seeking out pleasantries with the crowd as well as members of the fielding side. He used to bait the masses on the famous hill at Sydney by calling for the 12th man to bring him a glass of water. It was all part of the pantomime, of course.

I reckon it would have made his trip had there been WANTED posters slapped on billboards all over Australia that year. But he didn't have to leave the pavilion of their premier cricket grounds to discover he went down about as well as gherkin and ice cream sandwiches to your average Aussie. Legend has it that after taking exception to one on-field exchange, Jardine marched into the home dressing room to remonstrate with the opposition. He claimed he had heard one of them call him a 'pommie bastard' under their breath. He was met at the door by Vic Richardson, Australia's vice-captain, who is said to have addressed the rest of the room with: 'Alright, which one of you bastards called this bastard a bastard?' Just about the right tone, that. What goes on, on the pitch, stays on the pitch – unless the stump microphones are turned on, of course.

Bradman was the major draw card for a couple of decades of Ashes conflict, and what an anomaly he was in the history of our great game. Name any team you want, any decade you want and there is no-one to come close to what he did on the world stage. At 20 years of age he became the youngest player to score an Ashes hundred, and from that point forth he made records tumble like dominoes down a hill.

At Headingley in 1930, he scored 309 runs in a day. That must have felt like one man against 11 for that particular England team. When he took over the captaincy for the 1936–37 series, he became the first man in history to lead a team to victory having been two Tests down. With this Clark Kent-esque figure around there was not much room for others to breathe.

Len Hutton registered the highest individual Ashes score of 364 at the Oval in 1938, in England's whopping innings-and-579-runs victory, but still Bradman's Australia held the urn. The great Wally Hammond went on into his 40s in his bid to finally overthrow him. As Jack Hobbs said: 'The Don was too good: he spoilt the game.'

In his final series, Bradman fronted the 1948 'Invincibles' – what a team they were. Not only did they win the Ashes 4–0 that summer, they also went 34 matches undefeated on the tour, led by fearsome fast bowlers like Ray Lindwall and Keith Miller. In the 1950–51 series that followed, attendance figures were down by more than 25% on the previous one down under. Although my old mate Warnie sports the nickname 'Hollywood' it is fair to say that Bradman was exactly that. As soon as Australia's A-list performer hung up his boots, folk appeared less keen to turn out. And what a way to go – bowled by a googly from Eric Hollies second ball in his final Test innings when only requiring four runs to finish with an average in three figures. No matter how you dress it up those numbers are absolutely mind-boggling.

The Thorn between Two Roses

It was right at the start of my Lancashire career that I witnessed Brian Statham and Fred Trueman on opposite sides doing battle. But what a partnership they formed when thrust together, though. Statham was like a greyhound: smooth, graceful, lean and hungry. At the other end was this big Yorkshireman who possessed a classical action, an extrovert character, an admirable competitive streak and that commonly-recurring fast-bowling feature: a huge backside.

Brian was my first captain at Old Trafford, although it was partly his injury that led to my first XI debut at home to Middlesex in 1965. It would be a fair summary to suggest that he was a cricketer who got himself bowling fit by doing exactly that – bowling. There was no pre-season fitness regime to adhere to. No hill runs or swim sessions down the local baths. It was just a case of rocking up ready to play.

If Brian came back from an England winter tour, the first we tended to see of him was on the eve of the first match of the season, and when I say eve I mean eve. If we opened up on a Saturday, he would stroll into Old Trafford on the Friday, reacquaint himself with us all, chew the fat in the dressing room for an hour or so before pinning the team for the following day up on the board.

But like the rest of us he was a product of the age. There was no expectation of scoring 12 in a bleep test back then. A test of one's fitness was whether you had the stamina to be able to send down 25 overs in a day. He would take off his sweater in late April and answer that with unerring displays of high quality seam bowling. Brian was a very special bowler, who mastered a consistent line and length, and controlled the movement of the ball like it was on a string.

These days the late, great Brian has an end named after him at Old Trafford. It was fitting tribute to his efforts on behalf of the club and his impact as a Test bowler with England.

It was all a show with Fred. He played up to his own caricature with real skill. So much so that the fable of how good he was began years before he packed up. The trick for him was to make you think he was even better than he was, and his record meant he was intimidating enough before he opened his mouth.

One classic story comes from the 1952 Test series between England and India when one of the Indian batsmen was being rather meticulous over the positioning of the sight-screen. The umpire, getting a little agitated by the delay, inquired: 'Where *do* you want it?'

'Between me and Mr Trueman,' came the clever reply.

Wireless Wonders

My first memories of Ashes cricket were not from watching but from listening on the wireless to the efforts of Jim Laker in 1956. Of course, we all know of that famous match when he took 19 wickets, and subsequently I have studied the fields that were set. It was quite an extraordinary way that Australia played, and you are talking about uncovered pitches in those days, obviously.

Without doubt England exploited the dampness superbly, yet it is extraordinary that one chap in any era could get 19 wickets. Tony Lock, the left-arm spinner, would have been apoplectic that he ended up with just one in those conditions. They were a fine spin double act Laker and Lock even if they weren't necessarily bosom buddies away from cricket.

To see how Laker tried to get his wickets was quite an eye-opener. Alan Oakman was stood like a predator at leg slip, a position which has really gone out of the modern game, and the spin that Laker got combined with the accuracy made it a really attacking position from which to snare batsmen.

I came to know Jim because he was a commentator on the BBC's television coverage of the Sunday League alongside Peter Walker. Frank Bough was also around at that time, and they were a nice little commentary team. Jim also happened to be a really good friend of Jack Simmons. They were both off-spinners of course and Jack was one of the most gregarious fellows you could meet. The pair of them used to talk about the art of off-spin and other things for hours.

But it was actually Ray Illingworth, of the players I played with and against, that reminded me of most of Jim in that when he bowled he stood nice and tall in delivery. Accuracy was your main ally in the days of uncovered wickets because if you kept things tight the natural variation in a pitch would sometimes reward you by allowing the ball to spit this way or that.

I never tire of watching the cine reel of that 1956 performance at Old Trafford. It looks pretty clear to me that the Australians had no real idea of how to play that type of gripping off-spin where the ball does something off the pitch, off a decent length.

Fielders were stood all around, circling for their chance of an inside edge or a false defensive shot. One of the things that makes me chuckle from watching that back, though, is that a wicket did not encourage French kisses or gropes of each other's backsides; it was just a simple pat on the back or a nod of approval with your head. Sometimes if players got really carried away they might give each other a handshake.

But there was certainly no going down on your hands and knees kissing the turf, beating the badge on your chest or tonguing short-leg's helmet. There were no advertising logos to point towards the cameras either. The only name on any of your clothing might have been the nametag sewn into your shirt by your wife or mother. The most extravagant Laker seemed to get was to smile, and hitch up his pants in that 1950s fashion, as if to say he was ready for business.

It was really peculiar to England that the regulations meant you would play on uncovered pitches. Teams would come over and find it extremely difficult whereas an English player would develop a technique on these uncovered surfaces. Through the middle of the 20th century there was a fashion for fast-medium bowlers who were deadly accurate and hit the seam. Now, as a batsman that meant you had to play at most deliveries and if you weren't used to it jagging this way and that you were in danger of being dismissed.

But it all came about from England losing the first Test at Lord's, a match that the Australian fast bowler Keith Miller dominated. England's response was telling. Out went their own attack spearhead Frank Tyson, as attention turned to spin. With Lock and Laker together it was an obvious tactic. Some of the Australian party believed it was a tactic that was tantamount to cheating. But I don't see how preparing pitches to suit your own purpose can be called that. With the bilateral nature of Test cricket it seems eminently sensible to make use of any home advantage going.

We have reflected on Bradman's freakish numbers but two Laker statistics from '56 will stand the test of time, I am sure. To claim 19 wickets in one game, and 46 in an Ashes series is astonishing. It is fair to say that numerically at least Laker contributed more than any other Englishman to victory over Australia. Yet, in losing down under two-and-a-half years later, the urn was relinquished once more and stayed in the land of the didgeridoo for the entire 1960s.

It might have been different, according to good old Fiery Fred. I'll let two classic pieces of sledgehammer wit tell the story. England led the 1962–63 series, you see, courtesy of Trueman's eight wickets at the MCG. But two crucial slip catches went down. The first, by the Rev David Shepherd, was greeted by Trueman exclaiming: 'Kid yourself it's a Sunday, Rev, and put your hands together.' The next, by Colin Cowdrey, came with an apology to the bowler: 'Sorry, Fred, I should have kept my legs together.' To which, the great man replied: 'No, but your mother should have.'

Under Ted Dexter's captaincy, England drew more than Rolf Harris at his marker-pen doodling best, but in 1964 their most significant result was a defeat at Headingley that put Australia ahead. Disagreement on the best tactical policy in the field led to Australia's Peter Burge swashbuckling his team home with a big hundred.

The match I remember most clearly, though, is the fourth Test at Old Trafford that followed. Australia captain Bobby Simpson scored his maiden Test hundred, a whopping 311 to be exact, and the stand-out aspect from an England perspective was the fact that they opted to leave Trueman out on a featherbed, despite trailing with two matches remaining. It was a result of the Dexter–Trueman bust-up in Leeds, and meant they gave debuts to Fred Rumsey and Tom Cartwright.

As Simpson just batted and batted it was bleedingly obvious that they had come up with the wrong team. I guess the Simpson innings stuck in my mind both because it was at Old Trafford and also because he was the professional at my club Accrington.

What a fabulous cricketer Simpson was: a more than handy leg-spinner and one of the best slip catchers not just in Ashes tussles but that the world has ever seen. However, his main forte was as an opening batsman.

Later in life he became such an influence as a coach. He followed me in the role at Lancashire although he didn't stick around very long. He had a lengthy association with the area, from the time that he played in the leagues and coached us youngsters, and we had exchanged views on a few things when he had been over in the past as coach of Australia. It was an unbelievable job he did from 1986 to 1996. When he took over, Australia had not won a Test series for three years, and by the time he had finished they were celebrating four consecutive Ashes victories and a place in the final of the 1996 World Cup.

It was during the 1991 season that he got in touch to inquire about another Australian who also played for our dear Accrington. One Shane Warne.

'How's young Warne going?' he asked.

'He's not doing great, if I'm honest,' I told him.

'I thought he must be pissin' 'em out,' Bob said.

'Well, no he's not.'

'Right, get him to ring me. I'll tell him where to bowl.'

These days it is a privilege to sit in a commentary box next to Warne. Earlier connections in my career, meanwhile, take me right back to the 1930s through Gubby Allen, one of the central figures in the Bodyline fiasco, and a man who ran English cricket for a long time. He was Gubby to his very best friends but to most people he was most definitely Mr Allen. You can probably tell which camp I was in as an aspiring international player.

Having been called up in 1974 against India, my debut was at Lord's, and so I got in early the day before the match, and was wearing my pride and joy. Get this: the pride and joy of which I speak was a snazzy yellow leather jacket. I thought I was a right bobby dazzler as I turned up in this clobber, and displaying typical keenness of the new boy I was first in. I put my bag down and there was this chap sat on the table. I had no idea who he was. 'Alright,' I greeted him. 'How do?'

'Hullo,' came the rather authoritative reply.

'Nice day, isn't it?' I resumed, trying to break an uncomfortable silence, my tactic being to work out who the heck this bloke was, and what he was doing in the England dressing room, if I kept talking. 'See you decided to get here nice and early too.'

There was not much coming back from him at all, and what went through my mind was that this bloke had somehow wandered in uninvited. So I plucked up a bit of courage and warned: 'Listen, pal. I don't know if you realise this but you are sat in the England dressing room and they will all be coming up in a minute or two.'

'You've no idea who I am, have you?' he responded.

'No, can't say I have, sorry.'

'My name is Gubby. It's Gubby Allen.'

'How do you do?' I said, with a smile, which masked the fact that I remained none the wiser.

It took my more established team-mates to put me in the picture, and thankfully, he took my ignorance brilliantly. At night after play we would all be invited into the MCC committee room for a drink.

'I believe you have been told who I am now,' he said.

'Er, yes,' I answered rather sheepishly.

I was always careful to mind my manners around Gubby. He had that effect on you, which is quite a contrast to how one behaved around Alec Bedser, who was chairman of selectors at the time. Clocking me in my yellow jacket that week, he put me at ease with the blunt inquiry: 'What the f***'s that you've got on?'

I just couldn't see past this yellow fashion accessory being the dog's doodahs. It had been purchased from a bespoke gents' outfitters in Rawtenstall called Nobbutlads. Well, that's how it was hyphenated in local speak, as it stood for Nowt But Lads.

There was no girls' stuff on sale there, although being shiny yellow with these massive lapels I am sure a lass could get away with wearing something similar in 2013. Looking back it was quite hideous. But at the time I thought it was the business.

These days if you get picked for England, you turn up in the full suit for a Test match. Back then you were only kitted out afterwards, hence my turning up looking like a roadie for the Bay City Rollers. I was yet to receive my England jacket or indeed my MCC piping blazer that I would be sporting that following winter.

The 1970–71 Ashes series, the one which preceded my one and only tour as an England player, was a feisty affair and not just between the two teams. There was plenty of other niggle about too, and Ray Illingworth's men had broken relationships with a member of officialdom as well as some of the people that populated the stands.

All hell almost literally broke loose when a John Snow bouncer collided into Terry Jenner and knocked him senseless. The treatment given to one of their tail-enders incensed the Sydney crowd, who seemed keen on exacting their own retribution by rioting.

The umpire Lou Rowan certainly took exception to the short-pitched stuff sent down by Snow, whose staple argument on the matter during that series was that his deliveries were aimed at the armpit of the batsman and not at the head, and were therefore not technically bouncers at all. On one occasion when the subject matter came up, Rowan is said to have argued: 'Well, somebody's bowling them from this end and it's not me.'

Snow saw it his job to rough up opposing batsman. For him, it went with the territory as England's new-ball enforcer, and getting struck was just an occupational hazard for top-order batsmen. His intention was to spread uncertainty and apprehension in the Australian ranks and a haul of 31 wickets that series suggests he succeeded.

But his aggressive approach got this Mr Rowan interested throughout a niggly series and particularly when Jenner was peppered with rib-ticklers after coming in with Australia seven wickets down in the final Test at the SCG. When Jenner tried to wriggle out of the flight path of the third his misjudgement on length cost him dear and witnessed the ball being 'headed' into the covers.

It was not until a bloody Jenner had been escorted from the field, and Snow was preparing to send down his next delivery, that Rowan told him: 'That's a first warning.'

Such decisions are pretty arbitrary ones and you have to rely on the umpire's discretion. However, Snow was not the kind of man to take anything lying down and from what I knew of him was unlikely to merely accept a judgement without prior discussion. His argument as things got a little heated with the local official was that the delivery in question had been the first genuine bouncer he had sent down that over.

Unsurprisingly, Ray Illingworth, his captain, immediately offered his support. He was a very fine leader, Ray, and his teams would always know they had his full backing. As they stood arguing the toss, the first beer cans were lugged onto the field at the other end of the ground. And by the time the over was completed, it looked like the world's biggest New Year's Eve party had been going on at fine-leg.

And when Snow clasped his hat and sauntered off to the boundary along from that famous Sydney mound, the blood of the locals had not cooled. As I say, John was not a man to dodge confrontation, although it would take a far braver man than me to give it a touch of the Liam Gallaghers at that point. His 'come on, then' gestures were taken up by one have-a-go-zero who leapt the fence and grabbed him by the collar. Snow's remonstrations with this drunken chap amounted to him asking quite matter-of-factly what the hell he was doing. But it was the signal for the boozers behind him to unleash their tinnies and bottles once more.

Illingworth, again as befitted his position as leader, was first on the scene and ushered Snow away, and the rest of the England team off the field. Others might have questioned his actions – 'the game must go on' and all that – but he was a man of principle, so the players were all holed up in the away dressing room when Rowan entered to inquire: 'What's going on, Mr Illingworth? Is this team coming back onto the field or have you chosen to forfeit the match?'

With the Ashes in England's possession all bar the shouting it was a bit Hobson's Choice, really, wasn't it? Get back out there or hand Australia a drawn series. Illingworth insisted that a few minutes were given for things to calm down and so, with the ground swept of its debris, it was on with the show.

England left with smiles on their faces in relation to the series result but with scowls for Rowan, who did not give a single lbw against Australia in the series, a statistic that enraged the visiting players, including Illy.

This Rowan episode would have been one of the many instances that combined to move us towards neutral umpires in international cricket. Sure, the process of two home umpires officiating went on for another 20-odd years but in the end something had to give. Too often around the world touring teams would feel that they were playing against 13. For example, there was the popular theory that Javed Miandad had never been given out lbw in Pakistan. Now, as statistics go, that's quite extraordinary, and not strictly true. The facts were that it was not until the 10th year of him playing home Tests that he was first given out in that manner.

History suggests that Rowan was taken aback by Illy's attitude but if you are dealing with Raymond Illingworth you would simply not get the stiff upper lip that an Australian official might expect from an England captain. Indeed, Mr David Clark, the tour manager on that trip, expected the same thing – to be British about it and get on in the face of provocation. Earlier in the trip Clark had expressed his dislike of drawn matches and offered the suggestion that he would prefer to witness a 3–1 Australia victory than to see it end in stalemate.

It is fair to say that Clark's views and mine are diametrically opposed. Ray was exactly the same as me in his attitude and I am pretty sure I would have replicated every single one of his actions had I found myself in his position. In my time as England coach I would never do that stiff upper lip thing either, preferring to stick up for those under my charge, and remained desperately keen to win. During my England tenure, my attitude was always: 'You should never have appointed me if that was what you wanted.' I am just not that sort of bloke. If someone wronged me I would come back hard at them; it's the way I have always been, and not just on the cricket field.

Without doubt, that is how Illy has always been too. He will play hard and fair but if he is crossed then watch out because he will take matters into his own hands. There were distinct parallels to be drawn between Illingworth and Jardine, actually, as captains, and I would argue that there is a correlation that they were seen to be sticking up for their team out in the middle, taking the flak on behalf of the group, and that their teams were successful out there.

It needs strong leadership and a single-mindedness to win an away series in such a demanding and hostile environ-ment, and neither bloke would take a backward step. These guys revelled in being in charge and weren't about to let anyone else boss their teams around. In acting in this way they were showing their own individual characters, and neither would have found it easy to hide that in any case. The one thing that neither would accept was being pushed around. They had to be seen to be leading their players, not just the bloke who had an asterisk by his name in the score book.

For years there was always a suspicion that whatever coun-try you were in the appointed officials would favour the home team. Neutral umpires were necessary for the good of the global game but I believe we have now come full circle. I sit on the ICC panel that selects the officials for the elite level of the game and because of the way they are monitored centrally I am of the opinion that we can go back to home umpires standing in Test matches. Umpires across the globe are simply miles better and are more accountable for their decisions because of the presence of so much media coverage. Any mistakes are highlighted all around the world, and any real howlers would be struck down by the Decision Review System in most instances.

In the 1974–75 series there was a lovely chap called Tom Brooks umpiring. Jeff Thomson was a big no-ball merchant. He sent down loads of them, not that many of them were called as such, so when stood at the non-striker's end while batting we would monitor where he was landing. Of course, he was regularly landing over the line with his front foot but seldom was he called.

This situation had been the subject of debate in our dressing room and we decided that it should be a duty when out batting to emphasise his landing position to the man in the white coat. It entailed us drawing the line with our boots, making it highly visible, or running our bats down the crease to encourage attention being drawn to the area. The odd word didn't go amiss, either. 'Oh, he's close, really close, don't you think?'

You couldn't challenge the umpire back then, in contrast to the modern day when you can go right up to them and have a bit of a go. No, in ours it had to be a lot more subtle. Tom was a lovely bloke and he used to say in response: 'You guys play to this front foot rule so we tend to be a bit stricter with your lot.' It had always been a back foot rule before that, of course, and it was almost as if we were being punished for the rule change.

Conflict these days is dealt with a lot differently, and situations like Illy's England found themselves in would get nowhere near the levels of antagonism with the current procedures in place. Any grievances are recorded, and written down or emailed, considered by match referees, and then even higher up the ICC chain of authority if necessary. This diplomatic mechanism was something that those teams could have done with but it was still light years away.

Such was the disharmony that existed between John Snow in particular and the Australian public, that year, though, that one might have presumed he was kept away from the Test squad in 1974–75 for his own safety. There was a certain justification for branding him public enemy number one down under for his part in the victory there four years earlier.

So when our bristly, fiercely competitive villain turned up to do some television commentary during our tour, public enemy number one became a target for his adversaries from the stands once more. During the Test match at Perth, some of the local punters were so incensed by his presence that they literally tried to tear the scaffolding down to get to him. The gestures they made towards him suggested they wanted to shake him warmly – not by the hand, but by the throat. Put it this way, Snowy didn't look overly eager to clamber down to check out the theory that he was a wanted man.

My personal experience of the crowds down under was that the banter that flew about was mainly of a good-hearted nature. The infamous Bay 13 at the MCG was marvellous, actually, although not necessarily if you were the one posted in front of it on the boundary edge as Deadly Derek Underwood was on one occasion. It didn't last long, though, as he was soon protesting about his placement. 'I can't stand down there any longer,' he exclaimed. 'I really can't.'

Typically of the man, Tony Greig said he would go down there and stand up to it instead. It was a ritual for the Bay 13 lot to start throwing things at the fielders, and they didn't need a gallon on board to provide them with Dutch courage. Oh no, this lot could be loutish when stone cold sober. They just had to be in the mood for mischief, and if they were, and you were in range, then trouble was on the cards.

The bombardment normally began with lumps of ice. More often than not it went from single ice cubes, to handfuls of ice, finishing with the final assault of the whole esky. Now Greigy was not a man to back away from a challenge or at a point of confrontation, so he naturally started lugging these frozen missiles back with interest.

There was plenty of entertainment on offer aside from the cricket when you stepped into an Australian cricket ground in the 1970s. There was no Barmy Army around back then to amuse you with their songs, but this Australian lot didn't need any rivals to spar with because they used to find enough enjoyment in fighting amongst themselves. During the 1974–75 tour we got friendly with the stadium control police, whose radio room was adjacent to our dressing rooms.

So during our innings, we used to mill around in there, watch their surveillance, and listen to their officers reporting back on any shenanigans in the stands. It used to kick off regularly throughout a day's play, not just once or twice, and not just play stuff either. I am talking proper fights. Just for the sake of it, blokes used to throw things at each other, and it only took someone to react and all hell broke loose.

Remember those crowds were 95% Australian, so they weren't being wound up by Poms. Australians are aggressive people by nature and sometimes they just like to scrap. Watching the surveillance gave us a rare chance at seeing the Aussies lose at something that winter.

On the subject of crowd abuse, I suffered some minor incidents during my career, and tended not to react despite provocation. My general attitude was that they were looking for a rise out of you, and therefore refraining from a reaction would nip their game in the bud. Coming back with a quip only extended an unwanted interaction.

But the one time I did react was when I was struck on the back of the neck by a lump of cheese as I fielded on the boundary. Bending down, I scooped it up and held it between my fingers, looking at it incredulously. 'That's not very mature,' I said.

Sometimes the friction on the boundary edge is not one created by the public but the players with their behaviour. When Colin Croft was our overseas player at Lancashire we received several complaints from those situated in the Lady Subscribers' Stand of a rather disconcerting habit he had.

Nothing out of the ordinary, really, at least as far as fast bowlers go, but nevertheless something that upset the predominantly female spectators at fine leg. Between bowling overs, Colin would regain his breath in the deep and clear his pipes further by blowing his nose onto the grass without the use of a handkerchief.

Subsequently, as captain of the club, I was asked into a meeting to discuss the problem and find a suitable solution. You won't believe the one that we came up with – Colin switched from fine leg to third man, where his nasal ritual could be carried out in front of the popular side of the ground!

Chapter 2

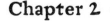

IN THE LINE OF DUTY

Playing in the Ashes would represent the pinnacle of any England cricketer's career and the opportunity to scale it came bang smack in the middle of mine. Nine years after my debut; and nine years before I retired.

My journey to the very peak of what English cricket has to offer began with a County Championship match on 12 June 1965, against Middlesex at Old Trafford, and has given me reason to chuckle every time I've heard the Half Man Half Biscuit song 'F***in' 'ell It's Fred Titmus' since. It's probably what I subconsciously thought at the start of every over he bowled to me in my maiden first-class innings.

Some late changes were made to the Lancashire team for that match, and an 18-year-old Lloyd, D, was one of the three call-ups, as much for a couple of impressive displays as a left-arm spinner in Second XI cricket at the start of that season as any ability I had shown with the willow in hand.

I arrived at the crease on the opening day with the scoreboard reading 140 for five, and although I failed to shift the '0' displayed under the number seven slot, I spent an age trying. So much so that I took a salt tablet for cramp before I was dismissed.

My lunging forward to counter Titmus's off-spin had taken its toll on my tense muscles, you see, because as a young player I was simply following advice from a more experienced colleague in Geoff Pullar. I was grateful for his input, too, as I sat waiting to go out to bat. Geoff's instructions were to get well forward but to make sure my bat was out in front of the pad to minimise the chance of an inside edge ricocheting up into the air for the preying close fielders. It was a practice I carried through faithfully, but good old Fred got me in the end, and claimed a further eight wickets besides during my debut match.

As starts to professional careers go, mine was fairly barren. Titmus bowled me in the first innings, and I was caught behind off the other spinner Don Bick for another blob in the second. In between, although I claimed a couple of wickets, I dropped nightwatchman Bick, who went on to score 55 and help Middlesex to a useful 77-run lead. After a pair, a costly miss like that in the field, and a modest start to my career with the ball, things could only get better, I suppose.

But while I might not have started as I meant to go on, I certainly finished strongly. To be honest, I had a fun-filled playing career, but it would be untrue to claim I loved every minute of it. Towards the end I lost the enjoyment of turning up for work, a trait that I previously took to be inherent.

It didn't help my batting that my eyes were no longer what they used to be, and if only I had gone to the optician's sooner to address a natural deterioration, I might have scored a few more runs in the couple of years when my enthusiasm for cricket waned. I knew I was not seeing the ball well enough either when batting or in the field, and as soon as I got a prescription things improved markedly. So much so that my tally for the summer of 1982 touched upon the 2,000-run mark in all competitions.

But a recurrence of the neck injury that was to rule me out of the final Ashes Test in 1974–75 hastened the end for me the following season. I missed half of it recuperating from its debilitating effects and by the time I did return the club had unearthed some exciting young talents to fill the void.

Amongst them was the swashbuckling Neil Fairbrother, whose performances persuaded me that the club no longer required my services. I notified them of my intention to retire well before the end of the campaign. Somewhat surprisingly, it did not dissuade them from picking me, however, and in contrast to my spluttering start, I went out with a real bang.

My final Lancashire appearance, at Wantage Road, Northampton, saw me open the batting with another left-hander, Graeme Fowler. We were of different generations but both of us hailed from Accrington, and we both hit hundreds in a drawn match with Northamptonshire. It was the perfect time to say goodbye.

Like all good stories, this career of mine had a happy ending, and there was ultimate contentment in the middle too when I was informed that I would be representing my country abroad. Not just anywhere, either.

When I was called up for my maiden England tour, in late August 1974, it is fair to say that I had limited travel experience behind me. I had never been out of Britain for a start, and the most exotic place I had visited on any type of excursion was North Wales. My mum and dad used to favour the Welsh coastline as the destination for our summer holidays, and we would always stay in one Methodist guest house or other. Firstly, because they were cheap and we were far from flush with cash. Secondly, because it gave my dad a chance to sing; one of his passions in life was singing.

The correspondence I had been waiting for to inform me of my selection in the 16-man party to tour Australia and New Zealand arrived while I was playing in a County Championship match for Lancashire against Nottinghamshire. It was in the form of an official letter from the Test and County Cricket Board, penned by Donald Carr. It was a bit like receiving a letter from the Queen: 'You have been selected to represent England on the MCC tour of Australia ... blah de blah de blah ...' In cricket terms it was akin to the royal seal of approval. After I'd confirmed my intention to travel – the letter asked whether I would like to go, and so I had to reply with something enthusiastic like 'Yeah, I'm up for that!' – the next thing required of me was to secure a passport. This was an opportunity to take part in the greatest series of them all for an England cricketer: the Ashes.

In those days you were given all your paraphernalia in one leather cricket bag: your England tour blazer, your MCC cap and sweater, and your shirts and trousers all tucked inside. There was no coloured clothing back then, of course, as one-day cricket in its infancy was played in whites, and there was no need for the Velcro pouch on the side to store your Oakleys, either.

However, some kind of goggles would have been pretty useful as it turned out, when we boarded our jumbo jet down under. A Qantas Airlines long-haul flight was quite something in the 1970s. Now, as a novice traveller in his mid-20s I confess I was a little bit wide-eyed. Those eyes were soon narrowing, mind, thanks to the tendency for folk to indulge in their filthy habits. These days it is easy to forget what it was like back then, whenever you travelled on an aeroplane. People would be lighting up their cigarettes all around you, so that when you sat down it was reminiscent of when the lights get switched on for the first time down the front at Blackpool. They would spark up the minute they'd parked their backsides and chain-smoke for the entire journey. Yes, the full 27 hours! Once onboard you couldn't see a bloody thing; it was like being sat in thick fog for a day.

Oh, did I forget to mention that contrary to the no-expense spared experience that our modern England Test cricketers have laid on for them – the reclining beds, personal gadgets and click-your-fingers waitress service – we were shoved at the back of the big bird to join in the economy chorus of coughing and wheezing? By the end of it we would have made Adele's voice sound like Shane MacGowan's.

It was comparable to being stood outside the front doors of a pub these days. Unfortunately, being up at 30,000 feet, we didn't have a *Hesketh Tavern* or a *Haworth Arms* to dive into for some fresh air. One of my pet hates is that – smokers loitering outside boozers, gobbing between drags on their fags. Never really understood where they're coming from, smokers. Partly due to the fact that I suffered from asthma as a kid, and therefore never felt inclined to try a cigarette, I suppose. I know some of you will be taking a drag as you're reading this and may find me a bit of a stick in the mud, but please allow a bloke his prejudices in the privacy of his own pages. In my estimation, it's a filthy habit and I probably couldn't afford to indulge in it either with the price of a packet of fags these days. Actually, why not go the whole hog on this? They should charge £50 per packet, of course. Then we could all pay less tax.

Anyway, I digress. So here we were, jetting off to represent our country, an international sports team, struggling for breath before take-off. Now take-off was an experience in itself for a flight virgin. Only once previously had I entered an aircraft and that was a sightseeing flight around the Blackpool Tower as a nipper. Never having been up properly before, I sat there considering how on earth we were going to manage it when next thing, this big bird set off like the clappers, and I got my answer. Like anything when you're trying it for the first time, it took some getting used to, and I just about had when we stopped off at Dusseldorf, Germany, to take some wood on board.

Peering through the smoke rings, and out of the window at healthier-looking clouds than hung around our beaks, I was spellbound by the whole experience, and almost delusional by the time we finally touched down. So imagine how I felt when they told me we had landed in 'Darwen'. 'Just down the road from me that, just beyond Blackburn,' I thought, 'and it's taken me more than a day to get here.' Fancy spending all that time to get a few miles down the road.

Rumour has it that Yorkshire used to do something similar for every pre-season tour during the 1960s – they'd set off from Leeds–Bradford Airport, get up to about 20,000 feet, U-turn just south of Sheffield, circle the region a few times to look down upon famous landmarks such as the white horse at Kilburn and arrive back in Leeds within the half-hour. 'Because if it's not in Yorkshire, it's not worth bloody going,' they used to say.

Goodness knows why Darwin in the Northern Territory was our first port of call but this was my first disembarkation down under. 'Cor blimey, these engines don't half get hot, do they?' I said as we clambered down onto the tarmac. It took seasoned traveller John Edrich to put me right: 'That heat you can feel's not the engines, you pillock, it's this bloody place!' You see, I was a bit wet behind the ears as a tourist and unaccustomed to anything other than cloud and mizzle for the first 18 years of my life, so the temperature was severe enough to really take me aback.

The previous England team that had travelled to Australia in 1970–71, under the captaincy of Ray Illingworth, had returned victorious, of course, one of the great (and rare) wins for an England team down under. John Snow was a key figure in that victory, as we know, but subsequently came under something of a cloud, and was not in our party. Another figure missing was Geoff Boycott, and it was his absence to which I owed my chance at international level.

Boycs had not been selected the previous summer, and although there were rumours surrounding his omission I never knew the official reason why. There were all kinds of suggestions made, conjecture in the newspapers that he had been dropped, other reports that he was preoccupied with the organisation of his benefit, but I never knew the truth, and why would I want to know? There was even persistent talk of him falling out with the then captain Mike Denness but I was not in a position to dwell on such matters. What interested me was doing well for England, having been selected as his direct replacement as opening batsman.

As far as I was concerned, he was just out of the reckoning, I had been picked, given the chance to fulfil a dream and play for my country, and everything else went over my head. I was concentrating on the business of scoring runs to better myself, focusing on that red, spherical leather object being hurled down at me from 22 yards – not analysing the personality clashes, or the torment he surprisingly suffered at the hands of the innocuous-looking swing bowler Solkar at the start of that series against India, that may have played some part in providing the initial opportunity.

I had made my maiden Test hundred against India during this initial spell of Boycs's absence, and followed that up with another in a limited-overs international match at the end of a troubled tour of England by Pakistan. Relations had become quite strained between the teams after the Pakistanis levelled accusations of skullduggery during the Lord's Test when Derek Underwood bowled them out. If there was any damp around, Deadly was well, deadly, and water had got under the covers. Persistent showers left a wet patch on the pitch, he kept hitting it and they simply couldn't cope. I was stood at short leg and it was like picking cherries.

Accusations that we were complicit in the state of the pitch were complete and utter nonsense. Pakistan had been ripped apart by Underwood in the first innings on a drying surface after a lengthy downpour on the opening day, and then after we batted to secure a 140-run lead, rain struck again when Pakistan came out to bat for a second time.

It was actually during the rest day of the match, the Sunday, that London was the subject of some major downpours and these continued into the Monday, which meant that when the temporary tent-like covering was removed, the pitch was discovered to be sodden. The rain had seeped through and in these conditions it was a different game altogether.

Deadly bagged a bundle of wickets with his idiosyncratic left-arm-round stuff – six to be precise – when the match finally resumed at around 5pm on the fourth evening. In plunging Pakistan from 192 for three half an hour into play to 226 all out, he took his innings haul to eight and provided match figures of 13 for 71, in addition to setting up a victory target of just 87 runs.

Dennis Amiss and I wiped 27 from that target before the close of play. But our efforts in 10 overs against the new ball were not the focus of attention that night, due to Pakistan manager Omar Kureishi's utter indignation. Kureishi put in an official complaint in which he accused MCC of 'negligence' and 'incompetence' in their attempts to cover the wicket. In those days, if it rained once the Test match was underway then the run-ups and edges of the square were protected but the pitch itself was exposed to the elements. On rest days, however, every effort was made to protect it from the elements, and Pakistan argued that they were entitled to be able to bat on a pitch in the same condition it had been in when stumps were drawn on the Saturday evening.

As it happened, we didn't get on again. Despite re-marking of the pitch during the final session on day five, the rain returned, and the contest, which had become more political than sporting, was abandoned as a draw and a three-Test series was on its way to a 0–0 stalemate. It was a series which bore few runs for me personally but the news I wanted to hear was delivered during a six-wicket win over Sir Garfield Sobers's Notts. That match concluded on 30 August, and I celebrated with 116 not out in the one-dayer against Pakistan in Nottingham the very next day.

Preparing for Battle

We felt almost from the moment we arrived that Australia were determined to show they were the better team and that they would avenge that defeat by Illingworth and Co four years earlier. And it is fair to say that we were caught on the hop by their line-up.

For a start, we did not anticipate Dennis Lillee being declared fit, and when he was, on the eve of the series, it undoubtedly gave the Australians a boost. The main thrust of the pre-series talk had been that Lillee was not going to play. He had suffered a serious back injury, spinal fractures that had caused him to be set in plaster from his backside to his shoulders for six whole weeks earlier in the year, and word was he wasn't going to be ready in time.

With him missing, we really didn't have anything to fear. Truth was that Australia were a little bit thin on the ground for fast bowlers. Or so we anticipated. They had Gary Gilmour and David Colley, the pairing who opened the bowling for New South Wales against us ahead of the first Test. Both had a couple of caps to their names – Colley's earned during the 1972 Ashes – while there was a recurring whisper doing the rounds that a chap called Thomson was in the mix too.

We had encountered two blokes of this surname during our four pre-series games – a bit of a beach bum, called Jeff, who sent down some fairly innocuous new-ball fare for Queensland, and who on his Test debut 12 months earlier against Pakistan had, by all accounts, gone around the park, finishing with match figures of nought for 110; and Alan Thomson, otherwise known as Froggy because of the way he sprang to the crease and bowled off the wrong foot, who had featured against England four years earlier when he got involved in a bouncer war with Snow. Because of his experience, we anticipated it would be the latter called up for the opener in Brisbane. But this hardly filled us with fear as his return for Victoria against us a fortnight earlier read 17-0-85-0.

We were hoodwinked, of course, as they wheeled out the man who would no longer be referred to as either Jeff or Thomson from that year forth. Following his selection he was forever known as Thommo and in tandem with Lillee ambushed us right good and proper. When he'd opened the bowling for Queensland against us in that first-class contest, he did no more than amble into the crease, under the express instruction of Australia captain Ian Chappell. He was merely playing to have a good look at us while being careful not to show anything of his true self – so that we didn't get accustomed to how freakishly fast he could send this ball down at you and would be caught unawares when the serious business began.

Facing up to Thommo was a real challenge not least because of his rather unique bowling action. In modern day cricket you will see batsmen such as Ian Bell and Eoin Morgan muttering to themselves: 'Watch the ball.' The television close-ups and slow-motion shots reveal that they mouth those words as the bowler runs up to the crease.

However, occasionally, you come up against bowlers that make it more difficult for you to be able to do that because of slight quirks in their actions. And then there was Thommo, who made it absolutely impossible because he didn't let you see it at all as he wound up to wang it down. With other people you knew where their hands were going and you could watch the ball all the way because it was visible. But with Thommo you just never saw it because the way he held it, with his body tilted backwards before uncoiling like a gargantuan spring, meant it remained behind him until the last nanosecond. His body shielded this arm that seemed to drag a yard behind the rest of him, and that, allied to the velocity he managed made him doubly difficult to face.

In that most wonderful of fast-bowling combinations, Thommo was the speed merchant, the unrefined paceman. Lillee, although a yard slower than the bowler the world had witnessed in the 1972 Ashes, was quick enough too, but a real artist in comparison to this laidback mop-head that had been plucked from the sticks. Because of his background there were some great tales about the young Thommo's early days.

For example, he didn't even have a run-up when he first started his professional career, never practised one during net sessions, just shuffled up and slung it down.

So much so that in that first Test at the Gabba, he sent down no-ball after no-ball (13 in the match) which triggered Chappell's presence on his shoulder as one early over progressed. Clearly struggling to get into a decent stride pattern, Thommo asked his elder: 'How many paces do I do, skipper?'

'What do you mean? I've no idea. Don't you know?'

'Nah, I've always walked back to where the tree is at this end – but they've cut it down!'

That's how much of a natural he was. These days fast bowlers carry tape measures among the essential items in their kit bags, mark their initials on the pitch with white-wash to identify their starting point, and do all sorts of other things besides to make sure they set off from the right place. It's precision. But there was nothing aesthetically pleasing about Thommo.

Make no mistake, with his dander up he was frighteningly quick, and described rather fittingly by one scribe as a one-man sonic boom. Even by fast bowlers' standards he was pretty raw as a cricketer – a guy who really was from the back of beyond. And in partnership with the recovered Lillee he made us England batsmen feel pretty raw too with regular blows to our bodies. They were a pretty gruesome twosome, who didn't seem overly bothered whatever the levels of pain they inflicted on opponents. Several of our party had to pay emergency visits to hospital during the six-match series, while I had to undergo a medical check that all was what it should be after an excruciating piece of physical assault in Perth. More of that later.

From my experience, Thommo hardly said a word on the field – I guess with the arsenal he packed in his right shoulder there was no need to – and he is even quieter now. Actually, a little known fact about him is that he slips over to Britain most summers, and lodges with his big mucker Mick Harford, the cricket-daft former professional footballer, while he does the rounds for a few weeks on the after-dinner speaking circuit, then heads back to Queensland and spends the rest of the year chilling out on his boat. You meet some great blokes in cricket and Thommo has to be up there for me. Although I am not so sure I appreciated him as an adversary on that trip 30-odd years ago!

Some suggested we were caught unawares by Australia after two wins and two comfortable draws against the state sides ahead of the first Test. Of course, we were without our own fast bowling nasty Snow, the scourge of the 1970–71 Aussies, and in terms of preparation for games it was nothing like what you might be used to reading about these days.

Let's just say that fitness was an interesting subject on my only England tour. There were no drills as such for fielding, practice was just day after day of netting. And when we weren't in the nets, we would be playing one of our many warm-up matches. We had landed in Australia in late October, and were involved in four four-day games between 1 and 25 November. That was 16 days' cricket out of 25 with all the travelling logistics such a huge country provides in between. It was gruelling work alright, especially for the bowlers as we were still on eight-ball overs under Australian regulations in the early 1970s.

Watching the lads now four decades later with their high energy drinks, their diet and nutritional advice, and a devotion to take care of themselves in their spare time, you can see how well equipped they are to combat such a schedule and environment but they are almost incomparable to our physical state back then. These days players undergo regular tests to make sure they are getting nowhere near the danger zone when it comes to hydration.

In contrast, we were frazzled and returned back home looking like pickled balloons. You see, we understood the need to get fluids on board but what we drank whenever there was a break in play – whether it be a formal drinks break, at lunch or at tea – was called a brown cow. A brown cow, would you believe, was an intriguing mixture of Coca-Cola and milk. We were necking this concoction like it had gone out of fashion at the end of every session. Put it this way, I am not sure you could call it a predecessor of Gatorade!

We simply knew no better. You only had to look at our daily routine when on county duty to see that we were technically still amateurs – certainly when comparing ourselves to the recent vintage to have come through that Old Trafford dressing room, like James Anderson – masquerading as professionals. Strength and conditioning would have amounted to an arm wrestle with your mates at the lunch table, while being careful not to knock over the beer bottles clumped in the middle.

Yes, for each home Lancashire county match, crates of Watneys Red Barrel would be emptied out at the start of the

40-minute interval and not many went back into those crates unopened at the end of it. That was a practice that carried on from the 1960s into the 1970s. Even on my Test debut, at Lord's, I supped a pint of shandy at lunch before resuming my first international innings. Could you imagine the furore now if one of England's top-order batters did that? It's the same game, but the world of cricket has changed.

Our modern lads are all tied into advertising whether it be through their personal gear or team-branded stuff – logos on all their equipment, the collars of their shirts, the pockets on their trousers, all of which is designed to keep you cool in these hot climates. They even wear vests underneath to regulate their body temperature and rate of perspiration. I ask you!

Forget skins. The only undergarments we wore were proper vests when we went to play at places like Liverpool or Southport (do you know how cold it gets at Aigburth in April?). And we didn't change our clobber drastically for our assignment down under, either. We wore flannels and these bloody great socks, made from thick wool that you might shove on if you were hiking through the Himalayas. Oh, and how could I forget the tour jumper? Nice and thick, MCC colours, cable knit. I was perspiring like a big black Alsatian.

And it wasn't just our attire that was inappropriate. Back in the day there was scant regard paid to what damage the sun might do to you. Skin cancer was not given a second thought, the world knew virtually nothing about it, and we all thought it was marvellous that whenever we weren't playing we could have a sunbathe. Even on the field, there were those of us rolling sleeves up to brown off the arms, and unbuttoning shirts desperately trying to improve the tan on the chest. There would never be any danger of us putting caps or hats on, so inevitably our foreheads looked like they had head-butted a Breville by the end of a day in the field. Protection from the sun is so matter of necessity these days – particularly in Australia with their 'slip, slap, slop' campaign – that you take it for granted. But in those days there was none of it. The result being that we scuttled around the place like lobsters clad in flannel.

Our fitness regime was monitored by Bernard Thomas, the physio. He would start by getting the fast bowlers stretched, which entailed the likes of Bob Willis and Mike Hendrick putting the back of one of their heels up on Bernard's shoulder, and Bernard raising up on his toes where he stood. There was a fair amount of stretching for everyone, in fact, but nowhere near the amount of physical activity players have become accustomed to as part of their preparation in subsequent years.

There was a lot of catching practice, particularly spiralling, high catches because in the thinner air the ball travels further and quicker. To lads like me who had not been down under before, looking into clear blue sky for a ball was quite a new experience, and took some adjustment. As a Lancashire lad I was more used to fielding in light drizzle. Despite the glare, however, nobody wore shades like your average endorsed 21st-century cricketer. We just squinted and got on with it.

Given the eventual 4–1 scoreline, you might anticipate a tale of misery being told of that 1974–75 tour – my only England tour as it happened – yet not a bit of it from my perspective. Although it was a chastening experience on the field, and there were some battered and bruised bodies by the end of it (mine among them), I recall it fondly. I made a bargain with myself to give it my best shot and enjoy it. In terms of touring, if not actual age, I was a young shaver and in addition to the cricket this was an adventure like none I had experienced before, and as it transpired none I would experience again (while a player at least). Even the chance to visit the vast sprawling mass that is Australia held an appeal for me.

Sure, things didn't start well. Mike Denness, our captain, suffered from pleurisy in the early days of the tour and that was a major disruption as we didn't see him for weeks. To dampen my personal enthusiasm, I broke my little finger in one of those darned fielding practices and missed the first Test, in Brisbane, where Thomson spectacularly deconstructed the façade that he was a fast-medium bowler fortunate to double his international caps. John Edrich broke a bone in his hand there at the Gabba and later at Sydney broke a rib. Dennis Amiss also fractured a finger in that first match, and a combination of their ailments meant I inherited one of English cricket's great statesmen as a room-mate.

Colin Cowdrey was the equivalent of cricket royalty. He was into his 40s and very much winding down his career at that stage – as the fact that he turned up looking rather lavish in a pinstripe suit, and his warm-up at the MCG, walking around the boundary edge as adopted conductor of the brass band, testify. A real gentleman, it was an honour to spend time with him; not that everyone held him in the same regard. Indeed, after one day's play during that Test, we were making our way out to the cars waiting for us at the back of the ground, when this little lad with his autograph book addressed Colin in a most uncouth manner. 'Hey, Cowdrey, you podgy f***er,' he said. 'Sign us this!'

'Oh, marvellous!' Colin said, in his archetypal English gent's voice. 'Absolutely charming!'

Rooming with PF, as he was subsequently dubbed on that tour, was almost a throwback to the era of gentlemen and players. Although mild-mannered and warm, his record and standing in the English game was slightly intimidating, and there was also some awkward history between us for me to get over when we were thrust together upon his arrival down under. You see, sharing a room with Colin took me back to an incident that had occurred in county cricket a good few years earlier. I had not really engaged with him since this particular occurrence on the field in a match between Lancashire and Kent in the mid-1960s.

Back in that era, county teams did not tend to travel with a twelfth man in tow to away matches. You went with your XI, and, in the event that somebody got injured, you simply borrowed a player from the home team. This role of loanee was one I fulfilled from time to time when Brian Statham was captain of Lancashire – it was not to be sniffed at for an aspiring young cricketer, particularly given the toffee involved. Doing 'twelfths' paid a few bob as a match fee, and in most instances, there was sod all to do to earn it. Unfortunately, however, this was not the case when Kent came to Southport for a County Championship match in 1967, and Muggins here was on duty.

Called on to the field as a substitute for what was a relatively short passage of play, I promptly dropped two catches

– one at mid-on and one at mid-off – to besmirch my reputation with all and sundry but most notably the esteemed leader of the opposition.

'Tell me about your twelfth man,' Cowdrey said to Statham later that evening. 'What *exactly* is his role in the game?'

Fair enough question, I suppose. I was a hopeful 20-year-old all-rounder in those days, not that he would have been interested by the actual answer to what effectively was a rhetorical question. Now, seven years on, we were top-order team-mates – human targets at Lillee and Thomson's coconut shy.

Felled by the Cracker at the WACA

Talking of coconuts reminds me of the most painful experience I ever had on a cricket field. Even if you have not seen the footage in question, you will no doubt be aware of it, so please remember to wince in sympathy in all the right places, and we'll go through it here for old time's sake.

Remember this was an era of uncovered pitches and facing some of those great West Indies fast bowlers was like hanging out the washing on the Siegfried Line. But of all the blows I took, never was I in as much discomfort as that day during the second Test in Perth when, sadly, I lost most of my genitals.

Thankfully this loss proved only temporary and they were returned to me some minutes later, having been found in 77 different parts, the other side of my protective box. They had migrated south (and every other compass point imaginable for that matter) the instant that a 3,000 mph Thomson thunderbolt shattered this plastic protector, turning it into some kind of medieval torture implement.

For the particular delivery in question, I got myself too square on and immediately knew there was trouble looming, hoping beyond hope that I would get some bat on ball as it climbed above stump level. Alas, no such luck. One of cricket's more interesting facts is that the first testicular guard was used in 1874, yet it took another 100 years for the first helmets to be worn. A relatively short time, I guess, for blokes to work out that their brains could also play an important part in their lives.

Of course, we are now so used to seeing blokes head out into the middle for gladiatorial combat with every piece of body armour imaginable. But we certainly didn't have things like chest guards or arm guards back then. You would have something resembling a thigh pad, although they were nowhere near the thickness of the ones you see in kitbags down your local club these days. These things were a bit flimsy to say the least. But being that way meant you had the chance to slide a *Reader's Digest* or your spare socks down there too to provide extra protection.

Yes, the sight of batsmen wearing helmets was still in its infancy, I wasn't using one, and I might as well not have been sporting anything between my legs either for the good it did. This pink litesome was completely useless for the job it was supposed to do. If you can't remember what these litesomes looked like, here's a reminder: you can still see them in use these days in bathrooms up and down the country – you know, those plastic things you keep your soap in.

Nowadays batsmen are much better protected around the groin but this flimsy thing did more harm than good. Because it was full of breath holes it splintered on impact and concertinaed my knackers. Suddenly, everything that was supposed to be on the inside was now on the outside. If you want to get a tad more graphic, imagine a cactus growing the wrong way out of its pot. Then consider for a moment how that might feel … Was it any wonder that I jack-knifed straight onto my head? Talk about being doubled up in pain. I lose my voice every November in memory of that cracker in the knacker.

Number one priority once back in the dressing room was to release my master of ceremonies from its snare: a pretty unforgiving job for Bernard Thomas, who certainly hadn't signed up for that kind of thing when agreeing to be England team physio. We didn't have any medical staff travelling with us in those days, though, so suffice to say I was very grateful for Bernard's delicate handling of the situation. To be frank, such was the stinging sensation, I wouldn't have minded a personal visit from the Fremantle Doctor but in the end had to settle for an hour or two of ice treatment once back in the dressing room. 'Can you take the pain away but leave the swelling?' I'd pleaded with Bernard upon retiring hurt.

You know as an England opener in Australia that you are going to cop some, and the crowd at the WACA turned gladiatorial, egging their evil henchmen on the next morning when I resumed my innings. The hairs stood up on the back of your neck walking to the crease anticipating a serious going over. A combination of Perth's extra bounce – even these days batsmen can leave the ball on length in the knowledge that slightly short deliveries will sail over the top of the stumps – and eight-ball overs meant there were plenty of bumpers, as Cowdrey was so fond of calling them, to contend with, and although I didn't score a mountain of runs – there were very few scoring opportunities against a backdrop of chin music – I was quite proud of sticking it out for six hours in that match against such sustained hostility.

There was no getting away from the fact that batting out there was hellish demanding. I would stop short of saying frightening but it was a real challenge facing someone as rapid as Thommo. As a collective, we just couldn't handle that pace.

Australia were ultra-aggressive with the ball, the tactic of targeting the body of the batsman a good one on such bouncy surfaces. But in one way we only had ourselves to blame. Or, more accurately, one of our own to blame.

No series brings out good cricket tales, or indeed good cricket myths, like an Ashes series, and Dennis Lillee would have you know in playground parlance that 'it was the Poms what started it.' One adopted Pom, actually – that lovable giant Tony Greig, whose decision to bounce Lillee in the first innings of that first Test in Brisbane had repercussions for the rest of us over the coming weeks.

As Lillee regained his feet and brushed past Greig, having been caught behind attempting to hook, he told him: 'Just remember who started this.' No matter who started it, it is fair to say that the Australians finished it, although, to his immense credit, Greig never took a single backwards step following this confrontation. He always played in the same positive manner and was forever the showman, signalling his own fours whenever he opened those big shoulders of his, much to the chagrin of his Australian adversaries.

Greigy was the one player within our ranks who took them on with success, and what a totally brilliant guy to play with he was. The cricket was always colourful whenever he was one of the protagonists, a fact that Lillee did not seem to appreciate, particularly when he uppercut to the fence and then dropped down or leant forward to wave his right hand to the audience like the conductor of an orchestra.

That he was out there able to antagonise at the Gabba was chiefly down to one man. A chap by the name of Clem Jones. There were all kinds of storms sweeping around Queensland in the build-up to the first Test, and Jones, the mayor of Brisbane, actually doubled up as the groundsman to get the pitch fit for purpose.

The square had been that wet that as the countdown to the first ball being sent down got closer, no-one really knew which strip we were due to play on. Eventually they produced this pitch that became visible the day before, and we practised along from it before attending a mayoral reception that night.

One heck of a surprise was delivered when we did because here was Jones, the same chap that we had witnessed slaving away in a cork hat, pair of shorts and vest by day, now dressed resplendent in chain, robes, the works. Quite a job share was that one. In fact, when it came to Brisbane in the 1970s he was chief cook and bottle washer too. He knew everything and everyone all around the city, it seemed, and his name was to be known around the world to others subsequently thanks to the naming of the Clem Jones Stand.

In defence of Greig's goading, Lillee could be a feisty bugger at the best of times, and was prone to react to the slightest provocation. Take the time when Pakistan batsman Javed Miandad bumped into him mid-pitch in a Test match at Perth, while taking a single to fine-leg. Lillee's response was to follow his opponent to the non-striker's end and administer a kick up the arse.

A number of his contemporaries would no doubt have been lined up behind him and would have put the boot in a good deal harder given half the chance – let's just say Javed was as popular as gherkin and ice cream sandwiches – but it emphasised that Dennis just could not resist a skirmish.

He was close to wearing Javed's bat as a cravat in that incident, and might have done but for umpire Tony Crafter's positioning between the two men. In the end the only damage done was to Lillee's pocket – he was fined $120 and banned for two matches.

Whichever way you dress it up, a number of us would live to regret Greigy's bravado. Some of my own words came back to haunt me, too. When I look back I really wish I hadn't offered the wisecrack that I could play Thomson with my knob end. Obviously I never meant it!

Being struck amidships is not something you forget. There are few things that leave me speechless but that was one of them, and even blows down below from other bowlers cannot compare to one from Thommo. My old mate Mike Selvey did double me over in a county match at Lord's once, so I thought it only right to pop into the Middlesex dressing room after play to allay fears he might have done any serious damage.

'Don't worry, Selve,' I grinned. 'Compared to Thommo, you were a pleasure.'

Verbals played their part in that 1974–75 series but mainly away from the ground, believe it or not. Every evening Australian television seemed to be screening interviews with one Aussie player or another in which they would spell out exactly how they were going to crush us Poms. The most memorable was when Thommo came on one night on the eve of the first Test and matter-of-factly exclaimed: 'I like to see blood on the pitch.' We were in a team meeting and it is fair to say there was the odd intake of breath as he declared a preference for hitting opponents rather than getting them out.

As an opening batsman I always liked to keep relations with those hurling that leather sphere down at me at the speed of light on an even keel. Dennis Amiss and I tried to maintain a certain friendliness for self-preservation as much as anything else. So I was at odds with the response drawn when Lillee walked into bat one day and got struck on the elbow by a Greig bouncer first ball. 'Well bowled, give him another,' squawked Keith Fletcher from gully.

I cringed as Lillee turned 90 degrees and retaliated with: 'It'll be your f***ing turn soon!' Funnily enough, Fletch was given a right working over when he came in. He would have been left in no doubt what lay in store for him, though, following another episode of the Dennis Lillee TV Show that evening. During an interview on the news, he was asked about the progress of the match, and to assess the position Australia found themselves in – most probably answering something such as 'we'll bloody crush 'em' – before finally being quizzed on what the opposition were like.

'The Poms are a good set of blokes, I get on with all of 'em,' he said, before looking right into the camera lens. 'Except that little weasel Fletcher, that is. I know you're watching, Fletcher, and you might as well know I am going to sort you out tomorrow.'

Fletch would have been forgiven for wishing that tomorrow had never come as Lillee roared into him next day. Picture the scene as Fletch awaited his punishment – no helmet, no visor, no body armour. Just the MCC navy blue cap sat on the top of his head as Lillee sent down the full artillery. Bouncer after bouncer was fended off or dodged in expert fashion until one short one failed to get up as much as the rest and finally located its target, hitting him straight on the head, flooring our number five batsman in the process, and sending the ball bouncing to Ross Edwards at cover.

'Blimey, he's only gone and knocked St George off his 'orse,' gasped Geoff Arnold, in reference to the emblem on the front of the MCC caps, as we sat in the dressing room watching the drama unfold.

One of the weird things in cricket is seeing the pseudo-pleasure people get when a team-mate gets sconned. Sounds vindictive, doesn't it? But it's not, really. It's similar to self-preservation. Quite simply, if someone else is being hit, you're thankful. Because it means it's not you.

I've never met anyone who likes being hit by a cricket ball. One bloke came close to challenging that theory, actually, although like may still be too strong a word. A certain Brian Close used to chest balls down like a brick outhouse of a centre-half. Trouble was these leather balls were made for cricket not football and were being propelled down the pitch by some of the planet's most hostile fast bowlers.

The most famous Close combat came in 1976 when, at the age of 45, he stood up to those West Indies firebrands Michael Holding, Wayne Daniel and Andy Roberts for the best part of three hours in a Test match at Old Trafford. It was in the second innings, in a hopeless cause, and proved to be the last of his England career, but what bravery this bloke showed.

Talk about bulldog spirit. Brian was as tough as old boots, and would literally put his body on the line if he thought doing so would enhance the chances of winning the game. And that was not limited to him wearing a few bouncers while batting, either. Here was a man who seemed to have no limit to his pain threshold, one who was brave enough to offer himself up as a human ricochet during that series against the Windies. Legend has it that during that series defeat, Close came up with an unusual and rather masochistic tactic in search of a wicket for England.

'I will field at short-leg when Derek Underwood is bowling to Clive Lloyd,' he announced at a team meeting. 'When Lloyd sweeps, the ball will hit me, and the other close-in fielders can catch the rebounds.' If you know anything of the man, you will realise he was deadly serious.

Some lads talk a better game than they play. Back in 1989, a number of years after I had retired from first-class cricket, I was still playing for my beloved Accrington in the Lancashire League. We reached the semi-final stage of the Worsley Cup and were drawn away at Todmorden, whose overseas professional at the time was the Sri Lankan all-rounder Ravi Ratnayeke.

He was a handy cricketer was Ratnayeke but had hardly pulled up any trees in the league that summer and we knew it. He was certainly not a player to put the wind up us. So we remained unperturbed about him coming across our path. However, when we arrived at Centre Vale in late morning, Ravi was nowhere to be seen.

His absence was explained a few minutes later when a beanpole West Indian strolled across the ground as our lads knocked up. There was a lot of mouthing of 'who's that?' around our group as he sauntered past with his kit. I had clocked him a long way off. Huge, supremely athletic, he was the new kid on the block as far as fast bowling in the Caribbean went. It was Ian Bishop, who had made his Test debut within the previous 12 months.

It turned out that, with Ratnayeke injured, Todmorden had hired Bishop from Derbyshire for the day. Now as business transactions go, this was a fairly impressive one.

Bishop flew in to the crease and got the ball through at a fair old lick, but our opening pair of Nick Marsh and Andrew Barker, elder brother of Warwickshire's left-arm swing bowler Keith Barker, resisted manfully to keep him at bay. Todmorden did not make a breakthrough until we had 63 on the board, in fact, and that put our wicketkeeper Billy Rawstron on the verge of going in.

Billy was our number four and confident enough to declare in the privacy of our own dressing room that, in his estimable opinion, this 21-year-old Adonis from Trinidad was not as quick as some others were making out. He even shunned the notion of wearing a helmet, a ploy I believed was unwise when confronted with a paceman of Bishop's velocity. He upped the ante by declaring if his West Indian adversary had the audacity to bounce him, he would be hooking. Oh dear, Billy.

At 71 for two, it was time for Billy's boasts to be put to the test. We'd heard the theory; now it was going to be put into practice.

You have probably guessed by this point that our hero was going to get the trouble he was asking for. Some lads reckon the cricket gods will not allow you to get away with saying stuff like that without having your words put to the test, and sure enough Bish obliged by unleashing one of his heat-seeking missiles. It kissed our Billy on the lips just as he was deciding that a cross-bat shot was the order of the day – careering him straight into the wooden stuff behind him in the process.

A sniff of the smelling salts later and Billy declared: 'Hey, I can't be out like that. I had completed my shot.'

As captain I thought I'd better put my young charge right as we escorted him from the field: 'Billy, you hadn't even started it. Now let's go and see a man about some teeth.'

Just to prove he was as mad as his pre-match talk suggested, our noble gloveman refused any treatment until our task was completed, so he went out and took his place on the other side of the stumps for the second half of the match, blood oozing from his mouth, looking like the lead character from a 1980s low-budget zombie flick. We won by 51 runs in no small part due to the efforts of our Rawstron. They breed 'em tough in Accrington, you know. Billy and I are living proof.

Exploding the Myth

Despite all of the pain inflicted, being on an Ashes tour was a great experience. The reality was that I was not good enough as an individual and neither was the team collectively, but being a part of a tour like that, travelling all over Australia on Ansett Airlines' internal flights, getting acquainted with the Australian way of life, and the subtle differences between the cities was a real career high and a great life experience. A tour like that was long and, against superior opposition, provided no respite. I know the current players talk about the length of tours, and the stretch of time they are expected to be away from home, but what you can't appreciate now is just how tightly the games were shoehorned into the schedule between late October and early February. Physically it was very demanding, particularly given the fact that we were still play-ing under the old Australian regulation of eight-ball overs.

Those eight-ball overs were an important dynamic in the flow of matches. Australia hit us hard with pace, and with a few deliveries an over sailing past your nose end, it felt as though we were being pinned down. At the start of an over, we knew that if we got through the first couple of deliveries from Lillee or Thomson there were still half-a-dozen more to come. Talk about dispiriting. On our side we only had Bob Willis with genuine speed, but his dodgy knees only allowed him one burst at full tilt. This in itself came with a caveat: if he over-stepped a couple of times he was suddenly looking at 10 balls before he got his breather, and his run-up was one of the longest the game has witnessed.

While aggression was one of the keys, if not *the* key component, of the captaincy of Ian Chappell – or Chappelli as he is more commonly known – the competitive edge never turned into abuse. Don't get me wrong, the will to win was unmistakable but you sensed he wanted it to be done fairly, even against the English. As a cricketer, I found him as honest as they came, and I am not sure he would have stood for unbridled nastiness from his players. I certainly respected him, and would call him 'captain' or 'skipper' as was the common practice towards the figurehead of your opposition in those times.

In fact, he was too generous on occasion, and I might have avoided my crisis in the Balkans had the Australians bothered to appeal when, on 17, I shaped up to a Thomson delivery; the extra bounce meant the ball got too big on me, and ran up the face of my bat on its way through to wicketkeeper Rod Marsh. I immediately went to put the bat under my arm – as English players you walked in those days – only to realise there was no appeal forthcoming. I waited another split second to listen for the 'HOWZEE?!' and the ball being thrown up in the air. But it never came. There was nothing, other than a 'well bowled Thommo' and so, as I had turned 270 degrees, there was nothing for it but to let out an apologetic cough and begin some phantom pitch prodding.

This respect for Chappell, held by our team collectively, was in no small part for what he had done for Australia since they had lost the urn in 1970–71. In 1972, they had come to England and earned a draw, and now he was going up a level. He had got this team together and it gelled beautifully – you could tell they were playing for their captain too. Didn't they flippin' just.

Like any other team during that generation they had financial issues with their governing body; they were not too enamoured with their appearance fees, because of the insubstantial proportion of the revenue generated from the huge crowds of that series ending up in their pockets. Chappelli's trick was arguably to spend as much time off the field batting for his men – negotiating better rates of remuneration – as he did on it.

Because once they crossed the white line, boy did those eleven men answer to his tune. They were supremely fit and a very well-balanced side. They had guys who carried out unheralded roles such as Max Walker, who, arms and legs akimbo, would run in and bowl all day. Walker possessed great stamina, a facet which allowed Chappell to rotate Lillee and Thomson at the other end. Then there was Ashley Mallett, a wonderfully steady bowler, who offered that spinner's gold – control. Although some of the edges from the short balls flew just out of reach, the Australian slip cordon caught just about everything that you would deem a chance, and so they were always going to beat us over a six-match series.

Although we had some feisty fighters, most notably Greig and Alan Knott, there was undoubtedly only one team in it, and despite the drawn third match, Melbourne's Boxing Day Test, going down to the wire with all three results still possible – Australia needed six runs, us two wickets – the only match we won was the last, and one of the two I missed.

Having begun the campaign late following that broken digit, I was forced back onto the sidelines and onto an early flight back to the UK, boarding it shortly after the second

MCG match had got underway. The injury, a long-standing one to my neck, was aggravated taking evasive action at short-leg in a game against New South Wales, and although I subsequently played in Adelaide, my pair of single-figure scores there were to be my last in Test cricket. So as I flew back to the UK nursing two damaged vertebrae, my team-mates cashed in. Thomson was ruled out of the series finale through injury and that other menace Lillee lasted half a dozen overs before breaking down. I believe it is called the law of the sod.

There were certainly no regrets, however. I left having experienced one victory over Australia that winter – top-scoring with 49 in the one-off one-day international on New Year's Day – and having forged some terrific friendships with our opponents. That token win was actually nothing like the limited-overs game as we now know it: there was barely a sole in attendance in the 90,000-capacity MCG, and it felt like a bit of a knockabout despite going down in the record books as a proper one-day international.

I would have to say that the Australians were a terrific set of blokes. Guys like Marsh, Lillee, Thomson, the Chappell brothers and Dougie Walters were all great company.

Walters was a figure of intrigue, and quite incredible for a professional sportsman. He was this kingpin player, talked about as if he was the new Bradman by his fellow country-men, and with a brilliant record in Australian conditions to give that hyperbole a semblance of justification. He averaged a touch under 58 on home soil but was not so terrific overseas, certainly not in England anyway, and had an average of under 40 to emphasise it. Neither was he the epitome of health, his lifestyle certainly not what you would expect from an inter-national-standard athlete.

Dougie was a chain smoker who worked for Rothmans, a company that was a big player in cricket at that time. Away from the pitch you never saw him without his fags, and that gave me the chance to play a few pranks. Wherever you went in Australia, you would be guaranteed to find a number of joke shops, and one of the items they sold were these explod-ing cigarette packets which were branded to look like real ones. Everywhere we travelled I would nip down to the near-est shop and stock up on half-a-dozen packets at a time, and then leave them strategically placed around the Australian dressing room.

Doug had a habit of leaving several packs lying around, so that at the end of each day's play he would come off the field and reach for one as he sat down. However, my trick of mixing in the fake ones with the real created a kind of Russian roulette, spreading them strategically all over the place, so that he would have no idea which were which. More often than not, he would pick up the joke set and they would explode in his hands.

To counter this, he devised a technique of flicking them from underneath rather than picking them up and setting them off. But, as with the best players, the best pranksters adapt and as the series went on, I roped more of their lads into my scheming. My later tactics were to get his real cigarettes and slip bangers into them too. In the end I reduced him to a nervous wreck.

I enjoyed socialising with the Australians and was one of the members of our team who indulged in one of the great established Ashes traditions: the post-match drink. These days it is limited to the actual end of the match, or even the end of the series, dependent on the views of the respective captains and coaches, but back then it was something that took place at the end of each and every day's play. Granted, some of our lads wouldn't participate at all, but the majority did.

The argument for not going into the opposition's changing room was that you were being asked to fraternise with the same blokes that had been trying to knock your block off just a matter of minutes earlier. 'Why on earth would I want to have a drink with him?' was the usual response from those hostile towards this after-hours get-together. Fair enough, it wasn't a three-line whip. But for my part, I enjoyed the chance to have a beer and a yarn for half an hour or so, a period which as much as anything allowed the masses that had filled the ground to get out.

Of course, international sportsmen shouldn't drink too much alcohol during matches, so we all made sure we had our brown cow (yum!) before knocking the froth off a bottle of VB with great chaps like Ross Edwards, Rick McCosker, Ian Redpath and Wally Edwards, whose entire three-Test career was encapsulated in that series, and who became Cricket Australia's chairman in late 2011.

I still see another of the group, the quiet off-spinner Mallett, on Ashes tours as he drinks in the same pubs around Adelaide. Then there was Walker, or Tangles as he was known due to his spaghetti junction of limbs on show when bowling, who is taken off so brilliantly in the Billy Birmingham tapes.

So Nearly Brearley

For the legendary 1981 Ashes, England might have had a different captain altogether, had I made a better fist of my return to the international stage. Yes, English cricket could be lauding the leadership skills of one D Lloyd rather than JM Brearley had history taken a slightly different course.

The 1974–75 Ashes had had its casualties when it came to future selection, myself amongst them naturally enough after a series book-ended by injuries and without a half-century on the shelf. It is fair to say that I was regarded as an ex-Test cricketer the moment I landed back on British soil. And I knew I had to do plenty to alter this opinion.

So it was back to concentrating on domestic matters in the summer of 1975, my third as Lancashire captain and the one that was to deliver the only trophy of my tenure. We faced Middlesex in the Gillette Cup final at Lord's, our fifth appearance in a showpiece one-day contest in six years. I had just returned from a broken bone in my right hand which had sidelined me for a month or so, and lifting the trophy in front of our mass of supporters down in the capital was one of my career highlights.

I guess being involved with, and indeed orchestrating, a successful one-day team meant my name was discussed from time to time by the selectors when it came to England squads. Indeed, ahead of the 1975 Ashes – shortened to four matches due to the presence in the calendar of the first World Cup – notice was provided of my standing not so far back in the pack when I was chosen in the MCC representative team to play against the touring Australians, forming an opening alliance with a young Graham Gooch. We put on a hundred for the first wicket but it was he rather than I that went on to get picked for the first Test at Edgbaston. He got a pair, and I am sure I could have matched that at the very least!

The 1970s was an era in which fast bowlers thrived and every county seemed to have a West Indian that they would unleash upon you. I remember the bush telegraph doing overtime when Andy Roberts was chosen to play for Hampshire's Second XI, for example.

At Lancashire we had Colin Croft but his ability to produce this deadly concoction of pace and hostility was not unconditional. Exasperatingly, Colin had to be in the right mood. It was frustrating for our lads at times to be fending off heat-seekers from the likes of Sylvester Clarke, Malcolm Marshall or Joel Garner, and then see Colin amble in to send down something only slightly warmer than medium.

He was up front about things, though, and was not easily stirred into aggression. The most notable occasion was on his County Championship debut when we played Warwickshire at Old Trafford. That meant a meeting with my erstwhile England opening partner Dennis Amiss, and I specifically asked Colin to rough him up with the new ball.

So imagine my surprise when, fists clenched and lip curled, I said to him: 'C'mon Col, lad, let's stick it up him,' and got the reply, 'I am not bowling today, m-a-a-a-n.'

'Eh? What do you mean not bowling? You're our overseas player, our hired hand, and you're an opening bowler.'

'Well, I only ever know after stepping onto the grass whether I want to bowl or not and today I am not bowling.'

Stubbornness is a decent northern trait and I for one was not for giving up easily, so I gave him the full spiel about owing me as captain, made a plea for him to do the right thing by the team, and even informed him: 'I'll decide when you bowl.' It was a moral victory when I got him to take the new ball as planned, although he won in the game of one-upmanship by operating at around 50% capacity.

We knew it to be half-speed because we saw him at full tilt on another occasion in Manchester, less than a month later, when he did fancy it. The presence of a certain Geoff Boycott and Yorkshire did something to stoke his competitive spirit, I would suggest. Perhaps my warning to Colin the night before the match in question that Boycott was the doyen of top-order batsmen, that no-one else was fit to lace his boots – not the great Viv, or the great Clive, or the great Gordon – and that he ate pace bowlers for breakfast had an effect?

'I can't see how we'll get him out,' I said in the course of that evening's team meeting.

Next morning, Colin sought me out and asked me, head tilted in the direction of where the Yorkshire players practised: 'Which the man Boycott?'

A nod in the direction of Yorkshire's finest was all it took. Colin's radar was in tune and in he went for the kill when opportunity presented itself. Boycott, Bill Athey and John Hampshire all fell in identical fashion – bowled Croft – as Yorkshire slumped to 18 for four.

If my ability to lead impressed the England hierarchy, it was more than should have been said for my batting. To be honest, there wasn't much fluency to my game in 1975 and although I scraped together 1,000 runs for the season, the tally included a solitary, painstaking hundred – against the champions Leicestershire at Blackpool. It took me 100 overs to register it, with the three figures acknowledged as Ray Illingworth completed a bungling drop from a steepler which came down at square-leg. It was unusual to witness such generosity from a Yorkshireman towards one of us red rose lot, and Raymond extended it further when he branded it the worst hundred he'd ever seen!

The following year, with Tony Greig now firmly ensconced at the helm of the England team, I had anticipated impressing in the middle order for Lancashire after shunting down a few places from opener. With the 1976–77 winter featuring an MCC tour to India and Sri Lanka, I recognised an opportunity to show that I could manoeuvre the ball around intelligently into the gaps in mid-innings, the period in which the spinners would be operating.

However, the attention I drew to myself was not for hitting out but getting hit once more. This time, right in the clock. Although I had already expressed a belief that close catchers could benefit from protective padding and helmets, and had even sported a self-made mask when fielding at short-leg, I still accepted that batsmanship was a pastime laced with risk. Over a dozen years as a professional cricketer, there had been ample opportunity to develop self-preservation techniques, without thought of wearing one of the crash helmet–visor combinations that had latterly come onto the market.

So all I had on when facing Northamptonshire's Bob Cottam was my Lancashire county cap. Bob, later bowling coach in the England set up of 1996–99 when I was coach, had worked up a fair old head of steam, yet being a happy hooker

I duly took him on when he dug one in. For me, there is no great recall of what happened next, although I was later informed I'd been out cold for five minutes after being struck flush in the face. I left Old Trafford for hospital, hit wicket, one of Cottam's 13 victims in the match. As my legs folded beneath me, I had slumped onto my stumps, apparently. There were no serious health repercussions from the blow but I was unable to bat in the second innings due to concussion.

The middle-order experiment continued for the next six weeks but I reverted to going in first midway through a match against the touring West Indians in June. I had been stumped for 48 in the first innings, and remained intent on playing my shots in the second, hitting 82 in a score of 230 for two declared. It was arguably an innings that would have stood out more but for my great mate Clive Lloyd's team knocking off the 192-run target I set them – in a single session!

I did make it on a flight back to Australia for the 1977 Centenary Test but only by virtue of being an ex-Ashes player rather than a current pick. Dozens of former England Test cricketers were flown over by Qantas, in fact, especially for this match, a celebration of 100 years of matches between the two sporting foes.

Again, the journey was quite an experience, with plenty of goings on. You can just imagine on an old jumbo jet with people walking around, loitering in the aisles, standing by the doors, it was chaotic. And all these ex-England players had been thrown together, so there were a few egos bounding about the cabin.

Arguably, the most memorable thing to happen on the flight was Bill Edrich getting off at the other end sporting a black eye and walking on crutches. He had developed gout on the way, and been in several scrapes besides.

In time-honoured fashion, and under Irish aviation laws, drink was taken during that behemoth of a transfer from English winter to Australian summer. Of course, it was all free grog from Qantas and there was a copious amount to be put away. The legendary John Arlott, who was travelling to commentate on the match for the BBC, had craftily found himself a stretch of four seats to spread out on, with the intension of having a snooze. Unfortunately, while he was laid out, Edrich fell on him and an almighty kerfuffle ensued.

In the scene I recall most easily from that flight, though, Bill was sitting, with Fred Trueman stood in front of him. Bill was a very well-spoken man and, in his rather plummy voice, and in no uncertain terms, informed Fred: 'I've got to tell you, Trueman, Alan Moss was a far better bowler than you.'

I'm not sure that Fred liked hearing that anyone was better than him. He might not have anything against Alan Moss but if he could have thrown Bill out of the plane it looked like he would have done. You can probably all imagine Fred's response. 'I've never bloody heard anything like that in all my life!'

Eddie Paynter, the former Lancashire batsman who starred in the Bodyline series, was the quietest and most sartorially elegant of this travelling group, dressed as he was in a full suit, shirt with pristine collars and a tie pin. It was like he was on a 24-hour silence, only breaking it when we passed over Germany with: 'Last time I was here, I was dropping bombs on the place.'

This return down under was an absolute hoot. Unlike the regulations for tours when you were forced to share, us old boys were treated to our own rooms in the Hilton in Melbourne where the one-off Test was played, the only exception to this being Gilbert Parkhouse and Eric Russell, who had to room together because they both suffered badly from arthritis and therefore couldn't put on their own socks. I guess, knowing how difficult it was to do their own encouraged them to aid the other. You can just picture it on a morning, can't you? 'Would you mind, old boy?'

I had always enjoyed the company of my seniors so this kind of trip was good fun, sharing experiences of Ashes past and having a laugh. I used to get on very well with Alec Bedser, who was the England team manager, and the man who effectively picked the side. He was nearly always good fun although occasionally he would get very serious about the game, particularly when harking back to yesteryear and how things were when he played the game.

In one team meeting, Alec happened to mention that our fast-bowling group, including Bob Willis, Mike Hendrick, Geoff Arnold and Chris Old, always seemed to be dogged by injury niggles, and that in his day this would never have occurred.

'I never used to be troubled by injury. Never got an injury … because I stayed in good shape bowling. I used to get bowling fit by bowling a lot of overs. I used to bowl 45 overs a day, and that's enough to get anyone fit,' he said.

Seemed by my calculations that if that many overs were coming down from one end it would have meant a good stretch of time in the middle for the batsmen too, so I couldn't resist interjecting with: 'You can't have been bowling so well, then, if you kept bowling 45 overs every day.

Couldn't you get anyone out?' Funny how the previous generation always knows better, isn't it? I didn't think they did when I played but I have since learned they do … Funny that, eh?

Alec enjoyed sharing a joke or two and while on tour he was required to front up and respond on behalf of the England cricket team whenever we were invited to official functions, dinners and the like. So, after a few engagements we knew the finale to his speech off by heart.

The Duke of Norfolk, a great supporter of English cricket, owned a racehorse that was trained by a chap by the name of Sid Furnell. Now Sid used to take his responsibility to report back on the progress of the particular nag very seriously, and would file detailed logs on its training schedule, food intake, its general well-being and most importantly its time trials around the stables.

But for a busy man like the Duke this was all a bit too much. Forget the diet, how the horse looked, how often it had been groomed, all he really wanted to know was how it was doing in its races. 'Could you be more concise?' he asked Sid. 'I don't have time to read all of this in-depth information, so please cut to the chase. Simply send me a brief note to inform me in the fewest words possible how things are going when it is in competitive action.

'Right you are, your grace, no problem.'

So, after the horse's next race, the Duke received a short but rather mystifying telegram. It read: 'S.F – S.F – S.F – S.F.'

What did S.F stand for? The only thing he could think of was Sid Furnell, so he gave him a ring to see if it was he who had sent the telegram. Of course, Sid confirmed that it was indeed his correspondence and that the message was his report of the performance from the previous evening's race.

'But what on earth does 'S.F – S.F – S.F – S.F' mean?' asked the Duke.

At this point, the entire touring party used to join in Alec's punchline: 'Started, farted, slipped and fell, see you Friday, Sid Furnell.'

The qualification for being offered a seat on the plane in March 1977 was a minimum of four Ashes caps, which meant I just met the criteria for this no-expense-spared trip to attend as a guest and watch the game. Somewhere at home I still possess the miniature bats with the autographs of all the great players gathered at the MCG for that match. Those signatures include that of Sir Donald Bradman, and these little bats went very nicely with a couple of others I have from the 1920s – one featuring the England and Australia teams and the other signed by players from Lancashire and Yorkshire. I am not a great hoarder of memorabilia but those kinds of things are cricket treasure as far as I'm concerned.

It was during our chill-out time at the Hilton Hotel pre-match that I believed my path had crossed once more with Thommo. Few men are as physically strong as him but one bloke did look just like him. A load of us were sat around the swimming pool one late afternoon when I noticed out the corner of my eye a figure tearing up this pool like an Olympian. He swam and swam and swam. Length after length he ploughed through, up and down, up and down. His marathon session certainly kept my attention.

'This bloke has been in here for about an hour,' I said to the other former Ashes performers.

'Don't you know who it is?' one of them countered.

'No. Not got a clue,' I said.

'It's Ray Lindwall.'

When he got out I had to double-take. The build of him was just like Thommo. His shoulders were immense, the size of a heavyweight boxer, and he could easily have been his body double. The only other cricketer who had a build similar from my experience was one FS Trueman.

But it was a man with a much slighter frame that dominated the match that week. Although it went down in history as the Centenary Test Match, Englishmen will forever refer to it simply as Derek Randall's Match.

England had plucked David Steele from nowhere during the shortened 1975 Ashes and here was another batsman with a personality that made a strong impression. Not since the third Test of that year, when supporters of the armed robber George Davis caused its abandonment, had an English dig-in demanded so much attention.

Faced with a record-busting target of 463, Randall strolled to the wicket at 28 for one singing 'The Sun Has Got His Hat On, Hip-Hip-Hip Hooray', and annoyed the hell out of Dennis Lillee and his cronies for the next seven-and-a-half hours. When Lillee hurled down a bouncer, Randall became more animated than my dog Tags when a squirrel hops over from the adjoining golf course and invades our garden, dodging this way and that, doffing his cap and even rolling onto his back. Talk about as daft as a brush. When his attempt at evasion failed and the ball struck him a meaty blow on the bonse, his response was: 'No good hitting me there, nothing to damage.'

It was quite a way to register a first Test half-century but although his theatrics drove Lillee potty, just as Greig had done two years previously, and his Test-best score of 174 was deemed worthy of the man-of-the-match, it all came in a losing cause as Australia triumphed by 45 runs in the one-off fixture, the last Ashes one between two full-strength teams for a while.

Some of the oomph was lost during the late 1970s due to the emergence of Kerry Packer and World Series Cricket, but as a player at that time you still wanted to be picked for your country. A single one-day appearance against Pakistan is all I managed between travelling home from the 1974–75 Ashes with my dicky neck and starting the 1980 summer, so despite scoring two Benson & Hedges Cup hundreds – against Derbyshire and Scotland – and an unbeaten 90 in a John Player Special League win over Gloucestershire as an opening batsman within a fortnight of the first international cricket of the season, it was nevertheless a surprise when I was recalled.

More so, when I was informed of the role they had in mind for me. They wanted me to be the old head at number seven. Oh, and if I acquitted myself okay, I would be under consideration to lead the team in the near future.

At the time there was an issue over who should be England captain, and a strong feeling that there was a lot on Ian Botham's plate at the age of 24. Although the choice of opposition for a fledgeling captain could hardly have been any stiffer than the West Indies, the selectors handed it to him regardless, while priming some older candidates, like myself, Keith Fletcher and Mike Brearley, via cricket's grapevine, of the opportunity that might present itself at a later date.

For the previous five years I had come to terms with being a former international batsman – that solitary limited-overs match against Pakistan in 1978 being all I had to show for my efforts – but any cricketer with pride never entirely gives up hope of forcing their way back in. So when I was handed my pleasant surprise at the age of 33, I was determined to make a good fist of it.

Alas, my last life as an England player spanned just two days – the length of a weather-interrupted opening match of the Prudential series at Headingley. West Indies had made 198 in their 55 overs on a day of weather interruptions and bad light. We had closed it 35–3 after 23 overs (yes, it was a one-dayer before you re-read the previous sentence) and therefore faced the prospect of knocking the lauded West Indies attack around at more than five runs per over for victory.

Beefy gave it some humpty for half-an-hour but his departure signalled my arrival in the middle with the scoreboard reading 81 for five. Malcolm Marshall was in some other district of Leeds with that red weapon in his hand – I never went that far on my holidays – as I mentally prepared myself for what I was about to receive.

I braced myself as he passed the pile of sawdust, picking up pace as he sped towards me. I've always been a fairly intuitive person and it was around that point that I considered he would not be steaming in like that if he was about to lob me a gentle half-volley. I second-guessed there would be no playing forward at all, and prepared myself for something pitching halfway down.

As this searing thunderbolt homed in at my body, I played what would best be described in an MCC coaching manual as the backward defensive jab. The ball smashed into my right forearm, causing it to swell up something rotten. Despite the pain and embarrassment I actually carried on, although not for long, despite my brother Clive appearing to be doing me a family favour by making an odd change to the attack. On came Gordon Greenidge with his medium pace, but instead of cashing in, I lost the lot, bowled for a single – Greenidge's first and only international wicket, and my final international action.

The injury prevented me playing in the next match at Lord's, you see, but it was not actually the point of impact that caused me the discomfort in the aftermath. Although I had been struck on the right arm, all the pain had transferred through to my left. It was extraordinary. Once the swelling had gone down in my right arm I resumed playing for Lancashire, but this discomfort in the other one would just not go away. Initially, the medics thought I had got tennis elbow and so administered a cortisone injection.

In those days, it was a pretty drastic thing was a cortisone jab, and one that meant you had four blokes on call to hold you down as it went in. It was a real case of 'X' marks the spot, and when this needle hit the spot, I almost hit the roof, I can tell you.

The upshot was that this injection made not a blind bit of difference, so eventually I went for an X-ray which provided a mind-boggling result. It showed that the impact of the blow I had received from Marshall had caused my left arm to jar down quickly, the by-product of which was that a piece of bone had chipped off inside it. In layman's terms the delivery had hit me that hard that the impact reverberated up one arm, through my neck and into my left elbow. It was fractured in a couple of places and led to me having surgery. Not the keyhole variety you may be au fait with in the second decade of the 21st century, mind. Oh no, this was an operation 1980s style. It was like a trip down the high street for the local butcher to have a go with his cleaver, and I have a rather exaggerated scar as a keepsake.

When I went for the injection in Manchester, Mr Glass, the surgeon, prepared me for the worst.

'This will be quite sore,' he warned. 'Should we have a sherry?'

He had one and I had one. It was like something you would see in a 1950s film. As a devotee of BBC's *The Fast Show*, this episode reminded me of one of my favourite sketches involving those old-school doctors Charles and Sheridan.

'Is it time for a brandy, Sheridan?'

'Twenty-nine minutes past six, Charles. No, I don't think so.'

'Oh, is that all it is? Goodness me, no.'

'I've actually come with some rather sad news, Charles. Poor old Bunny Armstrong-Miller popped his clogs last night.'

'Oh, that's terrible news. I could do with a brandy. Is it that time?'

'6.30. Yessss.'

They spend the next two minutes reminiscing about the past 40–45 years. Just about everything they talk about happened 40–45 years ago. It's priceless. What a pairing that Paul Whitehouse and Harry Enfield are. In fact, if you've not seen the two doctors in action put this book down now and go and have a look on YouTube. Simply type in '40–45 years' and hey bingo. That sketch gets me every time.

So my last England days were followed by this comedy injury with serious consequences. I am honest enough to confess that even though I knew what I was about as a captain after five seasons in charge of Lancashire, and was in decent enough touch on the county scene, I should never have been picked again.

No Limits for
My Sky Mates

It is fair to say that Mike Brearley was a captain who knew how to get the very best out of his men and the very best out of his very best man at that. Few international leaders have been able to match Brearley's motivational skills, and when it came to stirring Ian Botham into action he was masterful.

Botham had a wonderful relationship with Australia. He certainly relished playing against them and they seemed to admire the way he played the game too, even when his performances meant their own team would suffer. And in that series of 1981 boy did he make them suffer – even from positions most would have considered impregnable.

Free from the burden of captaincy after Brearley's return from a sabbatical of psycho-analytical studies, Beefy was able to express his extraordinary individual talent without inhibition. There are those of us close to him that would back the theory that his Beefcakes is at his best when he doesn't have to think too much, and with Brearley back to exercise the grey matter from the third Test onwards it sparked an unforgettable fightback.

One down with four to play, the transformation came in the nick of time. Of course, we all know what happened next after England, dismissed for 174, were asked to follow-on in Leeds. The miracle of Headingley remains an iconic landmark for cricket. Years like 1981 are not only remembered in cricket but in the sporting pantheon of both countries – and it is for matches as special as that one.

The appeal of tussling with the old enemy has never dipped from my experience, and so when the intensity is at its height, it engages the interest of the entire nation. Some things have the potential to capture the imagination of the uninitiated, to grab an audience beyond their usual limits, and the Ashes is one of them. Folk tend to go with the flow, and when a groundswell of interest develops, it takes others along who would not normally have any interest whatsoever.

It has certainly stood the test of time because people still go on about 1981 thirty-odd years later. In cricket parlance we still talk about 1932–33 and Bodyline; 1948 and the Invincibles; 1956 and Laker. You get iconic games, iconic series and iconic players. It gets folk knighthoods, does the Ashes, and that perhaps shows how this particular series transcends its sport.

All these other series come and go, they are unbelievably important in their own right, and we have been witness to some great drama in series with South Africa and India, both in winning and losing causes, over the past couple of decades. But there is something about the Ashes that draws out that extra effort, that extra intrigue, that extra appeal. There is no doubt about that through the ages.

Never more so than when Beefy opened his shoulders towards the end of an England second innings disrupted by bad light in Leeds. It was during that stoppage that the famous Ladbrokes odds were flashed up on the electronic scoreboard, encouraging Dennis Lillee and Rod Marsh to have their 500–1 bet on England. You'd be banned for years if you did that kind of thing these days but there was no jiggery-pokery going on; no suggestion that they were doing anything other than busting a gut trying to win.

Those two both liked a punt and they would have thought no further than the fact that Australia had won the game. Well, you couldn't argue with the fact that they'd won 9/10ths of it. Or even 99/100ths of it, if you like. They then came across somebody who objected to their thinking, replied with 'oh no you haven't' and then rolled his sleeves up and got busy changing the situation.

It was one of those games that you are wiser about as a spectator rather than being involved in it. From the sidelines you would probably recognise the fact that Botham was taking the game away from the Australians with his audacious strokeplay. But because Australia were in the heat of the battle, and possessed some quality bowlers, they would have thought: 'So what, he's getting out any minute.'

They would have dismissed the notion that he could carry on playing like that for the length of time that he did, but almost in a flash he set the game up for England. In that situation, self-doubt gnaws at the opposition and somebody with their tail up is not going to die wondering. When playing in that carefree manner players can give their best performance, and that is what IT Botham gave. It was his very best – an unbeaten 149 off just 148 deliveries.

For Australia the momentum had developed too vigorously. How do you stop a landslide? The answer is you can't. So even though that unbridled hitting only provided England with a 129-run lead when they were dismissed for 356 on the fifth morning, the task ahead was too great for the Aussies.

It is incredible to think that England defended such a modest score. A total of 130 is really nothing but it's quite surprising how tricky a target like that can be and how often teams fail to knock it off. When I think back to the characters involved, I can see that dressing room in my mind, even though I wasn't there. The game had been set up, and the England players would have been pawing around like caged lions wanting to get out to give it a go on that final day.

You need leaders in that situation, and I am sure that the lead on this occasion would have come from Bob Willis. You had the studious guy as captain in Brearley, Botham would have been swept along with the anti-establishment nature of his innings, but the one who drove the team on to the finishing line, after Australia sauntered to 56 for one, was Willis.

When you talk about bowling combinations in Ashes history, you have to have Botham and Willis right up there. They were absolutely magnificent together in that 1981 series.

Beefy rightly gets the majority of the praise for the backs-to-the-wall performances, starting at Headingley, but please don't neglect Willis's role in proceedings. I just wish the lads that play for England now would understand just how good a bowler he was. Bob was this massive bloke, as fit as a fiddle with an outrageous mop of hair. Remember he took in excess of 300 Test wickets too, and had serious wheels in his pomp.

He was hampered by injuries and you only have to look at his knees to see how much trouble and pain he went through to perform for his country. Again, it was not this delicate stuff when it came to the surgery being done. None of this arthroscopy business – you know, having a little look into the joint with a micro camera to assess what work was needed – it was simply machete at the ready.

In fact, if he rolled his trouser leg up for you he could hoodwink you into believing that he owed the local heavy mob a few grand. He has these unsightly gashes across both knees that make it look as if someone has hit him with a shovel, and a blunt shovel at that.

If you made a list of the best 10 English fast bowlers of all time Bob would be in it, no question, and the way he bounded in from the Kirkstall Lane End made it look as though someone was pushing him down the hill. There was such momentum about him and such purpose that he was unstoppable. You will not see many better fast-bowling performances than his eight for 43 in that 18-run win anywhere in the world. When he castled Ray Bright with a fast, straight delivery it completed only the second Test win after following on in more than 100 years.

Those of us on the county circuit obviously didn't see all this develop first hand but just as with players in other Ashes years we would follow it on the BBC, via live coverage on either the television or radio, as best we could. In special series you get special performances. Both teams raise their bars and you get the best of the lot soaring above it.

Just like the series two dozen years later, you could not take your eyes off the action for fear of missing something monumental. The great protagonists Beefy and Willis were so up for it, as the very best habitually tend to be for England v Australia clashes, and next up it was a spell of five for one by the former at Edgbaston that was to thrill a typically rowdy crowd and seal another astonishing, against-the-odds victory.

As things turned out, there were only two playing seasons left for me after that memorable year of 1981 and, in the penultimate one, I was involved in an extraordinary County Championship match at Southport which involved quite a turnaround in fortunes for Lancashire to triumph.

Warwickshire had not built quite as impregnable a position as Australia had at Headingley 12 months earlier but they had manoeuvred into a spectacular position from which to lose the game nevertheless.

I have good reason to remember Alvin Kallicharan and Geoff Humpage's record fourth-wicket stand of 470 because I was the bowler that ended it. I have plenty else besides to remember from this game, too, including the fact that shortly after being dismissed in Lancashire's first innings I was employed as a runner for Graeme Fowler, my opening partner, who had pulled a muscle. He went on to score 126 with me doing the donkey work over 22 yards.

Foxy also had a runner in the second innings but this time I was at the other end running my own runs. Warwickshire had declared immediately upon Humpage's dismissal on 523 for four, and we got to within 109 runs of their score when Clive Lloyd halted our efforts and asked Warwickshire to bat for a second time. They did so with disastrous effect on a beautiful morning seemingly made for batting as unheralded West Indian Leslie Leopold McFarlane tore through them with six for 59.

It meant we were left with a couple of sessions to knock off 226, and did so without losing a wicket, Foxy completing a second hundred of the match despite being unable to run and me chipping in with 88 not out at the other end, a score that took my total of first-class runs for the season past 1,000 with one day left in July.

I had been involved in the middle for almost the entire contest – for you statisticians out there I became only the fourth man in Test history to remain on the field for an entire match when I scored an undefeated double hundred against India at Edgbaston in 1974 – and I am not sure you would have forecast a 10-wicket win for Lancashire at any point during the first two-thirds of it. It wasn't quite a Lillee and Marsh 500–1 punt, but you would have got decent odds on a home win.

I would also have told you it was a decent bet that Clive Lloyd would strangle a young Steve O'Shaughnessy during my penultimate season as a professional. Now Clive was a pretty laidback kind of a bloke, and a very respected captain. But I am not sure how laidback he remained after an incident in our home fixture against Northamptonshire in 1982. Graeme Fowler and I were opening the batting as usual and made it to stumps after negotiating a tricky half-hour or so on the second evening with the score 46 without loss.

That start to our second innings had given us a lead in excess of 100 and gave us the chance to push on towards a declaration in a bid to dismiss our opponents and seal victory.

When Foxy was dismissed early next morning, I looked up at the dressing room to see who was coming out to join me in the middle. My eyes told me that Clive was padded up and ready. Indeed he stood up in his laconic manner and grabbed his gloves, only for another figure to appear ahead of him on the steps of the pavilion. Our celebrated West Indies great had been usurped by O'Shaughnessy, who strode onto the grass with a real purpose.

Clive soon followed, which of course caused a major stir amongst the members. It half-crossed my mind that our captain might have been retiring me out. 'Blimey,' I thought, 'I've been scoring quicker than Fowler so far and it's still not good enough.' But no, this wasn't a quest to replace me, merely join me.

However, with the laws of the game stating that once an incoming batsman strays over the boundary edge onto the field of play he is technically 'in', Clive was forced back off.

The usual 'how's it going?' conversation passed between myself and young Shauny but I could not let it pass. I just had to know what on earth had just gone on. 'Why have you come in then, mate? Looked to me like Clive was on his way down the steps behind you. He didn't look best pleased, either.'

'Well, I don't know why,' Shauny countered. 'He told me I was number three last night.'

'Er, you might have been number three last night. But in the morning the nightwatchman goes back to his original position, and you're down on the card at number seven.'

'Well, that's not right in my book. If I was number three last night, I am still number three this morning,' he continued.

'I am not sure our Clive will see it like that,' I continued.

'Oh, eck,' Shauny said. 'Be best to give me wicket away then would it, and let him come in?'

'No, stick around out here as long as you can,' I rejoined. 'Cos looking at that angry face staring out the dressing room window, the longer you stay out here, the better it will be for your health.'

I got a hundred, he got 50, and the next time we saw Clive he was in a far better mood.

Chapter 3

THE HIGH FLIERS

The last four decades of Ashes cricket have produced some wonderful characters and the best of them have had that ability to empty bars. Some of them, like Botham and Flintoff, also possessed thirsts to drink them dry.

More cultured ones have also played their part, none more so from an English perspective, of course, than my Sky Sports colleague David Gower, or Lord Gower as he is otherwise known. His celebrations of victory in 1985 when he was captain would have been with a nice glass or two of Châteauneuf du Pape rather than a pint of best bitter, though.

Beefy tended to raise the eyebrows by doing things like walking to the crease and belting the first and third balls of his innings for six – as he did to Craig McDermott at Edgbaston – yet it was the volume of the good Lord's runs in that series that was instrumental in the 3–1 victory that summer.

Gower was one of the most laconic strokemakers the game has produced, and when he languidly guided the ball through the covers to the boundary, as he did so often that year, it was as though he was ordering a serf to re-locate to another parish. 'Be gone with you,' he might as well have said.

It is perhaps because of Beefy's prominence with the ball – he took 31 wickets in six Tests – that Gower's contributions are forgotten when you recall England claiming the Ashes back four years after that vintage 1981. In all, he scored 732 series runs, and the pair of them played in a third successful series out of four – the 1982–83 trip down under was hit by the rebel tour to South Africa, of course – in 1986–87.

That tour opened to the usual friendly welcome from our Aussie hosts. Those charming immigration officers – where do they dig them up from? – had only just snarled at the collection of passport photos when the recurring question was posed for the first time: 'Mike Gatting, is this the worst England team ever to reach these shores?'

When you break it all down, it's just another way of saying, 'G'day, ya pommie bastards,' I suppose. It's almost as if they like to put you firmly on the back foot as you leave the baggage hall.

Not that the 1986–87 tourists needed an inferiority complex. Our own writers were weighing in too. That was the tour of Martin Johnson's classic line in the *Independent*. 'There are only three things wrong with this England team,' Johnson wrote. 'They can't bat. They can't bowl. And they can't field.'

Results in the warm-up matches did not bode well. Gatt's men lost to Queensland and then very nearly to Western Australia. Typically, it was time for a bit of Beef. Word was that it was a pre-series pep talk from Botham that altered the mood, but he was always better with actions than words and he took things on a stage further when he hit a hundred on the opening day of the series at the Gabba.

England had not won a Test match and had lost eight between these two particular Ashes series of the 1980s, and so it was not going to be a tussle awash with confidence. In fact, Australia were in an even worse predicament in terms of recent results and it was only when the urn had been retained by the tourists that they got themselves on the scoreboard. Victory in the final Test at Sydney – rumour had it that Peter Taylor, their matchwinning spinner there, had been mistakenly selected ahead of namesake Mark Taylor, and could you imagine the furore if that happened now? – was their first in 15 attempts.

It was during this period, however, that Australia dug up some real tough cookies. Men's men like David Boon with his legendary capacity for cans on long-haul flights and big hairy-arsed fast bowlers like Merv Hughes. In contrast, under Gower once more, England were a pretty easy-going bunch, even allowing the Australians to have choice of ball during the 1989 series. They opted for a Duke over the big-seamed Reader but some wise guy suggested they actually used one with a magnet in and that England's batsmen's buckled pads attracted it. Nineteen of Terry Alderman's 41 wickets that year were lbw.

Australian cricket was very serious again, and there was no more Mr Nice Guy from Allan Border from 1989 onwards, that was for sure. He even refused to take a drink with Lord Gower during that tour (until the Ashes were back in his possession, that is). It is the only time I can recall an Australian team snubbing the social aspect of the rivalry. Two more stats from that 4–0 defeat for you before we move on: Boon necked 52 cans of beer on the incoming flight from Sydney, and England went through 29 different players. I challenge you to name them, and give you one to start with in the words of Ted Dexter: 'Who can forget Malcolm Devon?'

This one and the next few series are memorable from an England perspective for what went on off the field rather than on it. In 1990–91 the tourists only hit the heights when the good Lord and John Morris took to the air mid-match against Queensland to get a different view of Robin Smith's hundred. The management took a dim one of their prank, and that trip in the Tiger Moth cost £1,000 more than they had bargained for.

Phil Tufnell was as maverick a figure as Australia's Shane Warne, equally prone to excesses and transgressions. However, he lacked Warne's get-out-of-jail card ability on the field. My experience of Tuffers was that he was a great lad and a grand spinner. But his fielding and batting left him open to ridicule from the most vicious of Australian tongues. Banners on the grassy banks paid homage to the 'Phil Tufnell Fielding Academy' while he even chronicles his own cowardice when he looks back on his tail-end contributions during after-dinner speaking commitments.

According to the man himself, he endured a Perth moment just the same as mine. It was at the WACA and came after an altercation with McDermott when Australia were batting. Having just received a send-off from Tufnell, McDermott's response was clinical.

'You've got to bat on this in a minute – hospital food suit you?'

But the man intent on putting him in Fremantle General Infirmary is Hughes. One delivery has already seared past his chin to trigger the usual spitting and snarling from this moustachioed beast when another rises up and flicks the glove in the course of self-defence. The difference between my retribution and this incident is that the Aussies let off a ferocious appeal, and Tuffers in his own words decided to 'oil the wheels of justice'. Squeals of 'Ow, me thumb!' were enough to tell the umpire his original not out decision needed reviewing. Not sure it made him any friends out on the field, or indeed that his pitiful whining would have gained much sympathy back in the away dressing room either.

Like Tufnell, Warne liked a tab, a tot and other things beginning with 't' besides, but he did special things that earned him immunity. Such as sending down the most talked-about delivery in Test history – his first in a Test against England at Old Trafford in 1993 that started on middle-stump, drifted outside leg and then completed a handbrake turn to clip the top of off-stump. What a way to start your Ashes career. 'If it had been a cheese roll it would never have got past him,' chimed England captain Graham Gooch of the unlucky victim of the ball of the century, Mike Gatting.

No wonder poor Gatt had to double check that this ball had actually bowled him before trudging off. It was hard to recall anything even remotely comparable. How do you combat a bloke if in the back of your mind you know he can produce something like that? I am not sure any cricketer I have seen has managed to have such a psychological effect on opponents as Warne, and it arguably all snowballed from that one sublime delivery. From that moment on, he operated with a Reddy Brek glow.

Chapter 4

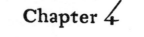

PREPARING FOR BATTLE

I was just a year into my job as England coach when I took on Australia for the first time in that capacity. It was fair to say that my initial summary of England's preparation for international cricket had not been positive due to the relationship of the counties with the national side. Of course, in those days we were no nearer to cracking the age-old chestnut of players rocking up on the eve of a Test match at one end of the country, having left a Championship match hours earlier at the other.

We were not only time deficient, either. Other top countries were beginning to invest in coaching resources, both in terms of staff numbers and technology, and this was a route I believed we needed to go down, too. One aid I persuaded the top brass to invest in was a software system called Statsmaster, a bank of sporting action which had been rolled out for Australian rugby clubs, and latterly developed for cricket.

Footage of previous matches was archived and could be viewed remotely on VHS – all compiled and edited by a university graduate who knew a bit about cricket and his way around technology, combining this knowledge of both as a pioneer amongst the sport's analysts. Imagine a pre-runner to digitally-downloaded recorded footage – reels upon reels of tape, for once not the red variety when it came to cricket administration – a kind of mobile visual library that allowed players to watch opponents they had only previously seen as a name on a scorecard.

It is only a couple of decades ago but there was obviously not the television coverage of cricket around the globe that exists today. Nowadays, guys can watch a mystery spinner like West Indies' Sunil Narine on their mobile phones before breakfast if they want. Back then, we had no such sneak previews of new kids on the block until this clever storage system came onto the market. It was a lot more cumbersome than anything one of our contemporary full-time analysts would use but the principle was the same. Press a few buttons here and tweak a few knobs there and, should you wish to know how many variations a bowler had sent down over the past month, bingo, the evidence was on your television screen.

We used it to build our own packages of where opposition players got out regularly or which were their favourite and most productive shots. The players were right into it as well, particularly the bowlers, who wanted to put what they were seeing into practice. They would carry these tapes around in their kitbags such was the importance to them of knowing how Sachin Tendulkar had been dismissed recently.

So drastically has the game advanced that the analyst now has a major input into a team's tactics, and they have become such experts that they can be in the ear of a captain or a coach, telling them: 'That man's wasted there at gully, you certainly don't need him, he's better off over here on the drive.' In the past, top cricketers would have dismissed advice from people like this, but the evidence is there to be deciphered and these people are leaders in their field. It's their job to find this kind of thing – recurring patterns in matches that the opposition has played. No hunches; there is physical evidence for their claims.

Moneyball, the analytical book on how the Oakland Athletics baseball team's management used statistics to improve their recruitment process, has gone on to be a major influence on sports like cricket too. All kinds of figures now come in and are stacked up to be used to influence your selection process. It means that traditional ways of picking people have been left behind, and some rise from out of left field. For example, when Lancashire signed Wayne White in 2013, *Moneyball* was at the heart of it. Peter Moores stacked up all his figures for what he was looking for in an all-rounder and came up with Wayne as his signing. Numbers told them that pound for pound he was the best option for them. It was not that they had seen something in him when they played against him previously, it was a signing made purely on statistics.

I viewed Statsmaster as an exciting addition after the board authorised its purchase, and also had a proposal passed to invest in digital cameras, to be placed around the net area at practice sessions, so that players could have instant access to their own techniques and acknowledge any faults that might be creeping in to their games. Seeing is believing, as they say, and having that hard evidence to show to players was a godsend for a coach. Tell them 100 times that something is askew and they will hear you but not always listen or be able to fully compute. Let them view what you're talking about with physical information and it is easier to address. These days, analysts can have a montage of a dismissed batsman's faults ready before he's parked his bum in the dressing room to take his pads off.

The counties stopped shy of investing £23,000 a head so that each of the 18 main grounds across the country had use of the library, but it was not long before all the Australian states had them. Thankfully, in England we are no longer sat on our heels when it comes to acquiring the best technology we can get our hands on. Each and every County Championship contest is recorded in some capacity these days, with some clubs having permanent cameras fixed at either end of the ground.

Of course, those cameras rarely film England players because the modern way is for them to feature in a limited capacity. We preserve our best in order that they give their best when it is required. Unfortunately, the system we had in place in the late 1990s hamstrung our challenge. And it was a gargantuan task before we considered how fit for purpose our team was.

The way we began the 1997 series suggested that we might have the personnel to win the Ashes back after a decade of doom. But, typically of the Aussies, they came back strongly in adversity and we nosedived as the volume of matches increased.

People will recall, and history will show those with memories foggier than the Tyne in early December, that we let a 1–0 lead slip. But what it will not show without delving beneath the surface were the performances and results of the county matches that the England players in those days were required to participate in between Tests. We had no real control over who played when or how often outside the six-match series, and it was to be forever thus while the counties held sway.

The traditional county system of players being employed by their clubs meant the only way we would ever get them a rest period was to dispatch chairman of selectors David Graveney cap in hand. It seems ludicrous now, and did to me at the time, that we had to beg to get our premier cricketers the time they needed to recuperate, or even to prepare properly for an international fixture. By the way, we rarely won a battle in this regard because the counties could not see beyond the fact that the individuals were paid to represent their club and that was where their principal loyalty should lie.

To be fair, the players seemed to view things in a similarly parochial way. Now not for one minute am I questioning any of the pride they had in playing for England. During my time as coach to the England team I recognised an immense amount of pride in every single player that walked out onto that field. But there was an inescapable feeling that playing international cricket was like being on a bit of a foreigner. That they had been loaned out from their day job. You only had to wander into our dressing room during a break in play to get that. Within five minutes the telly would be on and the lads would be crowded around flicking through Ceefax. 'How we getting on at Hove?' 'What's happening in the Roses match?' County matches had always been more important than England matches. It was just the way it was.

A shift towards the England team being pre-eminent only took place from the time that Duncan Fletcher took over onwards. The culture change was necessary because, let's face it, it's international cricket that pays the rent. England matches keep the counties going. It was a gradual process to change the thought process and ensure that the county stuff was preparation for England, not the other way round.

It was almost like the dynamic that exists in football where the fortunes of Arsenal, Manchester United, Chelsea and Liverpool seem to be more important to players than England, Scotland, Wales and Ireland. We've seen that development over a couple of decades and we are used to it now. But in rugby union it is quite the opposite and when the Six Nations comes around clubs very much take a back seat and the international weekends are very much the be all and end all of the game.

What a physical state our lot turned up in sometimes. Bowlers would rock up with jelly legs and want to, even need to, rest up rather than practise with their team-mates. It was rather comparable to international football these days in that players, at the time of reporting for duty, would be carrying niggling, albeit minor injuries. Of course, the current system in football is that the medical staff notify their counterparts within their international federation and the player is duly pulled out of the squad immediately or asked to undergo a full medical so that they can be ruled out. Only our players weren't pulled out or ruled out, they turned up and unless they were properly crocked would play.

Let's face it: firstly, they'd worked all their careers to play for England and weren't likely to give up their place lightly once established. Secondly, they were accustomed to the expectation of performing on the domestic circuit all week before joining up. It might have got us no nearer to that all-powerful Aussie outfit, but I bet some of the players now look back and wish they had been given the chance to have a go as fit as fleas rather than as knackered as nags.

The life of an England cricketer was so different then because of the dual demands. Central contracts have simplified things so much, to the point that I am sure that directors of cricket regard getting an established England player back these days as a real bonus. It is a contrast to when they used to see it as their right, which to all intents and purposes it was, because they were the ones coughing up the cash.

Nowadays, primary direction comes from Lord's, and if Andy Flower or Ashley Giles requires a player to report somewhere between series then off you go. Rather like other lines of work, you are answerable to your line manager, so if they tell you to turn up at 6am passport in hand at Gatwick for a flight to Germany it's a case of 'Ja, Herr. Drei säcke voll, Herr.'

Contrast that to when I was coach and arranged a team-bonding camp on the eve of the 1997 season. The purpose of this three-day get-together at the NatWest training premises in Oxfordshire was to foster spirit and create a comfortable environment for individuals to be able to express themselves. My concern was that whereas other teams like Australia and South Africa appeared tight units, we were thrown together from all over the shop. It felt like we were cricket's equivalent of the Barbarians at times – a feeling fuelled by the lads all wearing odd socks. We would then be sent into a lengthy Test series or dispatched on an overseas tour. How were we meant to feel as though we were all part of the same thing?

This short time away I had organised was designed to reinforce a culture of togetherness. It wasn't going to add any extra runs or wickets to our scorecards but it might help create a sense of united purpose to collect them.

The subsequent reaction of Graham Thorpe to this directive was no so much an indictment of him but the backdrop we were working against. He refused to attend, informing us that the time before the season began was his time, a time to rest with his family, and that he would resume all cricket-related activity when matches were on the horizon. A forceful phone call from the England and Wales Cricket Board's chief executive Tim Lamb resulted in his attendance, but you could understand the pressure these players were under at home and the sacrifices they made in cricket terms were two-fold as well.

I arranged for the squad to be addressed by Frank Dick, the former British Athletics Federation's director of coaching, who was carving out a reputation as a motivational speaker. He challenged our team to think about their own personal landscapes. Were they mountains or valleys? The first group, as the image suggested, were the ones striving upwards and achieving, while the latter lot were far more shallow, willing to dip their levels and coast at times for an easier life. He spoke about the key ingredients in good team ethic – trusting one another, and being defined by a collective attitude. Being stimulated to think about themselves in such positive terms and aspire to be achievers rather than slackers had a pleasing effect on the group.

This venture was undoubtedly a success. Our mistake, however, was to fill diaries with other 'new thinking' seminars and team-bonding challenges. Doing more of the same in every international break was not conducive to improving the atmosphere. Once in a blue moon they provided a jolt, but doing several a year diluted their impact considerably.

You will no doubt be aware that I was big into motivation through other mediums, and it's right that I encouraged the players to listen to and even sing 'Jerusalem' before we went out on the field. For Robert Croft, I secured a copy of 'Land of My Fathers'. There's nothing wrong with a bit of nationalistic pride as you prepare to do battle with the old foe.

They say a good percentage of sport is played in the mind and so I also made it my business to get those minds engaged more positively ahead of these meetings with Australia. Simple stuff it was, really. Like making a video montage of a player at his best, set to his favourite tune. Oasis more often than not, or a bit of U2, especially if Alan Mullally had had any influence.

Sky Sports could rustle these up in five minutes flat with all that info the lads give these days on their favourite artists, films and football teams, for on-screen graphics. But I diligently got them made up to the feelgood tunes, to play to the squad alongside blooper clips from the opposition. The Australian cricket team. Best in the world? They didn't look so good after a bit of Bumble editing, I'll tell you!

Sometimes opponents can be placed on too high a pedestal and this was one way to expose their humanity. We all make mistakes, don't we? Here was the proof.

Making your own players feel better about themselves and less intimidated by the 'oppo' equated to a few grand well spent in my opinion. But like other ventures to improve the atmosphere around the England team, it got kyboshed after just a couple of series. Trying to justify expenditure to counties that were driven by their own agendas was like pulling teeth, to be honest.

But there was an air of confidence about us when the Australians arrived that summer, and by the end of the Texaco Trophy that preceded the Test series, a fervour swept through the nation. We simply trounced them 3–0 in those one-dayers. Yes, three games to England, nil to Australia. It took some believing at the time that these all-powerful Australians could be whitewashed by anyone in either Test or limited-overs cricket.

A real energy ran through our team in that short series, exemplified by the way our lads threw themselves about in the field. The standard was back on a par with its highest point in my tenure – we had been very good during my first summer of 1996 when Chris Lewis, Nasser Hussain and Nick Knight tore in on singles and flung themselves full length this way and t'other – and a mobile team is always pleasing on the eye for a coach. We were exciting to watch, and in the middle match of the series, at the Oval, four of the six wickets we claimed were run-outs.

The inclusion of the Hollioake brothers really energised us during those three 50-over games. Adam took a couple of wickets and then raced us to our target with an unbeaten 60-odd in the first of the three, at Headingley, while Ben's precocious talent was first witnessed on the international stage a few days later, with the series already settled, at Lord's. There was a lot of conjecture about where young Ben would bat. Were we going to slip him down the order, hide him a bit, break him in gently? This was the gist of what we were being asked at press conferences in the pre-match build-up. Were we hell. He had been picked for his ability to bat at number three, and number three was where he would bat. How refreshing it was to witness a young England player display no fear and express himself, driving Glenn McGrath gracefully through mid-off and mid-on, flicking him elegantly for fours off his hip and hoisting Warne over deep midwicket for six. People who witnessed his 63 off 48 balls will not have forgotten it in a hurry.

Ben Hollioake was a really exciting player. Here was a true athlete, a talented sportsman, who had chosen cricket for his career path. He was only young, but he used that to his advantage in that debut match. There was not an inkling of him being afraid of failure. One of the reasons we liked him, and believed he was ready, was because he played on instinct, and there was no way we were going to slot him in at number eight, hide him away and potentially let him do nothing. Ben had a raw talent and we just wanted him to express that. Sure, there were a lot of rough edges noticeable in him, but oh boy what an athlete. What a flaming fielder he was. He was a great mover, with a great throw from the deep and he would have been a really special player. His bowling was a very useful work in progress too.

What a shame he was unable to fulfil that potential on the world stage. Could you imagine a side with him, Andrew Flintoff and Marcus Trescothick in their prime? We would have had the nucleus of a bloody good side. They weren't finished articles by any stretches of the imagination as we approached the Millennium but, given some time to develop, I believe that trio would have been the cornerstone of an England team with the ability to win a global trophy in limited-overs cricket.

If they had kept playing, and Ben had developed at the same kind of rate that Andrew and Marcus did, then can you imagine what an impact they would have made on our one-day cricket? There would have been dips in form for all of them because that is what happens when England Under-19 players of great ability get fast-tracked to full internationals before they have completed their full county cricket development, but if lads like that have the talent they tend to observe and feed off the better players they mix with, and England were probably one classy all-rounder away from being a really decent 50-over proposition.

John Abrahams, my former Lancashire team-mate, was coach and he would earmark a number of the players as potential full internationals. Marcus Trescothick's time would come slightly later but he had been identified as a really special talent since the days of England Under-14s, so it was almost inevitable that he would rise to the top once more. At that stage it had just been that things had not really worked out for him.

When he went back from the international stuff to Somerset, he found it difficult to secure a place in their first team, and finished up somewhere around seven or eight, and played as an all-rounder, when he did get in. The problem that he ran into was that he was away with England Under-

19s a lot and he was only a teenager, and the club needed a permanent and established opening batsman. They had just taken Peter Bowler, the experienced opening batsman, from Derbyshire, and also had Mark Lathwell around, which meant that Marcus did not push on as he might have done at that time. It was an unusual situation, I guess, because he was already on our radar but he was not playing first-class cricket like the other boys were.

I am sure that would be different now with the new dynamic that exists between the international and domestic game. A request from central office for a certain player to feature more prominently or regularly in a county team, while not guaranteed, would be much more likely to be accommodated than it was in our regime. Back in the 1990s, chairman of selectors David Graveney had to tiptoe around the counties, asking as politely as he could whether they would mind awfully if this or that happened, which normally drew a response that included the words sod and off. Counties held all the cards in those days as the ones that held the players' contracts, whereas now there is much more of a general understanding that England matters come first. After all, it is the money from the very top that underpins everything else.

Players are managed pretty well under the central contract mechanism, and my prediction is that cricket will get more and more like football where the manager dictates that star players are preserved for the most meaningful matches. I read an unbelievable quote following the 2012–13 Test match between India and England at Ahmedabad when the England coach Andy Flower fronted up and admitted to making a mistake.

'I've picked the wrong team,' he said.

I was flabbergasted by that because although I might be in Michael Atherton or Alec Stewart's ears offering my input it was they who picked the team, not me. There was no way I would be allowed to pick it. Could you imagine if I went to Atherton and told him: 'This is the XI you'll have out there today, lad.' Even if he used the politest language possible, the sentiment of his response would be something akin to 'Hey, pal, you can do one.'

We're talking about a completely different, completely new era, and a miles better era in my opinion. Graveney was, for me, a fabulous chairman of selectors, providing the squad of players that we wanted as captain and coach. But he just lacked the clout that his job required. It was only post-2000 and the handing out of the first batch of contracts that the chairman of selectors got some of the gravitas the role should carry. You also have to consider with Grav that it was only in his later years that he got anything more than expenses. His successor Geoff Miller is contracted in a full-time job. In my opinion, it always has been a full-time job, it just wasn't recognised as so when it came to things like annual salary.

False Dawn

There is seldom a correlation between what happens in one-dayers and Test matches but beating Australia in any format provided first-hand proof that they were not impregnable in that summer of 1997. Around that time, the late Bob

Woolmer, who was coach of South Africa, and I exchanged views on a number of subjects. Bob was keen on the Statsmaster programme for a start but typically of him he wanted it to do that little bit extra – his mind was always working around the minutiae of one subject or another – and attempted to design his own version. He later invested in the ready-made one.

In the course of our chats, however, Bob was fairly revealing. South Africa had just lost a home series to the Australians, and one of the surprising observations he made was that the winners of that series were more agile in the field and fitter than his team, one that prided itself on such areas. Australia's players were already in the practice of exercising shortly after being dismissed, or at the start of a day's play when they might not be expected to bat for several hours, lifting small weights in the gym rather than sitting around passing time in the dressing room. At the end of play it had become common practice to slip into warm-down sessions, or have a swim back at the team hotel. For cricketers developed in the northern leagues of England, the words warm and down were only used to describe the temperature of the post-match ale and the direction in which it was headed.

Nevertheless, Bob believed Australia could be beaten, and in the first Test at Edgbaston our team went about trying to prove him right. Birmingham is a great place to start a series, because of the crowd for one – they get quite partisan in the Eric Hollies Stand, so when you get on top the whole place feels like it's rocking, and I have always been one for home teams using whatever advantage they can get.

The conditions are also challenging for batsmen from overseas even if they have been in the country for a while because the ball tends to nip around first thing in the morning. One of the strengths of that particular England side was the new-ball skill of Darren Gough and Andrew Caddick. The reintroduction of Devon Malcolm for the first time in 18 months, following exclusion in the aftermath of an incident in South Africa under Ray Illingworth's watch, provided raw pace to boot.

It would be the other two that got the plaudits in future years as Duncan Fletcher began to turn things around at Test level but Devon was a seriously good fast bowler. He was the brunt of many people's gags because of his poor eyesight and jam jar glasses, but boy could he get the ball down the other end. In terms of sheer speed he was as quick as anything, and pace has always troubled even the best batsmen. As well as being an under-rated performer, I considered him to be an extremely good bloke.

Truly, we couldn't have started any better than we did at Edgbaston that morning. It went like a dream – talk about pinching yourself. The ball swung and Goughie played a major part in exploiting that, leading an attack that claimed eight Australian wickets before lunch. When things are in your favour, you need the bowlers to make the most of the atmospheric assistance. Inevitably, everyone expected Australia to come back twice as hard again after the interval and although they did fight in their stereotypical manner, doubling their score of 54 for the final two wickets, the positivity just snowballed. Courtesy of a sensational near-triple century partnership between Hussain and Graham Thorpe we were on course for a win inside four days.

Even though the dire situation shook the hopelessly-out-of-nick Mark Taylor into an innings of great character, a first Test hundred in more than 18 months – getting Australia to 327 for one, within 33 runs of us – ultimately was all in vain. The public reaction to us chasing down our modest fourth-innings target on the penultimate evening was fervent. Folk poured onto the outfield smiling from ear to ear.

If only it had been a one-Test series. Only joking …

But what happened next did have a certain inevitability about it, as Australia grabbed us by the short and curlies (sorry, I've lost my voice again … painful memories).

Glenn McGrath had been a notch or two down from his best in that opening match of six but because he was so consistent – chiefly down to his no-nonsense, simple, repetitive action – it was obvious he would not be down for long. During my time as England coach there was not a pace bowler that provided more furrowed brows or frustrated chunterings than McGrath. He was not the quickest nor the meanest, didn't jag it miles or swing it lavishly, but he was quick enough, aggressive enough and did enough to be in with a chance every ball. You simply couldn't take liberties with him because he was always at you, there or thereabouts, asking questions. Such a bowler preys on errors of judgement or loss of concentration by his opponents.

McGrath was as meek as anything off the field but get him across the boundary rope and it was the equivalent of giving Dr Jekyll a pint of his famous tipple. There have been plenty of Mr Hyde wannabes amongst our international fast-bowling brethren but this guy was the real deal. This mild-mannered chap suddenly became abusive, and close to losing it completely on occasion, once he got that new cherry in his hand. There have been few who have worn the Baggy Green to match his competitive streak – and that's saying something. It was incredible how often he courted conduct violations.

McGrath routed us in the next match at Lord's with eight for 38, but the rain-delayed start meant that it was not until the third day that our innings of 77 was completed. It did not break the team's spirit, however, and with the pitch becalmed, our top six, faced with a 136-run deficit, comfortably closed out the draw.

However, our optimism was swiftly deflated over the course of the next three matches – a trio of resounding defeats. Rarely can a Test series have been so spectacularly turned on its head as this one was. It seems lunacy to suggest that things might have ended up differently. BUT … if the completion of the turnaround hinged on one moment it was the one that came in the middle match in Leeds when we had Australia 50 for four. It was at that point in time that debutant Mike Smith was denied a maiden Test wicket by an uncharacteristic error from Graham Thorpe at slip. Matthew Elliott only had 29 to his name at the time, and his dismissal would have meant that half the Australians were back in the pavilion with 123 runs still required to get into credit. Elliott alone added a further 170.

Smith, Dewsbury-born but a prolific left-armer in county cricket with Gloucestershire, had been selected not as some ungenerous scribes suggested because of any selectorial bias from David Graveney, the West Country man heading our panel, but for his ability to move the ball through the air. He had taken 10 wickets in a recent County Championship match at Headingley, and was a decent horses-for-courses pick. Michael Atherton, as captain, was dubious whether he possessed a plan B and feared that his lack of height might make him hittable if the ball didn't swing, but all reports suggested that he got it to go regularly, and we even entrusted him to choose our ball from the box presented to us by match referee Cammie Smith.

I couldn't tell you why – unless perhaps the muggaticity reading was low in that pocket of West Yorkshire, or the air was distinctly unclammy at the Kirkstall Road End of Headingley – but it just did not get off the straight over those couple of days in July 1997, so the international wicket haul of AM Smith of Glos remained at zero, and we were all left to reflect on what might have been had Thorpe held on in the grabbers.

We did beat Australia again that series, in the final match at the Oval, and it has infuriated me since to hear people say that it was a dead rubber and that our opposition weren't trying their damnedest. Nonsense, of course they were. It was true that they had lost some other end-of-series games much to the ire of their coach Geoff Marsh. But one thing we all know about Australians is that they hate losing to the Poms, and equally we hate them beating us.

In previous series, England teams had lost 4–0 and not looked like winning games. Yet this time we had not only got one on the scoreboard but beaten them twice. A series defeat meant it did not count for a great deal in the overall scheme of things, but it was a great source of pride to have defeated the best Test team around on two occasions. Not enough credit was given for that, in my opinion. Having battled hard to beat Australia all summer, it was disappointing to hear people suggest that the result in the final match was only secured because our opposition had tossed it off, given things away because the series was over.

It just so happened that we caught them on an Oval pitch that suited us – a pitch that suited bowlers like Andy Caddick and Phil Tufnell. It was particularly pleasing to see Phil do well because Mark Waugh had done an interview in the build-up to that Test match in which he questioned his ability. He spoke too soon as it happened because Tuffers got him out with two absolute beauties.

It was a low-scoring match, and one for which, surprisingly, we did have ample time to prepare. The scheduling of the domestic fixtures meant we were able to get together in plenty of time. Intriguingly, the match itself only spanned three days but provided the kind of entertainment typical when ball dominates bat.

And the identity of the bowlers that dominated it for us might have surprised. In all Tufnell and Caddick shared 19 of the 20 wickets to fall, with Tufnell claiming match figures of 11 for 93. Yet when Australia, who took a 40-run lead on first innings, dismissed us for a second time for just 163, there would have been few in a packed Saturday crowd who would have given us a ballroom dance.

However, the pitch was crumbly and the crowd seemed to sense that they could play their part if they got behind the team. They literally roared Devon Malcolm into the crease and his early scalping of Matthew Elliott was just the start we required, catalysing Australia's downfall. There is something about chasing small targets that plays tricks on batting teams

– for some reason batsmen start doing things they would never usually dream of, or alternatively they stop playing their shots altogether.

Our matchwinners Tufnell and Caddick – Graham Thorpe and Mark Ramprakash had earlier given us an outside sniff with their work with the bat – were allegedly fragile characters but when in the mood they both became world beaters. With confidence up, impishly skipping into his delivery stride, Tufnell got plenty of revolutions on the ball, and this was one such occasion – the left-arm spinner that fizzed the ball onto the deteriorated surface rather than rolling it into the footmarks from over the wicket as was his wont when things weren't going so well. Caddick had lots of attributes comparable to Glenn McGrath, and sometimes produced performances to match. Overall, though, he lacked the consistency to sustain it.

The feeling when you dismiss an opposition team to win a match when you are defending only a 124-run target is euphoric, and the dressing room celebration reflected that. Australia had departed these shores once more with the little urn in their possession but the partying was boisterous. All apart from Tufnell, who ditched his usual jack-the-lad persona for an extended period of reflection, sat, towel draped over his bowed head, on a locker in the dressing room.

Earlier that summer on the back of those three Texaco Trophy wins, there was a real feeling of 'here we go'. But we had to walk before we could run and Shane Warne eventually had his say as he always seemed to in the end. He bowled fantastically well, as was his wont in English conditions, and our lads just couldn't handle him, as simple as that.

Warne didn't bowl many googlies that summer, nor during his career for that matter. Other bowlers had much better wrong 'uns and used them much more regularly. With Warne you might get one, maybe a couple a day tops. In fact, one of the greatest tributes you could pay my old mate is that batsmen knew exactly what he was about to send down – the cheeky chap would even let his opponents know his intentions on occasion and do exactly what he advised them he was going to – yet they still couldn't handle him.

He relied on a great flipper, superb control and an ability to really rip the regulation leg-spinner. To me, the latter quality was key. Warne was different to other leg-spinners because of the sheer number of revolutions he managed to get on the ball, and the by-product of giving it such a fizz was that deliveries would drift into you before pitching and then spin away. For a batsman, it was like facing an inswing bowler at times. The ball literally fizzed out of the hand and you could hear the seam whirring on its way down the pitch. Other nice leg-spinners who made it to the top level didn't have strength of wrist, and that is what made bowlers like Warne stand out. Others could roll the ball out nicely and get a little bit of spin but they simply could not create that same shape before it spat away. To be able to do that is just a God-given talent. You can't possibly teach someone to get that many revs on a ball on a journey of 22 yards. You can either do it or you can't.

Someone else that is able to get that ball going more than other practitioners of his art is Graeme Swann. Again, somehow when that ball comes out of his hand it's fizzing. Fizz always promotes dip in flight and that is what gets the best batsman out, as we see time and again in modern cricket.

Pleasant orthodox spinners, who almost offer the ball out of their hands rather than rip it, can do a job but they aren't threatening you. They might tie you down, and stop you scoring for a while, but they haven't got the weaponry of these special guys. A combination of spin, dip and bounce is what accounts for the very best players.

Although we talked about the need for an aggressive game plan to try to throw Warne, that is easier said than done when you have a once in a lifetime bowler to contend with, and we didn't have anyone with the confidence to step up and enact it. There was certainly no KP-like player to be able to take the game to him. I can recall Nasser Hussain trying to be proactive once, coming down the pitch to hit over the top and getting stumped. But that was an isolated dismissal because no-one else had the confidence to go head-on with one of the world's greatest ever bowlers.

Throughout the late 1990s, whenever we talked about balancing sides, we came back to a belief that we needed a five-man attack. But what we saw with Warne, and more recently with Swann for England, was that with a world-class spinner in your team you needed only four. If you work on the theory of having to bowl 90 overs in the day pretty much worldwide, you simply don't need five.

Your quality spinner bowls at one end for large chunks of the day while your three seamers are rotated from the other. With a guaranteed 25–30 overs of quality from your proven slow bowler, it is not such a burden for your other three and before you know it you have your full allocation of 90.

That has become the norm now but if the authorities were to ever look at rejigging Test cricket – to reduce it to four days of 105 overs a day, say – and force teams to adhere to faster over-rates, the whole strategy would have to change. You couldn't get away with four then, you would have to have another bowler. As things stand, the four bowlers selection route with the proven spinner amongst them allows you to lengthen your batting order, and to get in the 90 when you are only having to bowl 15 overs an hour maximum. When I was a county captain 30-odd years ago, we were penalised if we operated at under 18.

In terms of the make-up of the England team during my tenure, when Michael Atherton was captain he always wanted five bowlers to give himself plenty of options in the hunt for 20 wickets, and if you consider that Alec Stewart was a world class all-rounder as a wicketkeeper–batsman it was actually plausible to pick five. Then, when Alec took over the captaincy himself we had a couple of outstanding young all-rounders bursting onto the scene in Flintoff and Ben Hollioake.

I found that New Zealand was an interesting and challenging place to go and play a Test series, one that demanded the well-rounded attack of which Athers was so fond. Many of New Zealand's pitches have been drop-in ones over the years, inserted at grounds that are primarily designed for rugby union. These pitches tend to start damp in the morning session and dry out in the sun throughout the day. So you would want at least three seamers to rotate while the ball was jagging around early doors. Equally, after a couple of days baking in the sun, you would want a couple of decent twirlers to operate in tandem once the pitches naturally dried out. Once the moisture was sucked out in the heat, the pitches tend to spin, so Atherton's strategy of fielding a balanced attack of sufficient depth paid dividends. When you consider that two of the five bowlers would perhaps be Robert Croft, Craig White and/or Dominic Cork, all of whom could justifiably be termed all-rounders, the team had a good look about it.

Lessons in Leg-Spin

The subject of spin bowling occupied our thoughts in advance of the 1998–99 series down under. Which slow bowlers would we be taking with us? And how were we going to combat the threat posed by the inimitable Shane Warne?

Just 12 months earlier Phil Tufnell had contributed to England winning two Tests in an Ashes series for the first time in a dozen years with those Oval match figures of 11 for 93, but he was not selected for the tour down under, partly due to the change of captaincy.

Michael Atherton had always championed Tufnell despite his occasional off-field misdemeanours but his successor Alec Stewart did not push for his inclusion in the same way, and so we set off to Australia with a party that included two off-spinners, Robert Croft and Peter Such. The intention was for Croft to begin the tour as the first-choice tweaker and, if required, Such provided an experienced back-up. As it happened, Croft lost his place after just one under-par match whereas Such took his opportunity in much the way you would anticipate from a dedicated professional.

A shoulder injury had wrecked Warne's year, and indeed led to him missing the Test series in Pakistan, and his impending return loomed over us from the start of the tour. But even without Warne the Australians had much the more potent spin attack. Stuart MacGill would have been a shoo-in selection in most other eras but with Warne around had to be content with the second of the fiddles. For this particular series, however, he was the main man, and even when his rival returned, remained their primary leg spinner. It was his performances during this series that persuaded me unmistakably that this fantastic bowler would have doubled his Test wicket tally in another age.

For our part, our two off-spinner policy was made with Alan Mullally's size 15 boots in mind, the theory being that they would make use of the rough caused by the left-arm paceman's follow-through. But it is fair to say it did not work anywhere near as effectively as we had envisaged. Although big Al Mullall did okay and Such performed admirably enough to take five wickets in the second innings at Sydney, it was the Australians, through that excellent eccentric MacGill, who carried the greater threat.

We had travelled to Australia attempting to be as prepared as possible for facing high-quality wrist-spin. Peter Philpott was a man I knew well from my time in the Lancashire League and I considered him to be an expert coach on the art. To that end he had already lectured on the subject of leg-spin to emerging players in the ECB's development of excellence programme. He was in his sixties and possessed a rather impressive coaching CV, including coaching Warne and MacGill, the men we were scheduled to face.

I viewed preparation as key to the challenge of facing it in the middle, and so Peter's recruitment did not represent the full extent of our hired help. While Peter talked theory – the idea was to get the players to understand the thought processes behind it, and what the bowler was trying to do – Abdul Qadir, the former Pakistan leg-spinner, was drafted in to add some practical experiments.

Abdul could still operate to a good standard, and was therefore able to take things to a different level by bowling at our players in the nets. By that stage of his career, he couldn't run, and I hate to think what he would have been like in the field, but when it came to bowling he was still a genius. However, it remained slightly difficult to get meaningful, match-type preparation because in Australia all your net sessions are open affairs. You can't actually arrange private nets, and with so many members of the public watching, the players found practising against him restrictive. We just had to do our best in the limited time and limited capacity we had him for.

What Abdul did was to deconstruct leg-spin by bowling within the parameters of his action at reduced speed. By slowing the whole process down, so that he went through it at only half or quarter pace, it was like facing a bowler in slow motion until he reached the point of delivery. That effectively let our batsmen see how the hand, the fingers and the wrist worked in unison. Once the batsman got used to seeing the ball come out slowly, Abdul would build up his pace until it eventually came out properly. A top leg-spinner like him was able to disguise his intricacies at full speed, and for him to strip everything back down enabled our guys to train their brains and recognise what he was doing once he quickened back up.

Peter's work was more educational and revealed some intriguing information on Warne. We looked at his record in detail, and the research showed that those who had succeeded in duels with him tended to be those willing to take the game to him. It probably helped that the group in question were the best players going around at the time, with Brian Lara and Sachin Tendulkar the two most obvious examples.

Philpott simplified Warne's strategy, and made us see it from the bowler's perspective. It was all fairly straightforward, really. Warne's primary objective would be to go for two runs an over, which provided his captain with control and allowed pressure to come into the batsmen's thinking. If he succeeded in this target of limiting runs, the opposition were in his trap even without him taking a wicket early in his spell. Because if you sat in against him and scored at that rate, he would get you out eventually anyway, or McGrath might from the other end. Peter insisted that we needed to find ways of playing where we could score against him at a more reasonable rate.

Unfortunately, we didn't manage that during my time as coach but there was an England batsman who has prospered since – Kevin Pietersen. Most strikingly during his 158 at the Oval in 2005. Never in the time I have been coaching, or watching Warne admiringly from the commentary box, have I seen anybody take him apart like that. In Warne's mind – always awash with confidence – the KP manifesto to attack would have been okay because it increased the likelihood of triggering an error, and therefore a wicket. An aggressive bowler like Warne would have encouraged his attempts to keep hitting him across the line to deep midwicket.

Our employment of Qadir even on the most casual of terms was something of an unusual move. It was far from common practice for English cricket to get people in from other countries in those days. But I knew he was in Melbourne and he was delighted to come and aid our cause. We gave him a bob or two for doing it, and he had the enthusiasm to run in and bowl all day. In terms of attitude, he was just like Mushtaq Ahmed, or Mr Mushy as he is affectionately known within the current England set-up; full to the brim with love for the game.

We also had a young Chris Schofield out there too. Chris was someone I knew of from Lancashire, someone who as a teenager at the end of the previous season had taken eight wickets in a County Championship win over Gloucestershire. He was out in Australia on a scholarship, so we dragged him around the country with us whenever we could, both for his own development and as an aid to our batsmen in net practices.

As things transpired all this preparation before the series and between Test matches was not for Warne – well four-fifths of it was not anyway – but MacGill. So good a bowler was this New South Welshman that he actually had a better strike rate than Warne but they were never going to play two leg-spinners on a regular basis, and Warne was the very best of his breed, as well as being a fantastic slip fielder and more than useful tail-end batsman in his pomp. Unless it was absolutely ragging square, they would only ever pick one and let's face it: why would you need two when you have Warne?

He was far from your run-of-the-mill Test player was MacGill: a very clever chap whom you might readily call a character of difference within that Australian camp. Both highly intelligent and highly strung, players like him don't always fit into dressing room environments comfortably but when he was on the field, gee could he bowl.

In fact, after we dragged it back to 2–1 at Melbourne with a match to go, MacGill was at the centre of Australia's counter-punch in Sydney. They got us on a turning pitch there and it is now long enough ago for me to pose you a tricky quiz question. I will remind you that Warne came back from injury but can you recall who opened the bowling for Australia in this series-defining match? Before you start thinking about putting your answer on a postcard, I'll tell you. It was Colin 'Funky' Miller, who began with a few seamers before turning his hand to off-spin. It was only very late in his career that he started to send down a few spinners for Tasmania, and did so with incredible success, breaking Chuck Fleetwood-Smith's 63-year-old Sheffield Shield record of 60 wickets in a season, and raising the bar to 67, the previous winter.

The Sydney Cricket Ground had a reputation for producing spinning pitches, and Graham Gooch, our tour manager, walked out the day before the match to view the one they had designated for us to play on. His assessment was that it was 'filthy'. I am not sure the last time Australia had gone into a match with three spinners in their line-up but that is how they opted to go and we could now see why. Their plan was fairly transparent. Miller would send down seam-up stuff when the ball was new and then revert to his off-spinners later in the innings when it became softer.

With the conditions we were confronted with, we discussed playing more than one frontline spinner ourselves, and it is absolutely true that I proposed that we should pick Schofield. As soon as I saw the surface for myself, it struck me as the thing to do. The selectors would not have been expecting a raging turner like this when the original tour selections were made months earlier, and now found ourselves with all our eggs in one basket so to speak. I am not sure we envisaged ever playing both Croft and Such in the same match but that was our way forward now unless we did something left-field. I knew that getting Schofield in would give us some variation – the off-spinner turning the ball into the right-hander and Schofield turning it away. But I just couldn't get the idea past first base. Although he was effectively part of our tour group, he was still viewed as a young kid, and Alec Stewart just wouldn't entertain the idea. In the end, we included Ashley Giles, who had flown out ostensibly as a one-day squad player, in our matchday 12 but the final vote actually went to Alex Tudor.

So it was that we went in with just Such to bowl spin while Australia had Warne and MacGill paired together for the first time in that match. That meant they were always going to dominate us on a pitch that turned.

Australia also had a decent battery of quality fast bowlers in Glenn McGrath, Damien Fleming, Jason Gillespie and Paul Reiffel but our guys out-bowled them at the MCG in the penultimate Test on what I would say was an English-type track. There were some really fine performances, none better than that of Dean Headley on the final day, and victory in Melbourne had kept our hopes of sharing the series alive.

Although the Ashes prize had gone, it is fair to say that the prospect of a 2–2 scoreline meant we were still buzzing as a squad heading into the fifth Test. But our chance of securing it went in the second innings when Simon Taufel – the recently retired and very well-respected umpire, perhaps the best we had ever seen – made a bit of a bodge of a decision as a young third official.

Australia were 60 for two in their second innings when Michael Slater was run out going for two by a direct hit at the bowler's end from Headley. It was plain to see that he was a couple of inches short but when umpire Steve Dunne turned to television adjudication for the decision, instead of confirming that Slater was out, Taufel pressed the wrong button and confirmed he was in.

Having conceded a 102-run deficit on first innings, we would have been right back in the game. Particularly when you consider that Slater went on to get 123 of Australia's 184 all out. His strokeplay simply took the game away from us. Am I bitter? No! Absolutely not. It's not something that I ever think about. Honest!

With all those ifs and buts, and my Auntie having a fine pair of conkers, we could have drawn that series 2–2. However, we lost that final match by 98 runs, a relatively small margin and one that shows you that we had a really good team. We matched that crackerjack Aussie XI for sizeable periods of that series.

I have never changed my belief that England possessed some very fine players in the late 1990s, some guys that took on the world's best and excelled, but to their detriment they were always compared to their Ashes counterparts. The likes of Michael Atherton and Alec Stewart were subsequently left to bemoan the fact that they were up against that sensational

Australia team, one that was justifiably dubbed great. They were absolutely fantastic from start to finish, from one to 11.

At the core of their side were the Waughs, and as twins went they could hardly have been more different, certainly when you watched the way they played the game. Mark Waugh was one of the easiest players on the eye Test cricket has ever seen, with his graceful drives and flicks off the pads. Contrast that to his senior sibling Steve, who was possibly the steeliest cricketer of his generation, or any other for that matter, and was not interested in being aesthetically pleasing. For him it was all about getting the job done. A Cuprinol cricketer whose endgame was to do exactly what it said on the tin. Just looking at him, you knew that inside all he wanted to do was win.

Waugh was surrounded by tough guys, too. In later years, through my role as a commentator I got to know Mark Waugh quite well, and I would describe him as a real tough cookie himself. In the Waugh family, it was Steve who was seen as the abrasive one, the one that you wouldn't mess with, but Mark is also hellish hard. Mark always appeared more laid back and you had to dig deeper to find a lighter side with Steve. Brothers they may have been, but as characters they couldn't have been more different. Mark Waugh always enjoyed himself, got himself out and about, liked the social side, a bet on the horses, and it was perhaps reflected in the debonair manner in which he played when holding a cricket bat. Supremely gifted, he didn't seem to mind taking a chance or two. In contrast, Steve was calculated, serious and flinty. Steve was perhaps best described as beautifully ugly, a player you had to really prise away from the crease. He made you think that you literally had to knock him over to get his wicket. He would give you nothing. They possessed totally different techniques and totally different batting styles but they were equally intriguing to watch.

Steve was an utterly uncompromising character, who you felt would do anything within the spirit of the game to come out on top. As a captain, he was utterly uncompromising too. He played it as tough as anyone that I ever saw but neither would he take any shit occurring on the field unnecessarily. And that went for his own team as well as the opposition.

One of my memories of the 2001 Ashes series is of a young Matthew Hayden sledging – or should I say attempting to sledge – a couple of the England batsmen. Hayden was spouting off from his fielding position at gully. But there was no need for our guys to respond because the next voice came from the slips. 'If that's the best you can do, you best keep quiet.' It was Waugh. So typically Waugh.

Don't get me wrong, he was not shy of a word or two but believed in saying it in the right context and at an appropriate time. He was rather like Michael Atherton in that he would thrive on taking confrontation onto the field of play, generally raising his game a level when things became heated. I am not sure I have seen anyone feed off a verbal battle as much as he did when he got to the crease.

We sussed his liking, almost need, for a hostile chat, after a while, and decided to keep schtum on occasion. 'Not talking to me, eh? Well, I'll have to talk to myself then,' he would say, and then jabber away non-stop. He knew what he needed to perform at his optimum, and he did all he could to get into the necessary mindset.

Top Left: The little thing that causes us all to make such a big fuss. A replica of the Ashes urn; *Top Right:* Where it all started: the newspaper clipping mourning the death of English cricket in 1882; *Right:* Douglas Jardine, whose parentage was regularly brought into question by the Australian masses during 1932–33, with a wonderful look of single-mindedness in his eye.

In Affectionate Remembrance
OF
ENGLISH CRICKET,
WHICH DIED AT THE OVAL
ON
29th AUGUST, 1882,
Deeply lamented by a large circle of sorrowing friends and acquaintances.

———

R. I. P.

———

N.B.—The body will be cremated and the ashes taken to Australia.

Top: Bill Woodfull loses his bat countering the infamous Bodyline tactics adhered to by fast bowler Harold Larwood: note the leg slip, leg gully and short-leg fielders in place; *Bottom:* The great man known universally as The Don. Sir Donald Bradman, the greatest player in terms of statistics the game will ever produce, is applauded onto the field at Headingley, 1938.

Top: Jim Laker receives the two match balls with which he achieved near perfection at Old Trafford in 1956. No-one will ever come closer to taking all 20 wickets in a match; *Bottom Left:* I predict a riot: England fast bowler John Snow is man-handled by one of the crowd in the aftermath of flooring Terry Jenner with a short ball in Sydney, 1971. Ray Illingworth led his team off in protest; *Bottom Right:* Once more unto the breach: the great Colin Cowdrey and I step out in readiness to give the Australians a cheery 'good morning'.

Top: Think they call this a strategic time-out in modern cricket parlance. Jeff Thomson has just begun a crisis in the Balkans, and I am just taking a few seconds to plot my retaliation;
Bottom: Thommo in full flight: Tony Greig, one of the best men I played alongside, does well to deal with this thunderbolt at Sydney, January 1975.

Top Left: Fred Trueman was my absolute hero when it came to cricket commentary. He played the curmudgeonly Yorkshireman brilliantly on the airwaves; *Top Right:* The pigeon has landed: of all the players under my charge when I was England coach, Michael Atherton was the one who most relished the fight, but in Glenn McGrath he was punching against a fast-bowling heavyweight; *Bottom:* Knight in shining armour: Sir Ian Botham's finest hour as he turns around the Headingley Test of 1981. Bob Willis applied the coup de grâce with the ball.

Top: Mike Gatting looks on in disbelief after receiving the 'ball of the century' from Shane Warne at Old Trafford, 1993. In mathematical terms, the equation was simple: Warne = flippin' genius; *Bottom Left:* New kid on the block: Kevin Pietersen sweeping Warne during his flabbergasting 158 at the Oval in 2005. What an innings; *Middle Right:* This is *the* picture for me to sum up the Ashes rivalry. Andrew Flintoff consoles Brett Lee at Edgbaston, 2005, after one of the most pulsating contests imaginable; *Bottom Right:* Shane Warne has become a good mate, and someone I first came across in the early 1990s when he played for my club Accrington. He plays poker like he played cricket – he thinks he can win from any position.

Top Left: Armed with the technical advice of Latin Les, Michael Vaughan showed that, unlike the best Ashes series, *Strictly Come Dancing* did not have to be full of twists and turns; *Top Right:* Freddie's farewell: Andrew Flintoff's final contribution to Test cricket was to run out Ricky Ponting at the Oval in 2009. I signed him for Lancashire during my time as the county's coach; *Bottom:* Fancy dress day at the Gabba: if you look closely, all the Australians have come as multi-coloured bucket seats. England stacked-up 517 for one in their second innings to highlight the gulf in class between the teams.

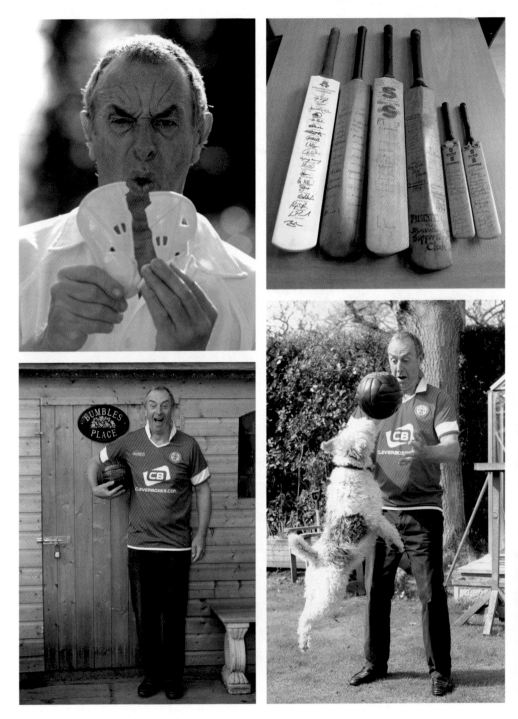

Top Left: I start losing my voice every time I set eyes on this damned thing. Just thinking back to the pain Thommo inflicted makes me wish I'd gone to an all girls' school; *Top Right:* I am not a big collector of memorabilia but these bats inscribed by all the Ashes heroes of yesteryear are special; *Bottom Left:* My second home. Every bloke needs a shed. Without one there would be no place on this earth for gubbins; *Bottom Right:* Two of the loves of my life: Tags and football. She's not bad in the air, is she? Whenever I am away on tour I'm like a kid in a sweet shop awaiting news of Accrington's progress. On, Stanley, on!

Legend has it that when Herschelle Gibbs put down a straightforward chance at Edgbaston in 1999, Steve's response was to tell his adversary: 'You've just dropped the World Cup, mate.' It was matter-of-fact, and planted the seed of doubt in the opposition. Had they really missed their chance? Well, ultimately, yes they had.

I hold my hand up here: I loved that play hard, have-a-beer-later attitude instilled by the Australians during this period. They wanted to win at all costs, even if it occasionally bordered on being too aggressive. That was what match referees are employed to police. It is they that determine things remain within the spirit of the game, and if an individual transgresses they should be punished accordingly.

But they always retained the dignity of the post-match handshake, looked you in the eye and said 'well played'. As a proud Englishman who hates losing, that proved a challenge. I noted at that time that the Australians dealt with the transformation from on-field warriors to bar-room chums a lot better. No-one better exemplified it than Waugh.

As with all Ashes series, it was customary to have a drink with your opposite number after play and at the end of that 1998–99 series I went in for a beer and chat with Australia's coach Geoff Marsh. We would have a drink at the end of every match, but Marsh reserved his greatest praise for the end of the series when he told me: 'We might have beaten you but you're getting closer.' Of course, it was of little consolation to hear him speak in complimentary tones about the qualities of our team but it was honourable and generous of him to recognise that they had been in a contest over a five-match series. What's more, it was evident that over the two previous series, one home, one away, we had been closer to the Australians in standard than England teams of the recent past.

We didn't leave the Australian dressing room until the wee small hours and many opposition coaches will have done the same in intervening years, drowning their sorrows, reflecting upon defeat. But while we were having a yarn, reminiscing about what had gone on, on the field, during those 20-odd days' play, chuckling at the flash points, marvelling at some of the outstanding performances, MacGill did something fairly inexplicable to alter the mood. Stood on the table in the middle of the room, he began playing the guitar and singing one of their songs.

It was a re-worded Midnight Oil song. You will probably know the original 'Beds Are Burning'. Well, MacGill's version had been doctored and included the line: 'The Poms don't like it when the ball is turning.' Mark Taylor was Australian captain at that time and he just quietly instructed his player to stop this performance and beckoned him down from up on high. 'You're just $1,000 lighter,' he told him quietly. 'Come down, there's a good lad.'

Atherton was not dissimilar to Steve Waugh in terms of toughness. He was at his best when the heat of the battle melted the tarmac. You only have to recall the incredible duel with Allan Donald at Trent Bridge in 1998, one of the great fast bowler–opening batsman confrontations of all time, or his marathon 10-hour innings of 185 not out to save a Test match in Johannesburg in 1995–96 as examples of it. When it was time to dig in for the cause, few men have been able to match his level of resolve. It is why Waugh nicknamed him 'The Cockroach'.

Conversely, Athers took no particular pride in scoring easy runs. Sometimes that extended not only to easy matches but to those you might term less-than-intense. In fact, it was on the 1998–99 Ashes tour that he made the first double hundred of his career, and he could not have cared less, really. It came in mid-December, between the third and fourth Tests, in a match against an Australia A team in Hobart, but he discredited it because he said that the opposition contained no bowlers.

To put you in the picture, they started with bowlers – of the calibre of Paul Reiffel, Michael Kasprowicz and Brendan Julian to be precise – all of whom played Test cricket. But he clearly felt the challenge receded when Reiffel broke down in his second over with the new ball, and became worthless to him when the frontline spinner Gavin Robertson was crocked before bowling a ball.

The Australian second string therefore had to muddle through with part-timers like Michael Bevan, Stuart Law and Darren Lehmann, and the medium-quick stuff of Greg Blewett. That was not a contest to inspire Athers, and he was actually at his worst when the cricket lost its va-va-voom. With both Alec Stewart and Nasser Hussain sitting out, he was captain of this particular match and opted, rather carelessly I believed at the time, to declare when we could have batted on in our second dig and ground the home team into the dirt.

Instead, he dangled a carrot by setting a fourth-day target of 376. I am not sure Blewett quibbled about putting the boot in during his unbeaten 213 that condemned us to a nine-wicket defeat with three-quarters of the final session unused.

It's fair to say Graham Gooch, the tour manager, and I were not best pleased with our interim captain that evening.

During this period, for all our ability, we had a habit of getting into good positions and either letting them slip completely, or allowing opponents off the hook in some way. We were too up and down, and that wreaked of fatigue to me. We had the talent within the squad but could not implement our plans or play at full tilt across an entire match let alone a short, three-match series. We were just so accustomed to lurching into games knackered rather than hitting the ground at speed that regular dips were inevitable.

The winter of 1996–97 – you will remember the one, we flippin' murdered Zimbabwe that year, didn't we? – highlighted this. Never mind the bungling in Bulawayo, I am talking about our failure to crack the world's worst jack.

Danny Morrison was theoretically the easiest scalp in international cricket, according to the statistics, with a world record 24 ducks. But we somehow contrived to disprove the theory on one afternoon and allowed him and the New Zealanders to escape defeat despite having all but half-an-hour of the final two sessions of the Auckland Test to dismiss either him or last-wicket partner Nathan Astle, and chase down what was, when he walked out to bat, a modest target.

They added 106 runs together, and administered a couple of metaphorical kicks in the biffs along the home straight to salvaging a draw. It was so frustrating watching a match that should have had a 'W' next to it in the record books. Instead it was accompanied by a big fat 'D' and had a tale to go with it. It was a sickening feeling to witness it.

Darren Gough, whose chest would barrel with pride during his best days and who was one of the individuals to set the early pace for us in the contest, was honest enough to confess that he had run out of gas. This was not an isolated occurrence for England players, and it was hardly their fault. The facts were blunt enough. We played too much, and the by-product of that was that we didn't concentrate enough time on getting lads physically fit for purpose.

Nor were we mentally as strong as others; Australia in particular. They were just used to winning, and it had given them deeper levels of resolve on the rare occasions they got into losing causes or, even rarer still, lost.

The Last Word

As a coach I sensed there was a definite psychological edge that Australia had over us during the 1990s. There was a simple explanation for it. Australia were used to winning and we were used to losing. As a group in Australia you have to be super tight because touring over there is like being on safari. The people, the media and the players hunt you down. When you're on safari the way to protect yourselves is to remain together in groups, so that you can't be attacked, can't be picked off in ones and twos by the preying beasts. A lion's technique is to try to isolate one or two from the group and that is how it feels when you're playing cricket in Australia. If they can get one outside of the group, they prey on him.

Australians are aggressive predators, who have tradition-ally homed in on the opposing captain and gone right for him. It is one of the key components in the process Steve Waugh used to call mental disintegration. People tend to associate that with sledging on the field but they are missing the point. It was a lot wider-reaching than just a few words. It's prowl-ing, looking at where you can recognise a weakness, and getting ready to pounce.

Sledging suggests something rather unsubtle, something rather off-the-cuff – as in the origin of the term 'as subtle as a sledgehammer'. But what Australia were masters of was planting seeds of doubt in the opposition ranks. For example, Justin Langer was the master of undermining opponents. He would wander up and engage in conversation, which before long turned into probing questions. He almost acted like a spy. It was what I would call gentle interrogation.

As you will appreciate by now, the crowd weren't shy of a word or two, either. In fact, there was an incident when Ian Healy was batting during the first Test that emphasised this point perfectly. Good old Angus Fraser was playing in this game – his penultimate Test as it transpired – and was field-ing down at fine leg. The locals at the Gabba were giving him some frightful stick, and Angus being Angus turned round and gave 'em plenty back.

Trouble was, that this was all taking place while the ball was in the air after Healy had played a hook shot, and instead of concentrating on getting underneath it, Gus was putting his all into this remonstration with the crowd. Tugging at the badge on his shirt he was, showing them the three lions, reminding them that neither had they played international

cricket, nor were they likely to be doing in the near future –
'you'll never have one of these' – as this catch steepled towards
him. Good old Gus, Healy only went on to top score with 134
from number seven.

Gus would no doubt remind you that we drew the game,
and that he actually had a decent record of not losing to
Australia. He only lost once in his final seven appearances
against them, and what a great team man he was. He was as
argumentative as hell, a right irascible sod, a throwback to
grumpy fast bowlers of the past, who tended to snap most
often with his close mucker and batting buddy Atherton.

Batting buddies became quite a popular thing in the following years and it is fair to say we experienced a few teething
problems, having started the idea off during my first years as
England coach. All the tail-enders were given top-order batsmen to pair up with as buddies in a bid to improve their ability to score runs. One of our problems was not getting enough
at the back end of innings compared to other teams, and I had
always been a believer in squeezing out anything extra from
the lower order you possibly could, as sometimes an extra 20
runs across a match can prove decisive.

Some of the partnerships worked well. I remember Mark
Ramprakash and Alex Tudor developing a good relationship
on that tour, and Stewart and Croft formed another good
pairing. In contrast, however, Fraser and Atherton only lasted
half a day before falling out. They had discussed the best way
to bat down the order and deconstructed Fraser's technique
when they came to the conclusion that it was best to agree to
disagree. 'Your technique's rubbish,' Atherton told him,
adding that he was never going to get any better, and the

whole exercise was therefore futile. Atherton couldn't be bothered investing any more of his time in what he saw as a hopeless cause.

That pair were always great fun guaranteed in the dressing room, batting their banter back and forth. Listening to them chuntering away was a real hoot. They were two of what I would consider to be a tremendous set of blokes. In my time with the England set-up they were no trouble at all. None whatsoever. There were flash points, of course, like when we managed to throw away the opening match of the one-day finals series against the Australians in Sydney. We had needed only 35 runs from eight overs with six wickets in hand, and in frustration I managed to smash Alan Mullally's stereo system to smithereens. I was so angry losing that match after we had Australia by the bollocks that I just completely lost it. But I did feel awful as big Al tried to mend the darned thing.

You see, despite being easy-going with our lads, I maintained the ability to move into the realms of volatility at times. But there were guidelines to keep things on an even keel. I always reminded the players that they were representing England, and to remember to behave appropriately. I also used to remind them that they had mortgages and families back at home, and that remembering these facts at all times would keep them out of trouble. Finally, I would tell them that whatever else they did or said, it was the team management and not them who picked the team.

Most of the misdemeanours were hardly misdemeanours at all. One of the biggest, in fact, was a collective failure to get into the dressing room for team talks at lunch and tea breaks because of the presence of the crowd entertainment at intervals. The lads loved watching these games of 'Chase The Sheila'. This was effectively a race around the boundary perimeter between the punters.

Proper, serious runners would be brought in to take part too but generally fans could have a go at what amounted to a 400-metre handicap. Participants were given staggered starting points depending on their ability, and it was one of the most non-PC events I have ever set eyes on. I recall one race featuring a chap with one leg (who was given a fairly substantial head start it must be stated) up against the New South Wales amateur cross country champion. He was the allotted athlete positioned at the back of the track, and there would always be a girl at the front – hence Chase The Sheila.

During breaks in play, I might have wanted to give the team a gee-up, just give them a 'well done' or impart something I had picked up from the previous session, but the lads so looked forward to this Sheila competition that I struggled to get them inside. You could forget tactical analysis when a race was on because everyone was busy picking their winner and waiting to see who would come out on top.

Even more ludicrous, however, was the scheduling that particular winter. In one of the odder itineraries the international cricket world has witnessed, the 1998–99 tour to Australia clashed with what was then called the Wills International Cup – a forerunner to the International Cricket Council's Champions Trophy, a tournament designed to raise funds for lesser nations. So although we were supposed to be down under for the Ashes – the most important series in our four-year cycle – I was in Bangladesh with a specialist one-day squad while the Test squad was heading for the main event. We simply couldn't be in two places at once so we had to pick two teams. I was coach so I had to go to Bangladesh, and I only joined up with the others once we got knocked out by South Africa, with Graeme Hick, who was called up as standby for Michael Atherton, joining me in transit.

You would just laugh these days at two international competitions going on at the same time and I recall sitting around the table at Lord's, asking how we were going to deal with the situation. Who would we send where? In the end we decided to split them into two entirely different squads, and so there was no crossover originally apart from myself as coach.

Historically there has always been an issue with the presence of the World Cup immediately after the Ashes but this now hampered our start. In 1999 it was not such an issue as the tournament was held in England, of course, giving us a four-month gap, but we were still contractually obliged to stick around and participate in a triangular tournament with the Australians and Sri Lanka when we were fatigued at the end of the winter. It was always thus for the Carlton & United Series or whatever they called it in subsequent years.

It was during that one-day triangular tournament that we experienced the furore over Muttiah Muralitharan's bowling action. Ross Emerson was umpire for our one-day international against the Sri Lankans at the Adelaide Oval, and word was that he was going to do him for a no-ball in the match. We had heard this rumour, but kept out of it as this was absolutely nothing to do with us. Emerson had already called Murali for throwing three years earlier and decided that he had seen something suspicious enough to enact a repeat from square-leg early on in our innings of 302 for three.

To be honest, the match descended into complete mayhem the moment Emerson followed through with his threat. There were all kinds of shenanigans going on. On the stump microphones Arjuna Ranatunga, the Sri Lanka captain, could be heard asking Emerson to stand back at the bowler's end. Emerson refused, telling him he was staying where he was while Murali was bowling. 'I'm running the game,' he told him, only to be challenged in no uncertain terms on that statement by the Sri Lankan captain: 'No, I'm running the game.' By the letter of the law, the umpire is within his rights to stand where he wants. But there is a way of doing things, and I'm not sure Ross chose the right one during that match on 23 January 1999.

Of course, I had a bit of previous when it came to Muralitharan, although I have always maintained there was a level of misapprehension in my comments made live on air at the Oval Test the previous summer. Simon Hughes had asked me in the immediate aftermath of a day's play what I thought about his action. My players in the dressing room weren't happy with it, I knew that, but I couldn't say it publicly, so instead, I simply said, 'If it's legal, we should be teaching it.'

There was a lot of conjecture about a number of bowlers' actions at that time but that comment didn't go down too well either with Sri Lanka or my bosses at the England and Wales Cricket Board. As far as I saw it, it was an issue for the ICC, and it was up to them to rule on legality. Thankfully they did come up with a 15-degree maximum flex in the bowling arm, which provided much greater clarity and less suspicion. In the aftermath of my comments the previous summer, however, I remained a bit of a public enemy number one to Sri Lankans.

There was all sorts going on during this thriller of a day-night match, which we ended up losing by one wicket. For example, the dressing rooms at the Adelaide Oval were side-on to the action, and there was not much room in the old pavilion there, the corridors on that side of the ground being quite narrow, so I happened to be sat there with my feet over the windowsill watching the game when there was a flood-light failure.

Down the corridor came shuffling a deputation from the Sri Lanka team, including a man who is now a very good friend of mine, Ranjit Fernando. All four members of the Sri Lankan management were suited and booted, and I was immediately curious as to where they were going. It didn't take me long to work that out as there was only one room in that direction – that of the match referee Peter van der Merwe.

A few minutes later they shuffled back past me without saying a word. Not long afterwards, I received a visit from Peter, who said: 'I'm afraid I'm going to have to put some-thing to you.'

'Oh, right, what's that then?'

'As we are all aware that floodlight over there has gone out,' he said, pointing across the oval. 'And there is a feeling within the Sri Lankan camp that you are responsible for it!'

'You what?' I roared. 'Where's the fuse box then?'

'Don't worry,' Peter resumed. 'That's the thing. It's 10 metres underground.'

Of course, we both laughed and got on with things. But that was a rare light-hearted moment on a very fraught day. At the height of the furore with Emerson, Ranatunga ordered his team off the field and made them stand at the side of the pitch before they eventually went back on – a 15-minute interim ensued while he spoke with high-ranking officials back in Sri Lanka on a mobile phone.

Indignation hung in the air that evening, and the whole thing was handled very badly. Whatever Ross Emerson wanted to do, he got it all wrong. Whether he considered Murali's action to be illegal or otherwise, he didn't put the correct processes into place. Since then, anything like that is no longer called on the field, but reported post-match, and dealt with in a process well documented by the authorities around the globe.

Thankfully, with the protocol well known to all and sundry, it is very rare that anyone gets the question mark of suspicion hanging over their heads. In fact, through the ages there have been very few bowlers who have been done for throwing, the Australian left-armer Ian Meckiff and Charlie Griffith, of West Indies, being ones that stand out.

The process is a lot more sensitive these days. With all the cameras around cricket grounds there is no real need to make a call on the field of play. If there is a dubious action that officials feel might be contravening the 15 degrees of straightening of the elbow joint in delivery, it is reported back to the relevant governing board and they are told to withdraw Player X from bowling in competitive matches until the action has been modified during a remedial phase. That to me is a far better way of doing it.

It was perhaps typical of the pattern of the tour that we lost the C & U Series finals to Australia despite being competitive. The dismissal in the first final at the SCG of Nasser Hussain – one of the players who came of age on the trip – lured out of his crease by the wily Warne, was another turning point for us. There were only a few months left in the job for me, and had suspected this as I wrote, but I had seen some of the things that were required to help improve England's Ashes teams of the future, and I listed them in my post-tour report. They included the establishment of a spin academy and a more professional cycle of rest, preparation and play. The cycle you might consider to have been implemented during the subsequent era of central contracts.

Chapter 5

DOGS OF WAUGH

Nasser Hussain – or Unlucky Alf as I knew him in his playing days – lived up to his nickname as the England captain to welcome Australia's 2001 vintage, a team that was up there with the 1948 Invincibles, Bradman et al. Ill fortune appeared to be his lot in life – if he avoided walking under a ladder a seagull would pap on his head, and as a batsman our Nasser was simply never out. He had endured this piece of bad luck, or that piece, been sawn off, caught off no-balls, and now as leader he had the misfortune of taking on the golden generation in their pomp.

This opposition was one that stacked up 16 consecutive Test match victories between November 1999 and February 2001, smashing the previous record of 11 set by those great West Indians of 1984.

Under the steely Steve Waugh, they had a killer instinct like never before. They were simply uncompromising in their quest to be the best. As character statements go, his refusal to succumb to a calf strain suffered in Manchester so that he could score a hundred on one leg at the Oval said it all. He was almost mocking the opposition: 'I don't even need to be able to stand up to get runs off you lot.' What a character he was.

I guess that process was all part of his mental disintegration process. We associate that phrase with words, of course, such as the Australian captain summoning a fielder to come and field at silly mid-off when Nasser was on strike, letting everyone within earshot know 'I want you to get right under his nose', and then positioning him 10 yards away on the drive. But being able to belittle the opposition physically in that way was quite something else. It's okay saying stuff but the big challenge is always to be able to back your quips up with actions.

Perhaps the funniest altercation, however, is one that took place at the Oval during the 2001 Ashes when Jimmy Ormond was selected to lead England's attack. Ormond was undoubtedly a fine county seamer with a sound career record but the Australians wasted no time in reading him his fortune on his debut.

'F*** me, look who it is. Mate, what are you doing out here? There's no way you are good enough to play for England,' Mark Waugh unceremoniously told him.

'Maybe not, but at least I'm the best player in my family.'

What a gold-dust comeback, and one of the few moments of triumph in a one-on-one contest for an Englishman over an Australian that summer.

Had it not been for a generous declaration by stand-in captain Adam Gilchrist at Headingley, Mark Butcher would have been denied another. Butcher was someone with the right temperament to succeed, and played wonderfully well for his unbeaten 173 after Australia's modus operandi – to go for wins first and foremost, and worry about things going wrong later – was applied. Without the rain, though, they would not have had a sniff. This team had secured the Ashes inside 11 days of cricket and only their fixation with winning led to a victory target of 315 being set in Leeds.

They seemed to have gone up another notch since their previous visit, and the size of the task when you played them was put into context when you finally got Damien Martyn out. Just when you were flagging, in walked Adam Gilchrist at number seven. He just used to smash it everywhere. From what I have gathered over the years, no one ever told him that they wanted him to play this way. There were no instructions to be up-tempo, to take the game away from the opposition, he just played like that, so they let him get on with it.

He is one of the players from my lifetime that changed the game. What a brilliant cricketer. People talk about looking for Eric, as in Eric Cantona, when looking for an individual whose brilliance can make all the difference. English cricket spent two decades looking for Botham. But nowadays we are looking for Gilchrist, particularly in one-day cricket.

There are a number of England wicketkeepers who are fantastic batsmen, and we have tried several of them as opening batsman – Matt Prior, Steven Davies and Phil Mustard – while looking for our own Adam. But such was his brilliant record as a batter in all formats, you won't be plucking another Gilly out of the pack. Whether he opened in one-day internationals or came in five down in Test matches he was a free licence player. He might lie dormant for two or three knocks. Then boom! He'd won the game in a flash, thanks a lot, see you later. His impact on the world scene was similar to that of Sanath Jayasuriya around the 1996 World Cup, and because of it all other teams were on the lookout for this multi-skilled gloveman. Brendon McCullum, of New Zealand, is probably the closest to him.

Useless Tosser gets the V-sign

Good old Nass was the kind of player who finished his career with few regrets. But if he had to nominate one it might just be his decision to ask Australia to bat first at the start of the 2002–03 Ashes. Not that his good friends in the Sky box ever remind him of his blunder at the Gabba – honest!

Things couldn't have gone much worse, really, what with Australia piling up 362 for two and England losing their young strike bowler Simon Jones to that horrific knee injury incurred while fielding. It is not the kind of start you want to make when you are already peeing uphill into the wind.

For England to spoil Steve Waugh's farewell party they needed all the cards to fall into place. And the customary taunting of the Poms coincided with the start of the tour when Sydney's *Daily Telegraph* produced the headline: 'Is there anyone in England that can play cricket?'

Woah, easy fellas! There was one chap who most definitely could play because he ended up the man of the series, albeit in a losing cause. It was no mean feat by Michael Vaughan to register three hundreds in a side that was losing regularly, and if an opening batsman was playing like that against that standard of bowling attack he had to be a quality player. In that situation, no matter how much the Australian public love to hate the English, there has to be a level of begrudging admiration from them, and we saw it in just the same way that they had responded to other recent standout performers among Ashes opponents like Darren Gough in the mid-90s.

That winter was monumental for Vaughan, the high point of a career that was cruelly disrupted and ultimately curtailed by a knee injury. There could have been plenty more success for him but for that problem, and although he didn't make a great fuss about it I am sure it prevented him hitting those heights of 633 runs for 10 times out again. In my mind's eye I still have that image of him pulling for four – flipping the ball over the leg-side with what looks like a wand.

My friendship with him – you may have noticed our tendency to make fun on Twitter – began on that tour but was really one that started through me getting to know his parents Dee and Graham. When Michael was tucked up in bed between plundering runs all over Australia and cementing his position as the number one batsman in the world, we would socialise in the hotel bars, most notably being threatened with eviction from one very late at night.

There we were, with Brett Lee strumming his guitar and singing, all having a drink or two when we were asked to leave by the hotel concierge. Me, one of the commentators, Lee, Australia's opening bowler, and Vaughan's parents were having a real ding dong do when the ultimatum was made: shut up or ship out. Ironically, the complaint about an 'infernal racket' had come from one of the travelling British press.

Vaughan was the premier batsman in the world at that time on merit, and came to be the world's best captain for a period too. Not many people can have laid claim to holding both those titles but I believe he was one who could with justification. There is no doubt that his injuries hampered him and things do get tough when you get a really bad injury.

We had witnessed this kind of thing with Ian Botham and his back. Although both men played on for quite some time they were never the players they were previously. Sure, their skill meant they were good enough to carry on for a while, but ultimately they were incapacitated – unfit for business at the highest level.

Vaughan was very shrewd from a tactical perspective and like his successors Andrew Strauss and Alastair Cook led as a player initially. That always helps when someone takes over the captaincy because if you can do your primary job within the side it tends to take the others along with you naturally. Tactically he would be quite innovative and decisive. And there was a lot of honesty in his leadership, and that meant he could be tough with them as well. I know that Jimmy Anderson once went to him and told him he wasn't speaking to him. 'Do I look like I'm bothered?' was Vaughan's simple reply. As a captain he was comfortable in his own skin and didn't allow the job to consume him.

There was drama in the home dressing room too that series, not least in the final Test at the Sydney Cricket Ground when Steve Waugh fought to save his career. Although his Australian team already had things in the bag and were on course for a whitewash, there was immense pressure on him in that series finale. Was it going to be his last Test? Was it going to be his last international appearance? These were questions with real substance and the reaction of the crowd when he got to his half-century on the second day told you, 'He is our man.' Undoubtedly, he was Sydney's Steven, not just Steve Waugh, Australian cricket captain, during the week when his Test future was on the line.

The match situation made it an even trickier innings for a bloke out of nick but from a position of 56 for three he counter-punched brilliantly. The place erupted during that knock and I had honestly never previously heard a noise like it. It seemed to beat the Sachin Tendulkar-inspired cacophonies I had been party to around India.

Trademark cuts clumped high over gully to the boundary were greeted with the most raucous cheers. It was strokes like these – hardly classical efforts from the textbook – that got Waugh going again. For a while during the series it had appeared like he was playing from memory, but he soon began to spread the field and got a pretty special ovation mid-innings when he got to 10,000 Test runs.

It was as if the second day of this particular Test was scripted. It certainly had perfect timing about it as he preyed on a tiring England attack in the final session. Waugh got up to 87 with three overs left, and then got himself into the 90s in the penultimate over. When he required six runs from the final eight deliveries of the evening, he took a single off Matthew Hoggard, and Adam Gilchrist set the tone for the finale by looking to play the ball out rather than score from it. Even then there was a twist as Waugh tucked off-spinner Richard Dawson away for three with three balls to go. Once again, Gilchrist played his part by taking a single to the leg-side.

Murmurs built to a crescendo in anticipation of the moment and with Waugh on strike to the final ball of day, Nasser Hussain indulged in a few mind games by chewing the cud for a minute or two with Dawson. Waugh would have expected that, of course, and provided the perfect response when he drove square for four.

A massive buzz engulfed the ground as he celebrated his 29th Test hundred, equalling Bradman's total in his 156th appearance. It drew a well-earned handshake from England wicketkeeper Alec Stewart – a man whose own Ashes career was at an end. He must have been sick of the sight of him but he knew something of the willpower necessary to keep going in that situation.

Waugh's personal achievement actually deflected from England's effort in that match, and victory gave something for the Barmies to cheer about. There was a section of about 5,000 of them that never stopped bouncing on that final day as Andrew Caddick bowled England to victory. Caddick's performance also gave rise to an interesting quiz question. Namely, who claimed 10 wickets in a Test and was never picked again?

Freddie Downs Em

The 2005 English summer contained not only one of the best Ashes but one of the best Test series you could ever hope to witness and, from an England perspective, was all about one man. A man, as it happens, I witnessed emerge from adolescence at Old Trafford.

Andrew 'Freddie' Flintoff was immense across those five epic matches, confirming beyond doubt that he had fulfilled a healthy proportion of the infinite potential he appeared to have from the moment I first saw him as a boy. During my time as Lancashire coach, he was a diamond player in the youth set-up at Old Trafford, and so it was a natural progression when he got to the age of 17 that we wanted to sign him for the senior squad.

It is not as though we discovered him; he wasn't unearthed from a Lancashire League, Bolton League or a Northern League club as such. Andrew had such obvious ability that he stood out a mile from being very young and had been within the Lancashire youth system for years, progressing through all the age group sides.

His natural progression was to move into men's cricket, and it was there for all to see that he had the physical attributes to compete at that level. He was a big, tall, slim lad with powerful shoulders – a physique that meant he did not look out of place lined up alongside the blokes.

Such was his prowess with Lancashire's under-age sides, however, that others around the county circuit knew about him too, and when Geoff Ogden and I turned up at his house in Preston to sit down with him and his mum and dad, he had already had a distinctly good offer from Northamptonshire. In fact, they were keen enough on him to offer him the chance to further his education down there, facilitating his move into a sixth form at one of the best schools in the county, one which I am sure he and his family found attractive. But despite the temptation of the deal at Wantage Road, I am sure he made the right decision in the end by committing to Lancashire.

It was my duty as first-team coach at Old Trafford to go in person along with Geoff, who was chairman of the club's cricket committee, meet the family and make the formal offer of a contract.

Whenever I carried out these signing visits, I always told the young players the same thing: 'You've got a great opportunity to go to the very top with us.' Because for any lad being signed by a club the size of Lancashire, that's true.

'This is your opportunity and yours alone,' I used to tell them.

During my spiel regarding what they might expect, I used to turn the tables on them and ask what their ambitions were. If they answered conservatively by talking of breaking into the second team, I used to cut them dead.

'Your challenge is not to get into the second XI, it is to get Michael Atherton and John Crawley out of that first team. Start thinking like that, then you'll be progressing, and eventually you might play for England.'

Once I had them focused on serious longer-term targets, I used to tell them how much they were going to earn if they broke into and established themselves in the Lancashire first team. That kind of money was always appealing but would be some way down the line and dependent on the individual's desire to progress, of course. Initially, however, they would not be on very much. 'Everyone starts on this same level,' I used to warn them.

Generally, this was more than acceptable for any aspiring cricketer straight out of the GCSE examination hall. But I will never forget signing a lad from up near Settle called Paul Ridgway, who was the exception to the rule.

At the same time Paul was coming through at Old Trafford, he was working down a quarry. So when, sat in his front room with his mum and dad drinking tea, I informed him of his prospects and starting salary of £8,000, I was met with a sharp interjection.

'But he gets £14,000 as things stand,' his mum piped up.

'Ah, yes, but when he plays for England, he'll earn a whole lot more, won't he? You won't have to worry about his starting wage then.'

My modus operandi in these recruitment meetings was to warn lads of the hard work ahead but also make clear the riches they could expect if they were successful. In years to come, Paul Ridgway would have told you that playing for Lancashire beat hammering away down the quarry any day of the week, but unfortunately he failed to make the grade. Not because of any lack of talent but quite simply because he got injured. He was a grand lad, who raced in and let the ball go as fast as he could – just as one would imagine a quarry-man would. He used to get redder and redder with every delivery hurled down but, sadly, like a number of young fast bowlers during the transition from teens to twenties, he succumbed to back injuries.

In some regards, Andrew Flintoff didn't change much throughout his 15 years playing professional cricket. But in others, he was distinctly different. For example, he was always very quiet as a lad, and quite reserved when playing. Shortly before that visit to his house in 1994, I went to see him play for St Anne's against Leyland when Malcolm Marshall opened the bowling and Andrew opened the batting.

Nowadays, when folk recall Flintoff they talk of his exuberance, his swagger, his unmistakable self-confidence. But there were nerves from him that afternoon, not so much due to the presence of the great West Indies fast bowler but my presence on the boundary edge. Malcolm cleaned him up in just a few deliveries but it didn't matter; let's face it, Malcolm Marshall cleaned up plenty in his time and Andrew was always going to fulfil his dream of playing at the top level. Runs from him would have been nice to watch but the truth was that the decision had already been made.

It is also hard to believe now – given his reputation as a bit of a hell-raiser – but for a year or two after he put pen to that professional contract with Lancashire he was an absolute teetotaller. I saw a lot of him in his early career as I was also involved with England Under-19s, and he never went near the booze. Things were happening quickly for him in terms of personal achievement, and he was fully engaged in making a success of himself.

As a consequence of that rapid progress, however, a lot was expected of him and I was one of the first to fall into the trap of demanding too much of his all-round talents. Because of his physicality and his ability to get the ball through at a decent pace as a fast bowler, we actually ended up bowling him too much; unfortunately it was not until later that I real-ised this. In a quest to get every ounce of talent out of him that we could, we asked him to do more than his body might have been ready for. All we saw at the time was this big strapping lad who would hit the keeper's gloves at a decent lick.

Flintoff had star quality but his team-mates weren't shabby by any stretch of the imagination. In the couple of years he had with England Under-19s – our policy was to pick all players two years young so that we would get a couple of summers out of the best in their age groups – Marcus Trescothick, Anthony McGrath, Vikram Solanki and Owais Shah were all team-mates. So he was amongst a very talented batch.

By his final year, however, there were already concerns developing about the effects of fast bowling on his back. Due to the number of overs he had sent down as a kid, Andrew had a bit of a split physicality. One look at his back showed you that it was not developing evenly. Half of it looked like the back of a man and the other half a boy. Certain sections of him were over-developed due to the demands placed upon him and others were unmistakably those of a gangly lad. My theory was that we had to build him up so that he could cope with the requirements of a seam-bowling all-rounder, and I made those thoughts known to the medical staff and physios.

But their counter-argument was quite to the contrary. We had to deconstruct him; work backwards to alleviate some of the pressure on his body. They reasoned that we ought to take his age – he was still a teenager, remember – as the primary guide and not be fooled by his appearance. As such, I was instructed not to bowl him as much, and he did have a period, after bowling far too much previously, when he bowled very little and played pretty much as a specialist batsman. The intention of this reduction in workload was to allow his back to develop evenly. Only when it was considered that he had a greater physical maturity, a few months later, did we increase his workload to all-rounder status once more.

Some things never changed with him, though. Even in his teenage years, Flintoff had that problem with his front foot when he bowled – it landed at a funny angle and his entire body weight went across it. That's some force on impact. Ideally, a bowler's foot points down the pitch but he could never get to a point where he felt comfortable doing that. Heaven knows he tried, and lots of different people used different methods to try to get his feet to plant in a different way but it just never happened. During Duncan Fletcher's England reign, there was a sustained effort to ease the pressure, and Andrew used to walk through his action in practice to try to make subtle changes to it. But no matter how perfect it looked when he delivered in the slowest of motion, whenever it came to ball one of a match, that foot angled awkwardly again.

It is not as though Andrew was a unique case. There have been other international bowlers who have had similar problems. Jimmy Anderson always splayed his front foot and when someone feels that is natural you are never going to stop it successfully. Tinkering is usually carried out to guard against potential injury but normally blokes come to realise they are how they are, and although parts of their action might not be textbook it is the way they bowl.

Lasith Malinga, of Sri Lanka, is another example of some-one who, despite railing against convention, has prospered. International players of the past have also had their quirks. Australia's Max Walker was arms and legs akimbo. You have to concede that you can't stop some things, and that doing so could have a negative effect.

So Andrew bowled with his front leg braced, and did so fantastically well. In fact, when he first played for Lancashire, wicketkeeper Warren Hegg said that he had to stand further back to him than he did to Wasim Akram, such was the pace he generated even then. Let's be honest, being compared to Wasim in any capacity is some compliment.

There was a lot of goodwill towards Andrew too when he first entered the first-team dressing room at Old Trafford. As a young man he fitted in perfectly with everyone, including the established players like Akram, Neil Fairbrother and Mike Atherton. That Lancashire team, which also included my eldest lad Graham, Ian Austin and Peter Martin, had an absolute ball. They were a good team, a successful team and boy did they enjoy themselves. They all loved Freddie to bits, so it's a bit sad that he seems to have fallen out with Athers in recent years. Guess it goes with the territory when you cross the divide from player to broadcaster or writer.

But he did show his true colours when personal tragedy struck our family, and Graham's wife Sharon passed away in 2011. Andrew came up from where he lives down in Surrey to the funeral and that showed he remains a very caring lad.

Even in the heat of battle he displayed empathy to others, and we saw that most graphically during that 2005 Ashes series. That embrace with Brett Lee immediately after the narrowest of victories was clinched will go down in British sport's annals.

His huge frame and immense power should not detract from his caring nature. It was no surprise to me when, while training with Barry McGuigan and his son Shane for his professional boxing debut against Richard Dawson in November 2012, he knocked down a sparring partner at the Monkstown Boxing Club in Belfast, and immediately stopped for fear that he had hurt him, bending over his opponent to ask if he was okay.

Apparently, Barry had to remind him sternly: 'This is a hurt game. You don't ask them if they're alright. Hit 'em again!'

People might feel that the boxing lark was some kind of publicity stunt. Not a bit of it, in my mind. In a newspaper interview before this maiden bout, Andrew said that cricket was a distant past for him and that he couldn't handle not playing. Because of the way he left the game, I can see why he has thrown himself into other areas and can relate to it.

He pushed cricket right to the back of his mind because he was not involved in it anymore, and he couldn't be even if he wanted to, given the state of his knee. Concentrating on other things away from his previous career was a kind of defence mechanism, I guess.

But he still turns up to play for the Professional Cricketers' Association's Legends team now and again, and when he does it is obvious what he misses most from cricket. It's the camaraderie of the dressing room. To some degree we all miss the banter when we pack up, and Andrew was old school in his appreciation of it – someone who always got a kick out of the social side of the sport. You can see that he likes to meet up and have a chat with his mates. And he also brings mates from outside of cricket with him to the game.

Meeting up for these PCA games helps revive the great memories of your playing career. To some of the lads these get-togethers remain an incredibly important part of their lives, not to sate any competitive desire, but to indulge in their past.

Few cricketers have a past as rich as that of Flintoff. Sure, injuries meant that he couldn't achieve everything he wanted to but, good grief, he did a lot. Firstly, let's not forget he was a double Ashes winner and until recently there were not a lot who could lay claim to that kind of achievement. And it is fair to say that he won the second on one leg.

That was one Herculean effort yet it is the first of the two, in 2005, that will be the one he is remembered for rather than the second. Just like Sir Ian Botham is remembered for 1981 rather than 1985. Freddie's force of personality shone through, and seven years into his Test career he was undoubtedly at his peak. It was said that we had picked him too early for the top level but there was absolutely no doubt in my mind, as coach, nor in the mind of Alec Stewart, the England captain, that we were right to get him involved at the age of 20. Even with the benefit of hindsight, I would make absolutely the same decision now.

Flintoff was ready in 1998; red hot in 2005. Whenever he got on the field, he gave absolutely everything, one of those rare players who possessed the knack of getting the whole country behind him. And it truly felt like the entire nation was behind the effort of Michael Vaughan's England team that summer.

Although England had developed some decent momentum in the preceding 18 months, winning all seven Tests the previous summer between historic away series wins in the Caribbean and South Africa, nobody really knew how England would fare when the quality of the opposition went up another notch or two. Naturally, they fancied their chances of being competitive against Australia after developing such good form during the build-up, but you have to remember that those particular Australians were crackerjack, arguably the best of their country's rich heritage. The entire series turned out to be unmissable.

Normally when you go to a Test match for a day out, you can meet up with Arthur and Tommy, head off to the Guinness tent or the Champagne tent, depending on your tipple preference, chew the fat for an hour and hardly miss a thing. When you then dip back into the cricket the complexion of the game is unlikely to have changed too much from when you last left it.

But the 2005 Ashes was completely different – you couldn't take your eyes off five minutes of the cricket for fear of missing something seismic. It was no different in the Sky Sports and *Test Match Special* commentary boxes either, by the way. Usually when you finish your half-hour stints on the microphone you nip off for a coffee, chill out at the back of the box, read the paper or have a wander into the press box for a natter. In 2005, not a bit of it.

There was a little bit of a warning as to how compelling things were going to be, and what Australia could expect, in the one-off Twenty20 international which preceded the series. Twenty20 is supposed to be a lot of fun but the Australians didn't have any fun at all during this match down at the Rose Bowl, because England were all over them like a rash. Quite honestly, Australia were caught on the hop a little bit with that match.

Intent on enjoying themselves rather than taking things too seriously, some of the Australians sported retro gear – Jason Gillespie wore a Dennis Lillee style headband – yet joviality was confined to only one of the two teams. England remained deadly serious, and throughout their crushing 100-run win coach Duncan Fletcher just sat there, hidden behind his dark glasses, motionless. It had obviously been a plan to get right into the opposition, and unsettle them any way they could, and, regardless of his lack of expression, he would have got immense satisfaction that the plan had come together.

Twenty20 is a batsman's game but Darren Gough charged in that day in Southampton and struck Andrew Symonds in the chest with a bouncer. Those kinds of deliveries tell opponents that you mean business. When you get your retaliation in first, the other team are in no doubt what you are all about. Gough did not feature in the Tests, of course, but here was his contribution to the summer's work.

The real flag was put down by Steve Harmison during the first Test at Lord's, however, when having roughed up Australia's opening batsmen Matthew Hayden and Justin Langer in the opening exchanges of the first morning, he left a permanent mark with the blow to Ricky Ponting's face. It was a brute of a delivery that reared into the grille of the

Australian captain's helmet, the impact of which drew blood from his cheek, and later required the delicate hand of a plastic surgeon.

This was Australia's warning – Langer is said to have turned to his former Middlesex team-mate Andrew Strauss perplexed that no England fielders had rushed to Ponting's aid – with this bloody big fast bowler just stood there, hands on hips, looking mean and nasty, which is the total opposite of what he's like as a character. There was a look in his eye that said to me, 'There's a lot more to come yet.' I'd seen it first-hand from some of their brutes 30 years earlier!

Flintoff was the spearhead, the leading wicket-taker, but the assault Australia faced that summer was five-pronged and relentless from that point onwards. In Test cricket currency, the five of Flintoff, Harmison, Matthew Hoggard, Simon Jones and Ashley Giles were worth their weight in gold. As a quintet they represented an extremely formidable unit. There was simply no respite, no easy runs for Australia, whose batsmen were left in no doubt that they would be targeted and under siege.

Giles might have carried less obvious threat than other left-arm spinners through the ages but he was integral to England's attack as the holding player. His role was comparable to one that you see regularly in football: the man who sits in front of the back four directing the pace of the game; the bit of glue that holds everything together. As captain, Vaughan knew he could trust Giles to control an end for a prolonged period of time while he rotated his faster men from the other. If the Australians went after him, it was fraught with danger. You could not take any liberties with an attack like that.

As the series progressed, it appeared that the equation was simple – keep that attack together for the full series and England would win. But Australia, ahead after securing victory at Lord's, fought like mad too, which meant that even though England spent the lion's share of the five matches on top, they were all relatively close.

That all added to the mix, making it quite simply the best series we had seen for years. And a series like that has moments that you never forget; Ponting's wound at Lord's; his run-out at Trent Bridge; Geraint Jones holding that catch down the leg-side off Harmison to dismiss Michael Kasprowicz at Edgbaston and square the series in nailbiting fashion; Flintoff's double-wicket over earlier in that same match; Kevin Pietersen slog-sweeping Shane Warne for six during what was supposed to be a final-day rearguard at the Oval; and a barrow-load of others besides.

England started so well at Lord's with the ball but their efforts were soon put into context by that champion of fast bowlers Glenn McGrath, whose disciplined five for not-many on the first evening dictated the way that match was headed. McGrath and loose balls never did go together, so when he stood on one on the eve of the second match in Birmingham, the consequences were significant. Disruption can cause captains to act out of character or do unusual things, and perhaps that is why Ricky Ponting opted to insert England minutes later.

The way England played exposed any mistakes or misjudgements made by the Australians, and the decision by Ponting to bowl first was prominent among them. Sure, there was a little bit of cloud overhead but I wonder how many times he has thought back about that decision and concluded, 'We should have had a bat.' It amazes me, really, how often captains consider inserting the opposition. When we were in New Zealand in early 2013 my eyebrows migrated north when, on a beautiful day, with not a cloud in the sky, no breeze and with a great-looking pitch, both captains confirmed at the toss that they wanted to bowl first. Cyril Washbrook, the great old man of cricket, told me when I became Lancashire captain: 'If you win the toss and want to bowl, think again.' Traditional thinking has always been to pressurise your opposition by putting runs on the board. Yet, for some reason, having a bowl is becoming the modern way.

In this instance, impetus was suddenly with England once more and watching the first three sessions of that second Test was comparable to watching a benefit match. England scored at more than five runs per over in being dismissed for 407, which is a phenomenal rate even in a decade when run rates were sky-rocketing. In such a dramatic series that detail is easily lost but Marcus Trescothick, Kevin Pietersen and Andrew Flintoff were box office viewing that day.

In addition to seeing Flintoff's development up close, I knew Marcus well too from my brief period coaching the England Under-15s. It is fair to say that he was already a fine striker of the ball at that age but also living up to his county nickname Banger, so dubbed for his love of sausages. I had already marked him down as captaincy potential at the age of 15 and he had such a good eye that he was an accomplished strokemaker and slip fielder. But his eating habits were a worry. He was a big lad who scoffed said bangers with another of his favourite foods, crisps, washing them down with litres of lemonade.

His diet was something I took up with his parents, although it didn't seem to have any recognisable knock-on effect. I advised that he would have to become tougher and get stuck in on the field if he wanted to succeed in the long term. As a boy he worried too much about how far tea was away. This advice was not necessarily heeded but the penny dropped with him further down the line. His natural talent got him the opening but his attitude under Duncan Fletcher was spot on, and his fitness was never an issue once he became an established international player.

Nor was his ability to take the game to the new-ball bowlers. At Edgbaston he hit the first of three half-centuries in first innings of matches that series, a rapid 90 that set the tone for the way England wanted to play. Vaughan and Fletcher had given him the licence to whack it should he see fit, and Trescothick's brutality pre-lunch told the home fans that if the team was to go down it would do so fighting. When he belted one straight for six in Shane Warne's first over of the match, it told the packed house that the order of things was changing.

Moving the game on so swiftly provided Pietersen and Flintoff with the platform from which they could attack. It was Flintoff who led the way in terms of aerial bombardment – clearing the rope five times. He scored more than 400 runs across the series, yet when people reflect back on the 2005 Ashes what epitomised England's victory was the sight of him steaming in with the ball. He produced that irresistible late spell the following day, and despite his batting being brilliant, it was always when he bowled that he seemed to seize the moment.

Virtually every spell he sent down was spellbinding. It was the summer that confirmed Andrew as one of cricket's great showmen. Here was a character that could rise to any occasion and produce when the quality in the contest was at its peak. For years every English all-rounder had been bullied into submission by Beefy's shadow, but this was undoubtedly a moment when Flintoff applied a half-nelson to the past.

His presence was so powerful, like a leading man at the opera or a conductor of an orchestra, that it felt like he directed the drama. In front of these full houses, Flintoff would stand at slip – and this really is Bothamesque – gently loosen his limbs to show the crowd he was ready for another bowl, and a buzz would cascade around the ground. 'He's coming on again,' blokes would whisper to their mates.

For the Australian batsmen, it must have had a psychological effect. Flintoff would charge in for his first delivery with what must have felt like 20,000 people behind him. It was as if he surfed to the crease on waves of positivity, and it was never long after Australia developed a solid foundation that this loveable Lancastrian would come along and burst their dam.

On commentary, I likened him to a steam engine during that Edgbaston match. He would build up for half a dozen or so deliveries and then once into his stride it was all the Australian batsmen could do to repel him. He was relentless, and once chugging he never wanted to come off. He was forever pleading 'give me another' to Vaughan. As an opposition batter you just want to get rid of a bloke like that, see him off.

Even then there was no real respite. The quality of the rest of the attack that year meant there was no let-up in intensity when a change was made. Once Flintoff was withdrawn, you were greeted by Steve Harmison at his aggressive best with that trademark, nasty, steep bounce, or the explosive pace generated by Simon Jones's powerful upper body. England were simply relentless.

As fan, player, coach and commentator I'd seen various England teams of the past have good sessions followed by bad, but Vaughan's team were the first I could recall being on song all the time. As a captain or coach, if your team is right into the opposition during the first hour of a day's play, you want to see that replicated at five o'clock in the evening. It must have been a source of great satisfaction that Duncan Fletcher got that every time.

One of England's great triumphs throughout those five matches was to keep calm on the field, particularly in the face of Australia's failure in that regard. The biggest example of this was at Trent Bridge when Gary Pratt ran out Ricky Ponting during a short stint as 12th man. Ponting was furious as he left the field, sharing his feelings publicly with the raucous crowd and Fletcher, who sat motionless on the balcony, staring straight towards the middle of the pitch. The silver fox didn't twitch a muscle, although there was more than a hint of his lips pursing into a smile. It would be naughty to suggest he was puckering to blow him a kiss, or giving him a wink, behind those customary shades.

To be honest, there was no more winding up necessary. You see, that incident was, in a snapshot, a representation of the bigger picture. England subtly got to Australia, got right under their skin, in so many ways, and the lack of response showed a real toughness. England weren't going to get dragged into any kind of skirmish away from the business conducted in the middle. Nothing was going to alter England's focus in getting over the line.

Some argued it was written in the stars that England would win – just as in 1981 we had a dead Pope, a royal wedding and a victorious Liverpool team in the European Cup final – but the fundamental secret to success was nothing to do with fate. England prospered because of such strong direction from Fletcher and Vaughan.

Their pre-planning was spot on to the extent that even when Australia gained a substantial lead despite being bowled out for 210 in the first innings of the series, England were not dissuaded from playing the brand of cricket they had plumped for on the eve of the series. It took strong management from the coach and captain to maintain them on the same course and reinforcement to all the players that as a collective they were a force to be reckoned with.

It was not long before there was plenty of evidence to suggest that this particular England team was one without any real weak link. They were ferocious, and triumphed courtesy of an attitude I would describe as totally un-English. Whereas, previously, England teams had been told by their bosses at Lord's to get on with things, show some stiff upper lip, and turn the other cheek whenever confrontation occurred, this one had balls.

This one tore straight into the Australians, unafraid of guys with big reputations and big statures like Matthew Hayden. Standing up to him was akin to the Australians' tactic of targeting the opposition captain. You aim to destabilise the strongest facet in the opposing ranks. England had a right go at Hayden, which translated into basic language said: 'It doesn't matter how big you are, mate, you are in our sights.'

To be fair, it was obvious that Australia, in a funny way, really enjoyed the battle that summer. During the post-series debrief, Ricky Ponting graciously conceded that the fact they had found an opponent who really would stand up to them had been an inspiring challenge, and that his team unfortunately hadn't come up to the mark.

Ponting got some stick down under after that, his captaincy even coming under question from some, for being too nicey nicey. But don't underestimate Ponting. He was a thorough-bred competitor, not dissimilar to his non-nonsense predecessor Steve Waugh. Under the steely-eyed Waugh, Australia were always up for the battle, and would go hard at the opposition as a default. But the 2005 version were far from push-overs, and remember that they contained a healthy nucleus of the 2001 and 2002–03 sides.

The key for England was continuity. Until the final Test, their first choice XI stayed fit. There was no discernible weak link and Vaughan put his bowlers on in pairs and did serious damage. They were unrelenting in their endeavour to knock the other lot sideways; whenever they suffered a setback, their response was overwhelmingly positive.

But don't forget, Ponting didn't give an inch either. His rearguard hundred to save the third Test at Old Trafford was the ultimate captain's knock and, typical of the ebb and flow, ensured that Australia saved that match with one wicket intact.

Quite simply, it was the best series we've ever had and you will not better it, I am afraid. I am certain of that. Folk flocked from all over the country on the fifth morning in Manchester as if to prove it. Lancashire's offer of £10 tickets tempted thousands, and seeing the crowd of people locked out took me back to my playing days when we had queues snaking down the road for Gillette Cup semi-finals, and to the old photographs you would see adorning the walls inside Headingley and Old Trafford of the perimeter of the grounds teeming with wannabe spectators during the 1940s. This was a real throwback to the halcyon days of the past and those with tickets literally running for a seat once through the turnstiles.

Of course, just as in the previous win of the series in Birmingham, Flintoff was man of the match for the triumph in Nottingham which put England on the cusp of a first win over Australia in 18 years. Ponting would subsequently say when Australia returned home that their job was to unearth a Flintoff. England's original version could be found in the gardens of Number 10 Downing Street hours later, having earned a marathon sup.

But that would not have been possible, and the series would not have been as momentous as it was, without its grandstand finish. Step forward Kevin Pietersen. With his peacock hairdo it was obvious he craved being centre of attention, and he performed on the day all eyes were on the Oval.

It was a day that began with every TV and radio news bulletin headlining on cricket. Folk all around the country were talking about England's chance to bat out the final day for the draw they required. England v Australia, 12 September

2005, was the hottest show in town. Everyone wanted a ticket to witness the drama unfold.

Well, I say everyone wanted one. As it happened, I met a chap during that final morning of the series, immediately after he came through the turnstiles next to the Alec Stewart Gate. He was clutching his ticket, which would have cost him £60–£70. He spoke to me as I made my way from one of our Sky Sports TV trucks into the OCS stand, the building where the commentary box was housed.

'They're not starting on time, are they?' he asked, panic strewn over his face.

'Yes, I would think so.'

'Oh no! You're joking.'

Naturally, I asked him what the problem was.

'Oh, I'm not bothered about seeing them play,' he told me, clutching his ticket stub. 'I just want it to be over. We've got to win this.'

But he got his wish, and some fantastic entertainment to boot.

This was one of those scenarios that Des Lynam in his pomp would have relished – a real 'how do they do that?' moment. Pietersen whacked the great Warne against the spin into the stands, and this was the first time I had ever witnessed anyone render him powerless. Warne played over 100 Tests and I cannot recall others pongo-ing him over midwicket like that. It was simply unheard of.

Flintoff had got England to the finish line, pounding in relentlessly to claim five wickets during one memorable spell the previous day to keep Australia in arrears. But it was Pietersen's outstanding innings of 158, his first Test hundred, that got them over it and propelled him to superstardom. It was as good an innings as I've seen.

Early wickets for Australia on that final day ensured a fairly intense finale to the series despite the end result, and there were plenty of English nerves around the Oval as Pietersen counter-attacked in his now customary, outrageous fashion, primarily against Warne, one of the game's all-time greats. It is incredible to think that Warne took 40 wickets that series and still finished on the losing team.

From what I have witnessed from my privileged seat with Sky Sports, the trio of Kevin Pietersen, Brian Lara and Ricky Ponting have possessed that ability to get themselves in, and to then shift gears once they are 'in'. That is what so excited me about Pietersen when we first saw him emerge in the previous winter in South Africa, where he built his hundreds like a good middle-distance runner would plan a race. He does something similar in that he gets the pace of things before applying the acceleration on the home straight. His management of an innings is truly masterful.

There comes a time in every innings when you see he is about to move into another gear like the smoothest of motor cars. At the Oval that famous September afternoon he went into overdrive. Much later, during the winter of 2012–13, he showed that perfectly with his hundred in the Test match at Mumbai. Just a few days previously in Ahmedabad, he had not got a clue how to get started, and looked stuck in reverse to be honest. However, the best players are able to come up with something by way of reaction, and he did just that. By getting into the nets and working tirelessly on his defence, he realised what he needed to do to feel in on those surfaces.

Then in the match situation, you saw that once he got a measure of it all, he knew when to step on the gas. The reason that Mumbai innings was so special was because he gave the innings the impetus it lacked. I know England would have been fretting about one thing, because I would have been had I been their coach, and that was the rate of scoring amongst their top-order batsmen.

They had Nick Compton making his way in international cricket, Alastair Cook tends to play at a fairly sedate pace and Jonathan Trott is never much of an upgrade on steady, someone who gets into his own little world and is rarely shaken out of it. Their presence in a cluster meant that England's run rate was always going to have the potential to cause a problem.

When Pietersen arrived at the wicket at the Wankhede Stadium, the team run rate sat exactly at two, at 68 for two. But when he left after scoring 186 it was 3.4, and England had scored in excess of four runs per over while he was at the crease. He had moved the game on, and that in a nutshell is why he's so special.

He had smoothly gone through the gears, dictated terms to the Indian bowlers and spread the field. A sign of good batsmanship is when you can set the field for the opposition captain. So that the fielders are where you want them, not where he wants them, and recollections of that 158 against Warne are that he did exactly the same. It was like him saying: 'Yeah, I'm in now, and it's my turn. Watch this.'

He saved that Test by taking it away from Australia. Certainly, as a commentator I was making the point that survival was all well and good but you need to score runs to get yourself out of dangerous territory. In that instant it was necessary to take the game away from Australia both time-wise and run-wise, and that was not a straightforward task when faced with an attack of that quality. The equation is always to get the runs up and the time down, to a point where the opposition cannot win.

Australia dropped him of course during that innings, and Warnie was left to rue that missed opportunity when he was still in the teens. But they also threw everything at him to try to get him out, including Warne going around the wicket. Some people suggested that was negative. But oh no, not a bit of it. Warne was so clever at mind games as a bowler, and that was simply him playing on Pietersen's ego. 'Okay, have a go at this!' he was telling him. He was fizzing the ball into the rough outside leg stump, and challenging Pietersen to attack him. And he did.

It would be naive to assume that Warne had given up at that stage by bowling it out there from that angle – that he had somehow given up trying to get him out. Not a bit of it, he was simply trying harder. There was no negativity, he was just trying to get him out any way he could, and he was playing on the possibility that once set the biggest danger to Pietersen was himself.

The adrenaline was certainly pumping that afternoon and one of my favourite memories of it was when he was actually in the post-match interview on the field of play. 'I'm speechless,' he claimed, before rabitting on for the next 15 minutes about it. He is Marmite. There are still people on Twitter that tell you he shouldn't be in the England side, and Kevin has developed a love–hate relationship with fans of the game. Sure, he is never going to please all of the people all of the time but I won't have it when folk tell me he's no good, that he's too reckless. Just have a look at the figures. They speak for themselves. He has an unbelievable record. An average of 49 in half-a-dozen appearances short of 100 Tests.

Michael Vaughan is someone I have got to know even better in recent years because of his media work, primarily with *Test Match Special* whose commentary box is more often than not adjacent to that of Sky Sports, and I always recognised him as a good thinker about the game. He had been a brilliant player in his pomp, the number one batsman in the world, lest we forget, at a time when Sachin Tendulkar and Brian Lara were in their prime, who scored runs for fun against a really top-class Australian attack. And in 2005, he was in his prime as a captain. Everything seemed to move in rhythm for him when England were out in the field, which is more than you can say of his dancing.

Very enthusiastic is our Mick about foxtrotting and the like. Similar to those other groovers Darren Gough, Phil Tufnell and Mark Ramprakash, he was gripped by Saturday night fever for a while. And he gave that *Strictly Come Dancing* challenge a fair old do considering he has the turning circle of a World War I tank. By rights he should only have moved in straight lines – just toddled up and down, changed hands and come back again – and it would have been much more of a level playing field for him if they had made *Strictly* like a 100 metre race, with all the competitors laned off. So good on him that he managed all kinds of twists and turns.

To be honest, he started the series like Steve Harmison did at Brisbane six years earlier, and I have to take some credit for the improvement. I put a call in to Latin Les, who helped get him into shape, and we even roped in another of my Manchester acquaintances Carlos, an Argentinian rumba specialist, to put the finishing touches on things. Carlos's speciality is to make sure male dancers' facial expressions are bang on – the trick is to make them imagine they have just finished a session of colonic irrigation. One of the traps you can fall into, as you may have noticed from your telly, is that blokes allow themselves to look like they've just started the colonic.

Having studied Vaughan on *SCD*, I decided to enrol him into our Morris dancing team. It is still in its formative period but I am working on a collective from the cricket world. I like the attitude of Morris men. I was in the Cavendish Arms in Cartmel once when I met this group of lads with bells all over them, holding hankies and sticks. Just the sight of them had me giggling.

'Alright, lads, have you just been on?' I inquired as I stood at the bar waiting for my pint to be poured.

'No, not yet,' came their collective reply 'We're having a few beers first.'

'Be honest, would you do this sober?' one of them parped.

Actually, come to think of it …

A Sobering Reality

Talk about going from one extreme to the other. What a contrast the following series down under provided. Andrew Flintoff's team of 2006–07 were terrible. It really was a case of us going from our best to our worst. The disciplines of the team were poor, and there was no excuse for that really.

Sir Ian Beefalot gave it some serious welly on the sex, drugs and rock 'n' roll tour to New Zealand back in the day, but this England team did their best to make their behaviour as notorious. Of course, they got nailed 5–0, a subject which unsurprisingly Shane Warne brings up regularly whenever patriotism raises its head in our commentary box.

'When were that? I have very hazy recall, and I don't remember any of it,' I protest.

'Yeah, exactly the same as the team,' he responds.

Australia were ruthless in that 'revenge' series. They were careful not to use the word in the build-up but they were full tilt throughout the most-hyped England tour down under. Ticket sales reached new levels and so did the depths of despair for Flintoff and coach Duncan Fletcher. They turned up with blokes half-fit and a plan to replicate the 2005 winning side as near as damnit. But no Vaughan, no Marcus Trescothick, no Simon Jones meant one thing: no chance.

Two summers earlier we had seen how the tone was set for the series by a Steve Harmison delivery. The same could be said of the follow-up. Only this time there was nothing positive or menacing about it.

Every player visualises how they wish to start a big match, and I am sure big Steve would have had an image of the ball being pouched by his mate Freddie at second slip. Of course, that is exactly where it went. Although as I blurted out instantaneously on air: 'What usually happens when the ball flies there is it is followed by a big appeal.' Unfortunately, there was no bat involved.

As former cricketers you have to show some sympathy but Australia displayed none. No wonder by the time the Ashes had been won back in early December a few tourists sought refuge in a few stiff drinks.

Glasses raised at the end of that series provided me with one of my favourite memories from the game. To be there to witness the final goodbyes of Warne and Glenn McGrath in Sydney was so special. A memory I will never forget. It was not only a special moment for Australia but a special moment for the Ashes.

I had managed to get away from my perch up in the commentary box, and made my way down through the stands towards the boundary edge, taking my little camera with me. The pair of them were clutching their Baggy Green caps, acknowledging the rich applause of the home crowd as they left the arena for the final time. I don't think I've ever taken a better photograph, and this particular picture remains stored on my laptop computer.

Warnie has been a long-term pal because of the Accrington connection. Bobby Simpson had recommended him as over-seas professional in the early 1990s, and we soon learnt that he was a young man intent on enjoying himself, with an eye for the ladies. I'm pleased to report he didn't hook up with my daughter but the same could not be said for one of my daughter's mates. Thank goodness it wasn't our Sarah.

Ricky Ponting was part of that great Australian team, the youngster that came through it and who was around long enough to be on the wrong end of Ashes results once the pendulum had swung back England's way. When he came into the side he was surrounded by players like Gilchrist, the

Waughs, Warne and McGrath. Even this Aussie side had an average well into its thirties. But he seemed to take it on himself to inflict the primary damage at the start of the series, crashing 196 at Brisbane.

A fearless batsman, a truly fine player of the short ball, and a great competitor was our Ricky. When you recall him in your mind, he's always got that old Baggy Green on his head and he's gnarled beyond his years. To me, he looked like that when he first burst into the team. He was Australia's young fogey.

When he first came in from Tasmania, I looked for the influence of characters like David Boon, Jack Simmons, John Hampshire, Jack Bond and David Hughes on him. Tasmania always had an England coach in their early days of competing against the big boys of Australian state cricket, and it was an English influence that helped them gain their entrance into the Sheffield Shield in the late 1970s. As a batsman, Ricky was the complete player for me, whose greatest strength was arguably the fact that he was so difficult to dislodge at the start of an innings.

And he grew up fast as Australia's golden boy batsman. He was just 23 when, in my series as coach over there, he turned up one day with a black eye he had received late one night in the Bourbon & Beefsteak, a 24-hour cavorting institution in Sydney's Kings Cross.

The Australian Cricket Board were always good at teaching their players right from wrong and I never forget the way they dealt with that particular issue – they simply wheeled Ponting out in front of the press to explain himself. There was no-one there to hold his hand, one of their media personnel simply informed the gathered media that he was going to get help with whatever he needed – probably boxing lessons, by the look of him. There was none of this flannel that they were looking into the incident, they just dealt with it head on. I bet he looks upon that incident now as one that helped him grow up faster.

From a cricket perspective, even from a young age Ponting had that air about him that he deserved to be there, that he was good enough to be a Test cricketer. Given the standard of the team he had come into, and indeed the standard of the competition to break into it, to make it seem from the off that it was his stage was no mean feat. He just slotted in to the batting order like he'd been there forever. They got him in to bat at number six initially but it was not long before he was up to number three and once there he didn't relinquish the place until the very last year of his international career.

It is always a sign when you are moved out of your established position and when they eased him down to number four to bring in players like Rob Quiney and Peter Forrest the signs would have been clear to him that it was the beginning of the end. When he did finally go in late 2012, he would perhaps have reflected on the 2006–07 whitewash of England as his career high, but it would also go down on his personal record that he lost consecutive away series to England as Australia captain. I would maintain in his defence that those defeats were easy to explain away. On both tours, the other lot, England, were better.

Short of the Finishing Tape

Misery loves company they say, and for Ricky Ponting there will always be a pair of frustrating run-outs for him to agonise over when he reflects on his Ashes exploits in years to come. A nice bottle of Jimmy Boag's should help take the pain away, Rick. Always hits the spot for me.

Gary Pratt did him off the bench in Nottingham in 2005, of course, and he would have felt a right daft apeth after being left short of his ground again in one of the iconic moments of the following series, during England's push for victory at the Oval. You will no doubt recall Andrew Flintoff's slingshot from mid-on careering into its target at the batsmen's end after Michael Hussey had attempted to steal a single.

It was the moment that swung the contest firmly back in England's direction and triggered the sound of 20,000 people roaring approval as Flintoff stood arms aloft celebrating. Being left short of your ground is annoying enough without having to contend with the joy of others at your less than satisfactory fate.

Actually, even dusting yourself off and making for the dressing room to nothing but a solitary handclap and a hint of a cheer from the opposition can be a source of humiliation. It is something I experienced as captain of the MCC against Oxford University in the Parks one year.

Captain's privilege meant I paired myself at the top of the order with Bob Lanchbury, who played a dozen or so first-class matches for Worcestershire. Bob was a decent player and was at that time scoring lots of runs in the Birmingham

League. Batting with him, however, required good communication on your part because he was deaf. So, as we kitted up to go out to bat, Bob instructed me: 'Whenever you want to run, make sure you look directly at me when you are calling so that I can lip-read you.'

No bother, I thought. That will be easy enough. A few singles taken, a few overs seen off, and I was just beginning to feel 'in'. So when I cut to square cover, forcing the fielder to run round five yards to cut the ball off, I instinctively shouted 'yes' and set off for the other end. It struck me halfway down that Bob was not appearing in my eyeline, and a hopeful glance upwards was not met with any suggestion that he might be setting off any time soon.

Panic struck me as I realised I had failed to look up after striking the ball and now it was almost certainly too late. I witnessed for the first time Bob stood there, one hand leaning down on his bat handle, the other palm upwards pointing at me down the pitch, an accompaniment to his lips mouthing the word 'no'. About-turn necessary, I hurtled my way back from whence I came and got in a dive with half-pike that got me as swiftly as possible over the crease and into the usual concoction of mud and sawdust that resided in the vicinity – about a second too late.

Oh, the ignominy of it all, as I trudged off. It wasn't as if Bob hadn't warned me. He had been explicit with his instructions, and failing to adhere to them had cost me dear.

I was vexed enough with myself to alter the batting order for the second innings, leaving Bob up the top and demoting myself to the very last space on the scorecard in a bid to avoid any further calamity. This time, Bob provided more humour, only the joke wasn't on me this time. Early on in his second knock, a huge appeal went up for a caught behind, so loud that you might have heard it in Cambridge let alone Oxford.

Bob stood his ground but was given out by the umpire. 'Did you get a nick?' he was asked, once back in the visitors' dressing room. 'Yes,' he admitted. 'It was a definite edge. I just didn't think they had appealed!'

England most definitely did when Flintoff's arrow hit its target. One last hurrah with the ball would have been great but physically there was not much left on that final afternoon so a run-out that put the team on the cusp of another Ashes victory had to do. It's so sad when the body knocks on the door and says: 'No more'. Darren Gough, Dean Headley and Simon Jones had all experienced the call and now it was Flintoff being told that his troublesome knee was spent after a decade of top-level pounding. I had known him since a lad as Andrew, but to the people he was the warm, amiable and fearsome Freddie.

The summer of 2009 had some interesting venue choices to say the least, and although I liked the decision to give another Test to Chester-le-Street when West Indies were in town – Paul Allott says when he was at Durham University he could buy eight pints for a quid, and too many matches in London, where it's £4 for something so flat it could be served in envelopes and you part with the best part of a tenner for a lukewarm pie, is a put-off for a thrifty northerner like me – I was nowhere near as keen on the idea to open the Ashes in Wales.

Yes, I am very proud of my Welsh heritage, but if you can prove that any of the England management, the cricket people, agreed to that I will show my backside from the top of the Brecon Beacons. Just like in 1997 we should have got 'em at the Bull Ring first up. It was a wasted opportunity. Bit of a stronghold is Edgbaston, as we know, and it would have played into our hands and against the Australians.

Over the previous 12 months Jimmy Anderson had provided unmistakable proof that he swings both ways, and allowing him to duck it this way and that at the start of the five-match series would have been using home advantage. Inners and outers with pace and accuracy will test the very best, and with the Edgbaston surface prone to nibble a bit as well, Stuart Broad would have been a tricky proposition too. The players were pretty peeved that they would not be playing at all at Old Trafford or Trent Bridge, Broad's home and a bit of a home from home for Anderson over recent years.

The Major Match Group, who make the decisions on scheduling, at the time included former trade unionist Lord (Bill) Morris, Karen Earl, who ran a very successful sponsorship agency, John Pickup from the recreational game and Mike Vockins, the former chief executive of Worcestershire. All are delightful people, with some experience of the game, but none has ever run a Test match or been in charge of a major sports team. The selection, in addition to drawing accusations that it was a Welsh mafia stitch-up, also kyboshed any chance of developing early momentum.

But what was shown in grinding out that draw at the Swalec Stadium was that after a few months of disruption, England had got the right man as coach in Andy Flower. He is immensely proud and tough to boot, and his background in Zimbabwe clearly steeled him for any challenge. His first target after surprisingly losing the Test series in the Caribbean earlier that year was to mould the team into one that performed collectively. It was pretty obvious, I think, that England possessed quality players who had underachieved, but the challenge faced by Andrew Strauss and Flower was to change the culture of the team from individuals into a cohesive unit.

At that time, partly because of the slate being wiped clean under a new regime, and partly because a number of star men were coming back to fitness, there was a lot of scrapping for places. I have never gone along with the notion tripped out by selectors that 'you have to have consistency'. Hunger is what you want, and as the curtain opened on the 2009 summer five players were fighting for one batting position against the West Indies.

England played with great style in trouncing the reluctant tourists from the Caribbean. No weaknesses detectable and two crackerjacks in Andrew Flintoff and Kevin Pietersen both back in after injury. During the one-day series that preceded the arrival of the Australians to our shores, you could tell the players were in tune because the running between the wickets had Andy Flower stamped all over it, and the fielding looked panther-like.

Right venue or not, what a game down at Cardiff! Australia gave it everything and won nine-tenths of it but did not have that bit of magic to shift either Monty Panesar or James Anderson in that final session. Ricky Ponting must have been musing over absent friends, and surely Messrs McGrath or Warne would have done for either of them 'tout de suite'.

You had to admire the English rearguard on that final day when Paul Collingwood earned his nickname Brigadier

Block. The one blot on the landscape was the shenanigans involving England's 12th man Bilal Shafayat and the physio Steve McCaig. In my book, Ponting was quite right to comment that it was 'ordinary' behaviour when they encroached onto the field with drinks and gloves. Anderson, though, was having none of it and waved them away – or at least that's what it looked like. This is a fight to the finish and I will back myself, he seemed to say. They are all like that in Burnley on a Sunday evening.

The quality of the Australians' batting in that game was a lesson to all in terms of technique, concentration and responsibility, and perhaps England learned something of the need to bat time rather than force things on that slow surface. Collingwood's determination was a masterclass in attitude.

My epic moment, though, was the working over that Peter Siddle gave to Graeme Swann. For all of us who have been out there, this was the time that we felt envious of the custodians of Ashes cricket 2009. The smell of battle, the body-wrenching effort of the bowler, the battering and spirit of a batsman who is struggling to cope but will not yield IS the game.

We had a mystery blond turn up for the next match at Lord's. Apparently he had missed the first Test because he was playing cards in America, so it was a good job we kept it under wraps that there was a whist drive going off in St John's Wood. We would have hated for our Shane to have missed England's first win over Australia at headquarters for 75 years.

And what a way to complete it – a champion performance from a champion bloke on that final morning. You may have known him by one of his aliases – 'Pedalo Fred', 'IPL Fred', or 'Miss-the-bus Fred'. But when he was on it he was on it. Not the influence across the whole series that he was in 2005 but when England needed it most at Lord's, Flintoff delivered. There would have been more that answered yes than no if you had asked the Australians, 'Was he the reason that you lost the game?'

His every knee-jerking, side-straining stride kept the crowd spellbound as he charged in from the pavilion end. I have never known such a fervent Lord's audience and the fans, both English and Australian, stayed way beyond the presentation, reliving the morning glory of Fred. Yabba-dabba-do!

The Queen popped in to meet the teams on the second day, and after that kind of performance he should have been getting the summons to her place for an anointing. In consecutive home Ashes years he single-handedly lifted the status of Test cricket. Had the Queen Mother still been around he might have been invited for a tipple. I am not sure he would have refused.

For so long the F-factor had crippled England's bid to derail Australia. But fear no longer played its part, and those Aussies never could stomach a dose of our own F, Freddie. It was that week that he confirmed the end of the series would mark his farewell from Tests at the age of 31, and even the oppo let out a sigh of disappointment.

But at that juncture, Ponting knew he had it all to do. Australia appeared to have lost their mongrel – no, not one of their WAGs' dogs but their bite, their feistiness. Mitchell Johnson had been the leading wicket-taker in the world for a period not long before but was all over the place in English conditions. In fact, the only snarler related to the Australian camp was Johnson's mother, and she was snarling in the direction of his fiancée Jessica Bratich, a Perth-based karate champion. And as the late, great Peter Cook said: 'She lives f***ing miles away!'

Edgbaston has not exactly been Ponting's favourite venue either following his faux pas in 2005, and this visit seemed doomed to failure too when he found himself locked out of his own press conference. Had the door bolted on Australia's Ashes hopes? Well, the rain reduced the chances of them going 2–0 down after England worked a first-innings advantage in a vastly reduced contest. That was one of the least memorable Ashes Tests in memory, in fact, so much so that the thing I recall most readily is bursting into Muppets mode when it was revealed that Graham Manou was playing after Brad Haddin damaged a finger in the warm-up. As in *'man-ou, man-ou, doo doo de doo doo ...'*

Like all good dramas there was a twist around the corner, however, and the crushing defeat at Headingley provided England with two startling realities: how good Kevin Pietersen is and how vital Andrew Flintoff is to the team. Their dual absence through injury – KP would not feature after Lord's – was more crucial to the result than the pre-match disruption of being stood in the street in the early hours courtesy of a hotel fire alarm or Matt Prior going down in the warm-up like a sniper had shot him. It showed a good spirit between the teams – and England had credit in the bank from Edgbaston with the Haddin situation, remember – that the toss was delayed while Prior's back spasm was worked upon.

Defeat within eight sessions at Headingley would have appalled Flower because as coach you are accustomed to winning or losing but 'performance' is everything. England had been given an examination at a ground that can get bowler-friendly with the mere sighting of a cloud overhead, and they came up woefully short. It would not have been the defeat but the manner of it that furrowed the brow that evening.

Some might have suggested it gave credence to the leaked Justin Langer-prepared dossier that turned up in a Sunday newspaper on the third morning. Lest we forget, though, England were still ahead and had been when Langer's thoughts were put down on screen. These reports are standard procedure and England would have had one from John Buchanan, who had been signed up to do some 'consultancy' work. England wisely kept any such documentation locked away.

Using his vantage point in the Somerset dressing room, Langer dubbed England 'shallow' and claimed they had a 'sing when you're winning' attitude. In my opinion it was pretty run-of-the-mill stuff with a couple of glaring inaccuracies. I have always viewed James Anderson as a wholehearted performer, a real trier – certainly not a 'pussy' – and the way to bowl at Matt Prior is certainly not wide.

Prior's stock rose with every passing appearance that summer and the upcurve has rarely plateaued since. His wicketkeeping, previously under scrutiny, was clean and assured and for this a lot of credit was due to the unassuming Bruce French, the former England gloveman, who clearly found a way to connect with his charge and push him to the limits. I think we knew that series that Prior would get to the very top, and at the time of writing he is the world's best wicketkeeper–batsman by a long distance.

What followed proved to be a career-defining moment for many of the players, not least Jonathan Trott. It was Johnny Nash time after Leeds; as in 'There are More Questions than Answers'. Could Andrew Strauss lead from the front and seize a decisive moment? Could Alastair Cook battle with those technical gremlins and foil the new-ball attack? Could Ian Bell move from lovely player into a Ponting-like run machine? Could Paul Collingwood move from foil player to leader? Could Matt Prior rubber-stamp his position as England wicky for the next five years? Could Andrew Flintoff go out in a blaze of glory and get the T-shirt? Could Graeme Swann deliver when it really mattered? Was Stuart Broad the new Flintoff? Could Steve Harmison hit Australia with accuracy, pace and menace one last time? Could Jimmy Anderson produce one more match-winning spell?

To be fair, the players did their utmost to answer in the affirmative. But Trott's debut was a sensational piece of selection as well as performance. Trott did not have the same standing as some of the Australian batsmen – Simon Katich, Michael Hussey and Michael Clarke – but what he did show was that he possessed a sound game plan and an outstanding temperament. What a call it was by Ashley Giles, the selector who pushed his case for the final two Tests once it became clear that Ravi Bopara was in no nick.

Trott showed something of himself during that debut hundred that us English cricket followers have come to take for granted: he is unflappable when at the crease. And Broad's was a coming-of-age display on a tired, dry pitch.

Did anybody see Andy Flower at the end of the game? Thought not. He did pop out to give an interview during the celebrations and winced when asked about the open-top bus ride that some might have been expecting, but, typical of the way he operates, he was already thinking about the next series before the players had finished sipping champagne on the outfield. He had done such a remarkable job with those players in such a short space of time and he allowed them to enjoy their winning moment by withdrawing.

Naturally, there were two cricket events that the British public looked forward to with the greatest of relish in the autumn of 2010. One involved 11 men of England defending their crown against the same number from the rogue isle; the other was a celebration of my 473 years in the sport.

Even then, during 20 theatre show dates of *Start the Car* across the UK, in the company of co-host Peter Hayter, the *Mail on Sunday* cricket correspondent, I found the two subjects inseparable. The majority of the nice people who bought tickets – each of whom contributed a brick to the west wing extension at Bumble Towers – had a good laugh at my time as a player, coach and umpire, but most of all they wanted to know my opinion on what we could expect to see during England's attempt to win in Australia for only the second time since I featured in the mid-1970s.

As far as that particular series goes, and as you most definitely know by now, I have been there, read the team talk and worn the abdominal protector. There was even a rumour that I was close to being the first player in England v Australia matches to be dropped by the selectors on the controversial two-testicle rule post-Perth 1974. One that I quickly dispelled by insisting upon a medical. I am not sure if persuading them I still had three worked in my favour, but at least I got a few more caps and an after-dinner joke out of it.

Of course, every time I talk about the whack at the Waca it invokes tears of contrasting emotions. Plenty of them are tears of laughter from those sat in front of me, and it is a moment that defines my career. As I say at the start of the show, if Michael Aspel popped up with his Big Red Book, his opening gambit would be: 'Tonight, David Lloyd, this is your lite-some.' I've still got the offending article in 37 bits in my garage, as it happens, and take it on tour with me so that during the interval the audience get a closer look. They all tend to want to see it close up too – nowt as queer as folk, I guess.

The more studious cricket aficionados tend to get quite analytical with their questions, which are scribbled down during the 15-minute break and which I attempt to answer in the second half of the performance. They seek such in-depth insight as: 'Why is Kevin Pietersen such a knob?' That, I kid you not, was the first question of the opening night in Leamington Spa, and showed Jim from Pretoria to be one of life's deep thinkers. How do you go about answering a question like that? It was only an hour's performance.

A slight aside here. Our Kevin does tend to court negativity, and I am not sure why. I have always found him a decent lad. When we were out in New Zealand in early 2013, I spoke to him and told him that the builder we were using on our new house back home was called Jack and walked around on one leg practising his KP swivel shot with a cry of 'boom, boom'. I asked him whether there was any chance of this lad's hero providing a signed shirt. 'He thinks he's you,' I told him.

Kevin obviously had more serious matters concerning him and a couple of days later he was forced off the tour with a knee injury. Chances of the shirt gone then, or so I thought. 'Here, Bumble,' Stuart Broad said to me on the eve of the final Test in Auckland. 'KP left something for you before he got on the plane.' What a lovely gesture.

In general when you are on television, there are cues preparing you for what is coming up, but these Q & As with a live audience really put you on the spot. Particularly technical posers such as:

'Bumble, please consider the following scenario, choose your multiple choice answer and provide a reason for this choice ...'

Of course, you expect to be asked things like who was the best all-rounder you have ever come up against? Imran Khan or Sir Garfield Sobers. Or the nastiest fast bowler. No prizes for guessing that one. Or, who was the most explosive batsman? A certain West Indian gentleman with the surname Richards was pretty special, and it's a pleasure to recall some of the stuff that the great, snorting Viv did on the cricket field.

But, no, the question on this particular card was nothing like that.

It continued: 'What would you rather be attacked by: a horse-sized duck or 10 duck-sized horses?'

There you go. Not easy, is it? Put on the spot like that, pluses and minuses for each went spinning around my head. I am not sure there is a correct answer to something like that, Stu, of Staines.

At my age, memory questions do prove a bit of a struggle (you've done stuff, seen more stuff than the young 'uns, so of course you are going to forget some of it along the way), so you can imagine the trouble a question about one particular former Ashes captain posed in Manchester.

'Has Nasser Hussain ever bought a round of drinks?' asked Don Kiddick.

That was harsh from Don, really, so I confirmed he had even though I couldn't swear, hand on bible in court, that I'd been present on such an occasion.

Mostly, however, people were talking shop. What chance had England of emulating Mike Gatting's team of 1986–87 and actually winning the series down under? If I was a betting man – I am as it happens and enjoy winning the charity bets I have with Coral for good causes – I told them I would be putting money on a 3–1 away win. I was adamant that England were a better team, and good enough to be two matches better than Australia over the course of five. But I won't dwell on that for too long. After all, nobody likes a smart arse.

A few weeks later and we were thrust into the thick of the fiercest rivalry in international cricket. One in which standing your ground and bloody-mindedness combine to leave onlookers with sheer disbelief at what that combination cooks up. In terms of intensity, it beats the Ashes itself. Yes, I am talking about the 35-year feud between Sir Ian Botham and Ian Chappell.

I always got on very well with Chappell but the same cannot be said for Beefy, and putting them together is like throwing grenades around on Bonfire Night. As in, one almighty explosion is only ever seconds away. And I was witness to the reprise of one of the greatest bust-ups in sports history during the second Test of the 2010–11 Ashes. Yes, they re-enacted the spat of more than 30 years earlier that had led to fisticuffs, a chase and allegations of threats to do all sorts of bodily harm to one another.

We were leaving the ground at the Adelaide Oval one evening after play when the pair's paths crossed. Of course, as established commentators they are often in the same vicinity but for the good of world peace do everything they can to avoid each other. But on this particular occasion, with all the combi buses parked next to each other out the back of the ground, a meeting between the two was inevitable, and so it came to pass.

The Channel 9 bus and Sky Sports bus were parked adjacent to each other in the television compound, ours directly in front of theirs. People like Mark Taylor, Michael Slater and Big Ronnie, the Australian channel's floor manager, were milling around in this compound as we passed their bus to get to ours. Nasser Hussain and Beefy are with me, the designated driver, and as we turn round the front of the vehicles who should be leaning against the bonnet but Chappelli. Nasser and I both shuffle past and as Beefy follows, the former Australian captain muttered: 'C***.'

Of course, we all knew who this was aimed at, and it had the obvious effect on its target, who doesn't break stride towards our chariot but nevertheless replies with a booming: 'Oh, f*** off, you c***.'

As we reached our vehicle, however, it was clear that he was not going to let the provocation go. He threw his bag inside and turning round declared: 'Right, that's it, once and for all, come on.'

It took Big Ron, this huge unit of a man, to step across and plead: 'Come on, fellas, ease off now. We can't have this.'

That request meant the threat of a bare-knuckle dust-up was avoided but the obscenities continued through the open windows of the vans as we drove off. With expletives filling the air, Beefy was absolutely steaming mad.

In this kind of situation, timing is everything, and I simply couldn't resist.

'That went well, then, Beef.'

'Just f***ing wait 'til I get him on my own in a lift,' he retorted.

'But Beefy, he's a bloody pensioner. You've got to let it go.'

'There's no chance of that,' he warned. 'No chance.'

It took him two days to come down from the height of his anger, and to be fair it has been simmering for decades. That bar-room barney at the Melbourne Cricket Ground in the early months of 1977 is Ashes cricket gone mad. It was an incident that spiralled out of all control, and has reached a level like you have never seen. Just the sighting of one by the other is enough to have the veins bulging in their necks.

The silly thing about it is that we are talking about two of the great men of international cricket. Fantastic blokes, the pair of them, but there is a massive blind spot when it comes to each other. For everybody else it is an absolute hoot, although I am not sure anyone wanted the stand-off in Adelaide to escalate any further. They are both guys who will never back down, never give an inch to an opponent, and part of the problem is that their DNA is so similar. Unfortunately, in this scenario it is not possible for them both to be right. And in this instance, two rights definitely make a wrong.

Flower Power

Post 2009 Ashes I was in the same camp as others like Michael Vaughan and Michael Atherton in arguing that England should maintain a five-man attack. Easier said than done without a top-class performer like Flintoff to balance things, I grant you, but it just seemed like they needed that extra firepower if they were to beat teams regularly.

Like most things, however, this was an area that Andy Flower and his management think-tank got right and one which I concede I got wrong. The quality of the bowlers meant that four was plenty.

There were lots of other good calls being made too between 2009 and 2010–11. Flower made them into a selfless unit for the World Twenty20 in 2010, one of the chief reasons for their success in the Caribbean. That coaching phrase 'There is no "I" in team' can be so hard to achieve because players can get into a mindset of 'I will get some for me first and then kick on'. This usually comes with uncertainty in selection but Flower and Paul Collingwood had clear visions of what they wanted and managed to transmit that to the team. Yes, it was a surprise that Jimmy Anderson was left on the sidelines but the inclusion of Ryan Sidebottom was the right call.

I have seen England in all forms of the game and been involved since the 1960s but I'd never been able to say before that we were fitter and stronger, and out-fielded all-comers, in a global competition. Our blokes were in peak condition while those who had been lording it at the much-hyped Indian Premier League traipsed about like lummoxes. England's dynamism made the IPL seem like a series of beer matches while the World Twenty20 took on the mantle of the real deal.

Flower does not allow indecision. With him you choose your method and implement it. He has always been an uncompromising sort of character. When we played Zimbabwe they would warm up with a game of touch rugby before the start of play and he would be scrapping! Strauss's calm authority provided a perfect foil when it came to planning for the defence of the urn.

Of course, tough men had gone in search of the prize before – Nasser Hussain told us that when he plays Monopoly with his family he insists on being the iron and will not compromise even if the kids kick off, a startling revelation indeed – and it has made not a blind bit of difference. Australia poses the severest of tests for visiting cricket teams but despite their home advantage this soon turned into a reality check for Ricky Ponting and his team. Quite simply, he had to come to terms with the fact he did not have this flippin' great attack at his disposal any more. What that first drawn match at the Gabba confirmed to us was that while Australia would be competitive at times, and have the odd session in which they might dominate, England were the better team.

There were own goals everywhere you looked in Brisbane. First, in the build-up they had a big image of a right-handed Doug Bollinger at the Gabba. If it wasn't bad enough that someone had flipped a negative the wrong way around – Doug is a left-armer – he wasn't even going to be playing in the opening match.

Also, when I first toured Australia there wasn't much fuss when their supporters lugged beer bottles at you. Yet this time, with all their rules and regulations in place, the Barmy Army's trumpeter Billy was restricted in the parping of his instrument. He received a letter informing him of the correct protocol. He would not be allowed to play when he liked, rather at set intervals under their instruction. Land of the Didgeridoo? More like Land of the Didgeridon't.

Probably saved Billy a bob or two, though. All that playing must make a bloke thirsty, and Australia is not such a good place to get a thirst on these days, especially if you're a thrifty northerner. Exchange rates meant that a beer cost £6.50 – a beer, not a proper pint – which meant developing delaying tactics. Buy said drink and admire it for an hour before taking first sip was the way to go. No wonder folk were getting so fraught. On my first voyage into the Pig and Whistle – chosen hangout of the Barmies in Brisbane – two chaps were having a right old scrap. At those prices, I could only deduce it was a difference of opinion on whose turn it was to get to the bar.

I was pleased to get an invite from Shane Warne, aka Australia's Parky, to film clips for his Channel Nine chat show that week. It meant a few free pints of Guinness while the cameras rolled. From my experience, you've got to take advantage of any Australian hospitality because as soon as the cricket starts they get feisty. I was talking to Ian Healy, who was in hysterics about getting everybody to boo the Poms at one of the Aussies' official lunches. The humour is different over there and the locals are on a different wavelength to us. They just think it's funny to rub us English up the wrong way and wouldn't think twice about giving you a smack on the nose after a couple of pints. Hilarious, I am sure you'll agree.

There were a couple of notable feats from the opening day of the 2010–11 Ashes. Firstly, there was a new record set for the number of people 'milling around' at the toss. There must have been in excess of 100 out on the square before Ricky Ponting flicked up the coin – a mix of TV commentators and cameramen, radio people and assorted hangers on – which made me wonder what was stopping the rest of those in attendance swamping the outfield to get a closer look.

Then, there was a more acceptable 'I was there moment' when Peter Siddle took his hat-trick. The Aussies had bowled like drains for much of day one with Ben Hilfenhaus and Shane Watson's cunning plan after tea being to aim so wide of off-stump that the England batsmen couldn't hit them with a yard brush. But then along came Siddle to change the course of proceedings with a good line and length delivered with some menace. England's response to those basic disciplines was totally inadequate but did provide one of those great nerve-tingling experiences: the noise reverberating around the Gabba was amazing.

Put it this way, the atmosphere in the ground proved quite a contrast to that on the final couple of days of the match when England comfortably secured the draw. In fact, the silence was broken through an incident in the commentary box when Nasser Hussain landed a chair on Lord Gower's foot as they were switching over on the microphone. It sounded like he had been shot. Later, Gower said on air that he had a throbbing sensation. There's no answer to that, as Eric Morecambe would have said.

We saw what Alastair Cook was all about in England's second innings of 517 for one. Unfortunately, in addition to the double hundred, we were also witness to Ricky Ponting's behaviour when TV overruled his 'catch' against Cook. The stump microphones meant we could hear just how strongly he felt, directing his displeasure at Aleem Dar. In one way, Ricky was lucky this was a Test match and that cameras were pointed at the middle, because if it had happened when umpires like Cec Pepper, Syd Buller, Arthur Fagg, Bill Alley or Charlie Elliott were around his feet wouldn't have touched the floor with language like that. You swore at them at your peril.

Frustration was no doubt sparked by the lack of penetration with the ball, and they just couldn't seem to dig anyone up to alter that. In fact, the Australian chairman of selectors, Andrew Hilditch, could be seen power-walking in a tracksuit round the outfield for half an hour before play each day. Couldn't recall Ray Illingworth ever doing that! Could you imagine José Mourinho striding around the Bernabeu in a onesie while Real Madrid were warming up?

They were given notification of what they were missing rather cruelly during the second Test at Adelaide when the recalled Doug the Rug was stopped in his tracks as he ran in to bowl at Kevin Pietersen. Having aborted in his delivery stride, the Rug turned round to see a giant picture on the sightscreen of Shane Warne tucking into a Legend chicken burger. The spectre of Warne loomed large. He swears it's the best burger he's ever tasted but how Australia could have done with their bowling attack being beefed up.

It was all a bit too namby pamby. Mitchell Johnson was dropped and took the opportunity to show off his new 'wild-cat' body art. I liked the comment of the master, Richie Benaud. He said, in that wry way of his, he had never noticed a tattoo make anyone bowl better.

Seemed like the Aussies were doing everything they could to deflect attention from their on-field performance. Perhaps they thought wearing disguises would distract their opponents. Suddenly, we had Ricky with a new weave, and then Doug turned up with a hair regeneration of his own. But the England batsmen were never going to be intimidated by a man with a new squirrel on top of his previously exposed bald sphere. Statistics show that baldies do it better – just look at the records of Jonathan Trott and Matt Prior – so the message to Australian cricketers has to be 'just say no' when it comes to rugs.

Forget dodgy barnets, the stark truth of the tour was that any of England's back-up bowlers would have walked straight into Australia's team. It is not often in history that you would have said that the Aussies would have taken any one of them but I bet you they would have. Meanwhile, they had Ryan Harris – a sort of Mark Ealham with wheels – coming back from a chronic knee injury telling us he'd got through 13 overs and was fit for Adelaide.

In contrast, England's fast-bowling stocks were looking bountiful. Steve Finn bore an uncanny resemblance to Glenn McGrath while Ajmal Shahzad was a dead ringer for

Matthew Hoggard in his pomp. Finn has it all, height, pace and bounce, and if he can follow the advice of West Indies' deadly duo Courtney Walsh and Curtly Ambrose – who aimed at the wicketkeeper and allowed natural variation to do the rest – he will have a very decent international career. With his attributes of height and pace, getting it on a path to the gloveman just outside the off-stump means it passes the exact place where the batsman doesn't want to see it. Chris Tremlett is another who has everything when fit because of his massive frame. People tell me that he does not have menace but some of the nicest blokes in cricket have been fast bowlers: Michael Holding, Allan Donald, Brett Lee, Bob Willis and Andrew Flintoff among them. The list is endless, but in work gear these guys were ferocious. No sledging or slagging off the batsman. Just a look that told you I will make your stay out here so uncomfortable you will be shouting for your mum.

Australia's problem seemed to be that they had a glut of third seamers, and no strike bowlers, which meant that even after Johnson and Ben Hilfenhaus were axed post-Brisbane, their replacements Harris and Bollinger were forced to toil for long periods out in the middle. Not that they would have been as hot as us lot. You see, the Sky crew were forced to broadcast from the old changing rooms deep in the Sir Donald Bradman Stand. It was stifling in there with no air-con. Obviously, we didn't want to be seen as whingeing Poms so we got on with things. After all, it was not as if they'd had months to get ready for this Test. Stiff upper lip and all that.

Just as James Anderson cracked the game open with the ball on that first morning at the Adelaide Oval, so Kevin Pietersen took his opportunity to stamp his authority on things with a typically arrogant display of batting. England played some tellingly dismissive shots on days two and three and he played a lot of them. The Australians thought they'd indulge in a spot of bumper warfare, but he just played the short stuff as if it was in slow motion. And the way Xavier Doherty bowled suggested the Australian spinner needed the rest of the X-Men for support. It was pure savagery, and even though he got him in the end, the harsh reality was that KP had 227 to his name first. Australia couldn't possibly pick this bloke again. They'd probably have been better off with Tommy Docherty. The fact they plucked him out of the obscurity of the Sheffield Shield made Australia look like the old England.

Lots of bit-part offerings but no specialist class was Australia's problem. Shane Watson was out for twin half-centuries in the second Test, and that was another of their myriad of problems. He's a very correct player, but he is also what I would call a 'volunteering' opening batsman. He gets to his half-century, then he relaxes, so it didn't surprise me over this past winter that he was reintroduced in the middle order. Watson just hasn't got the mentality that players need to go in at the top – you need to be able to judge the pace, bounce, everything, and 50 is only a start. It might be handy in the middle order, but definitely not up top where you are the layer of the foundations.

Australia were suffocated by expectation perhaps, whereas England revelled in it. It was a spellbinding performance from Graeme Swann during that crushing innings victory. He was interviewed before the match and asked how he'd enjoy the pressure of bowling Australia out on a fifth-day pitch. 'Bring it on!' he said. There's always a cockiness about him, but in a really good way. He got through 41 overs of top-quality finger-spin that did not let the batsmen settle even when they were 'in'.

Adelaide is actually my favourite place in Australia, with its architecture and one building in particular, the Royal Oak public house. It was nice to reflect on an England victory over a few drinks there as the rain bucketed down (the heavens emptied South Australia's annual rainfall about an hour after England completed the job on the final morning, if you recall). I also enjoyed two dozen oysters at Adelaide's Oyster Bar that week. There is an honours board on the wall in said establishment, which claimed the world champion male oyster eater had guzzled 31 dozen in one sitting! It made my effort look positively Ryman League. I like my oysters, though. Gives you lead in your pencil. It's just a shame there was no one to write to out there.

Kevin Pietersen's ride in Shane Warne's Lamborghini raised a question or two. It could only be Kevin! Bit clumsy of him was that. Once he had posted on Twitter that he was heading for the Great Ocean Road, the cops were always going to be keeping an eye out, but him being pulled up represented a rare Aussie victory, and it's fair to say that it stood out in terms of poor judgement from the England camp. Stuart Broad's stomach injury at Adelaide felt like a big blow but England knew they had the strength in depth to cover. So much so that after plumping for Chris Tremlett in Perth because of his bounce, they even opted for Tim Bresnan over Steve Finn, who was leading wicket-taker in the series at the time, for the final two matches.

Even the global dash by Jimmy Anderson worked out okay. How times have changed. In my day, the labour ward was the last place a husband was allowed, and that was if your workplace was just up the road, not on the other side of the world. Try to sneak in and the midwife would say: 'You did your job nine months ago, now clear off!' But I understand that the modern generation guys feel they ought to be there, and want to be there no matter what.

As things turned out, England were not out-bowled by Australia in the defeat at Perth. It was just that the bloke called Mitchell Johnson, who had not long in the past been ranked number one bowler in Test cricket, turned up having previously been on the missing list. He'd done nothing different with his action, but his rhythm and aggression were there and most significantly he got the ball to swing. And it wasn't swinging from his arm, either, but in the last third of its journey, which is always so much more of a challenging proposition for a batsman.

England's bowlers still carried out their jobs effectively – bowling the opposition out on the first day of the Test is always job done in my book – there just weren't any runs to play with from the batsmen. I did think that on this particular Waca pitch, with its pace, England's leading batsmen might struggle and so it proved. Johnson's round-arm action means he is the one bowler whose deliveries do not tend to go over the top of the stumps, and he homed in on them like we had not seen before, winning lbw reviews and offering a constant threat.

Sure, England had lost to the old enemy, and you would rather see them win in my position, but the contest at Perth gave a snapshot of what Test cricket needs. If we are to take the very real threat of Twenty20 domination seriously, this is the sort of pitch needed to provide top entertainment. It's always been the case that thrilling surfaces like this – not a minefield, just good pace and bounce on offer to bring the fast bowlers into play – make for entertaining viewing. Yes, if batsmen get themselves in they can score runs, while spinners can get the ball to bounce but they have to work hard.

When you turn up at a ground you've played at and done well, you often have fond memories of the place. Of course, I've only got memories of Perth. Forget the fond. But Johnson loves the place. A record of 36 wickets in five Test appearances tells you why. And it was interesting that he attempted to completely downplay his efforts in the aftermath. Asked: 'Has it clicked for you, Mitch?' He said: 'No, it was the conditions!' In other words, he's quite comfortable in the surroundings of the Waca but he knows he might be totally different elsewhere the following week.

Ryan Harris looked to be coming good for them too after getting mileage in his legs over two Tests. In horse racing terms he needed two to get going, and has done over his career. Quite a few Aussies would select him in their Ashes XI for this year, but it was quite an eye-opening statistic that he took his 200th first-class wicket in March 2013 – a dozen years after his debut.

At least with Harris you could see what he had been picked for. I was still uncertain as to why Steve Smith turned up with his kitbag on his shoulder. Word was he was there to provide a bit of fun, to crack a joke or two in the dressing room, and improve team spirit. Well, how about some runs, mate?

When I think of the old Yorkshire team of the Sixties and people like Brian Close, Ray Illingworth, Fred Trueman and Geoff Boycott, I don't think they cracked many jokes but they got the job done pretty effectively. I am pretty certain England will refrain from chucking in Michael McIntyre and Jack Whitehall this coming winter.

If they were after a funny man then, not for the first time that winter, I considered they had perhaps plumped for the wrong man. Watching a bit of domestic cricket on the TV, I burst out laughing when I saw this Tommy Cooper bloke playing for South Australia. He plucked a couple of catches out of the air 'just like that' and I half expected him to come out to bat in a fez. Now, he would have added some levity to the dressing room. In fact, Australia would have been better served playing Simon Smith or even his amazing dancing bear and they would have had more chance of scoring runs than his namesake at number six. The whole of Australia seemed to be saying that Smith was not a number six – it was just a shame no-one stopped Hilditch on his pre-match jog to tell him. There was a pointed quote from Ricky Ponting in *The Australian* newspaper about Smith: 'The selectors feel that Steven Smith is our best No 6.' I took that to mean Ricky shared my view, and didn't.

Australia's all-out aggression in Perth was all very well but when they needed to change and play a spinner in Melbourne they did not. Interestingly, Nathan Hauritz was in form, but with the bat primarily, having just scored another hundred in state cricket. But they overlooked him and Michael Beer for the MCG, and I guess Ricky might have got his way after the selection success of the third match. It was interesting to hear him emphasise that this was 'my team'. He didn't want the spinner in Perth and got his way because the selectors wanted to leave out Johnson, apparently.

But you just knew things were not well within the Australian camp despite levelling things. Ponting played on despite his fractured little finger, having an injection in it to deaden the pain. To his credit, he knew they required his leadership and Greg Chappell, the head of the Australian selectors, provided a startling admission that they had nobody else who could captain the team. I should think that put Michael Clarke's nose right out of joint as the vice-captain.

According to certain television executives, it was irrelevant, however. There was a TV ad doing the rounds for a well-known mobile phone company in which Ricky Ponting was batting blindfolded to the slogan: 'We've got to give the Poms a chance.' It was amazing how dated it looked just a few days later when Australia were routed for 98 at the MCG.

There was a lot of talk about the pitch before that game, but if England had written to Cricket Australia and asked them for an early Christmas present in the preceding days this is what they would have requested. A little bit of moisture, a nice covering of grass, some cloud cover and a surface that might take a bit of spin towards the end. Happy Christmas, Andrew Strauss!

Anderson and Tremlett exploited the conditions brilliantly with the new ball and Tim Bresnan must have felt like he was bowling at Headingley. The Yorkshireman sent down a terrific spell, taking a leaf out of Peter Siddle's book and sticking to a disciplined, accurate line and length. Then, in the second innings, he got it tailing about with reverse swing. However, the best ploy of the lot was not by a bowler but by England captain Andrew Strauss, who put himself in at gully and told Graeme Swann to go round the wicket to Michael Clarke. Bingo.

Strauss grew in stature as a leader throughout his tenure. He was always going to be a major player for me, because when you hunt down the captain, you have a chance of catching the rest. Look at what England did to his opposite number Ponting over those first four matches – not to put too fine a point on it, they absolutely nailed him. Strauss, on the other hand, impressed on and off the field. And he reminded everyone, first and foremost those in the dressing room, that England still wanted to win 3–1 and not settle for taking the urn back via a draw.

My view was that Ponting was clearly leader of the Australian group still, and that despite being out of form he was old and wise enough to deal with both roles and succeed in dragging his country out of the doldrums. But in terms of the personal battle with Jonathan Trott – number three versus number three – there had been no contest. Hats off to Trott for that. First drop is such a specialist position, but he came in and made it his own 18 months earlier. He possesses an opener's technique and tremendous concentration. Before the series, cricket aficionados would have had Trott as second best to Australia's most famous Ricky but how wrong could you be? The days of England fretting about the number three position were over once Trott was given his chance.

Despite my feelings on Ponting's influence, however, I really wasn't sure what on earth he was doing around the

Australia team once he was ruled out of the final Test. He certainly shouldn't have been in the dressing room for this match while injured. Not one of the former cricketers and captains in the Sky Sports commentary box considered that a healthy situation. When you're in, you're in, and when you're out, you're out. If you don't adhere to this guidance you become like a spare Rick at a wedding. It was like he wanted to stand up and do the speech even though he was not best man. He sat there in his Aussie gear, and mates or no mates, he must have made Clarke feel uncomfortable. When the captain is ruled out, you've got to let the deputy take full control, and that means giving him the room to breathe.

Slightly different role, I know, but notice how adept Andy Flower is at distancing himself from the team. He always called the captain 'Andrew Strauss' or just 'Strauss', and refers to all players by surname. It's a respect thing, and the players had to refer to each other as 'Mr' at their pre-series boot camp in Bavaria. Once they got through that kind of discipline-busting schedule, a tour of Australia didn't seem so bad after all. But it also highlighted that Flower understands when his role starts and ends. He is for the team but not a part of the team.

England wouldn't have been inconvenienced at having a bowl first in that history-shaping match at the SCG which finished things off for them. It was about 18 or 19 degrees, so there was no movement, but when you are from Burnley that's almost tropical. Jimmy Anderson had what looked like a brand new pair of boots on and was slipping about during that first innings, and Billy Bowden busied himself, too, to hand out a warning for running on the wicket.

Anderson' s status as one of the best new-ball performers this country has produced was rubber-stamped when he completed a seven-wicket haul in Sydney to finish with 24 wickets in the series. He's a fabulous lad is Jimmy. I remember Duncan Fletcher saying to me that he found him a bit quiet and stand-offish, but I told him they're all like that in Burnley. Latterly, he has matured into a real leader of the attack, however, and always has words for the other bowlers. If the question to England upon arrival down under was: 'What have you got after the new ball?' well, the answer was that they had reverse swing led by this bloke.

What an exemplary team man he is, as is Matt Prior behind the stumps. Prior's 118 off 130 balls, from number eight, was a sensational hundred, and a totally selfless innings. It is not an easy discipline to bat in his regular position of number seven because before you know it you can be stuck with only the bowlers for company, but his attitude helps him out. He never gets static with the tail and that allows him to make the most of the scoring opportunities on offer. Here we were eulogising Ian Bell's ability to churn out a quality hundred from as low as number seven and then Prior trumps it.

It has to be said that good blokes appeared to be growing on trees for England in that first decade of the 21st century. And it was time to say goodbye to one of them in this match. What a great decision by Paul Collingwood to go on a high – perfectly timed and typical of the bloke. He is a yeoman and a stalwart is Colly, and the sort of character the English public take to. He is a 100 per cent rock-solid performer and it's good to go from Test cricket with great memories rather than people saying that he should have gone ages since. My mate

Warnie gave him some frightful stick about his MBE but having three Ashes series wins on your CV is pretty impressive for Dr Digin.

What struck me about this particular Ashes victory for England was that while we were saying goodbye to a proven international performer – a player who had known what it was like to beat Australia regularly; and there are not that many around, remember – our traditional enemy were rummaging in the bargain basement and getting excited at anything on offer. Like Barbra Streisand, a star was born in Usman Khawaja, but he only got 37! Anyone would have thought he was the new Bradman judging by the reaction. Splashed all over the papers for getting within range of a Test half-century. How times have changed, eh? Jason Gillespie scored an undefeated double hundred and was never picked again.

The game plan was all askew too from some of the new breed of Australian batsmen. The majority of them appeared to be trying to hit 10s, let alone sixes. Why don't they try to time the ball for four like their graceful predecessors Mark Waugh, Damien Martyn or Darren Lehmann? Those blokes guided it, but this lot thrash at it like they're trying to burst the damn thing. With the odd exception like Mike Hussey, it seemed they were caught up in Twenty20 mode. It smacked of a lifetime on bowling machines. They are for grooving shots, they don't teach finesse.

But don't take anything away from Andrew Strauss's team of 2010–11. Job done. Every single former England player would have wanted to be in the away dressing room. It really is the place to be after a triumph like that. You do your lap of honour and all that, but it hits you when you get back in there and reflect on what you've done with your mates. Remember that famous picture of Beefy in 1981 sitting there with a cigar? They're the moments you remember. For some of us those moments of glory were in Cup finals at Lord's, but this lot got to the very top of the world game.

To any young players seeking the secret of success I'd tell them to look no further than Alastair Cook and Matt Prior. Not too long ago people were saying Cook's front leg was too stiff, he couldn't play forward because of this bracing and the fact that his weight was all wrong. Well, not any more, now he has cruised past every other England batsman to have strapped pads on in terms of making hundreds. And Prior couldn't keep pigeons let alone keep wicket when he fell out of the team in 2008. He's a highly accomplished wicketkeeper now. Their secret? Hard work. Simple as that.

Of course, they have an excellent support staff in head coach Andy Flower; then there's David Saker, an Australian who paid his way to England for an interview because he wanted to be part of the set-up. Thing is, Troy Cooley did an equally good job with our bowlers in 2005 but he's not had success with Australia's, and it comes down to one thing really: the ability of the players. As I say, it is the willingness to graft that paid dividends for this England group, as exemplified by the likes of Cook and Prior, but they had the raw materials to start with.

As a proud Englishman, I was honoured to think this team represented us lot against Australia, and it also brought a bit of a lump to my throat to witness the incredible receptions the lads got from the Barmy Army. I know the more well-heeled tour groups get a bit hot under the collar at the noisy lot stealing the limelight, but fair do's. They don't leave you wondering which team they are backing. Normally things are pretty steady until mid-afternoon, but after the 4pm watershed when they're fully fuelled they can get pretty lively. Not on the final day, though. They were singing about 90 minutes before play started. The mind boggles at the thought of what they had for breakfast but the most important thing, ladies and gentlemen, was that we were not just bringing home the bacon, we were bringing home the whole pig! And the Aussies can keep the sharks, snakes and spiders! What a privilege it had been to call the action in that particular series.

The Special Ones

The world of cricket commentary has lost two great voices since the last Ashes series in Christopher Martin-Jenkins and Tony Greig. They were both absolute treasures to work with, and had such wonderfully distinctive broadcasting voices. They were also remarkably similar in one way: they could make you laugh without an ounce of effort on their part.

CMJ was an absolute doyen of commentators, of *Test Match Special*, and of the game in general. Whether he was making a point on air, or in print in his former role as cricket correspondent of the *Times* newspaper, you could not but notice his passion for the sport.

He was wonderful company and he had a great ally and friend in Mike Selvey, of the *Guardian*, the three of us often forming golfing parties while on tour. CMJ was wonderfully absent-minded, bordering on eccentric, and you would be regaled with dozens of warm stories about him if you wandered into the press box for a chat. Including occasions when he would pick up the TV remote and attempt to call his office for a chat. I kid you not.

But one of my favourite stories involving us all came in New Zealand on the 2007–08 tour. Selve used to gently egg CMJ on, knowing how easy it was to get him on to the hook, and give the rest of us a bloody good giggle. We were playing a round at the Millbrook Resort in Queenstown, and CMJ was on the tee swinging away, loosening up, ready for his round. Picture the scene: a beautiful golf course, with rolling hills in the background. 'Marvellous place this, isn't it?' CMJ commented, as we stood there waiting to get going. 'Did you know, it was designed by Ray Charles. You know, that famous New Zealand golfer.'

Selve, without batting an eyelid, maintaining the same rhythm in swinging his own club, carried on the conversation: 'Yes, and I believe there are a number of blind holes on this course.'

'So I understand,' CMJ replied.

He just carried on completely oblivious to the gag, and that was CMJ all over. It didn't matter a jot to him that it was Bob Charles, the left-handed Kiwi in question. Once you got to know him you realised this kind of faux pas was par for the course with him.

I was involved with *Test Match Special* after hanging my white coat up following three years as an umpire in the late 1980s and relished the camaraderie of that great broadcasting flagship. During one of the matches I was involved in, the Old

Trafford Test between England and India in 1990, the team were invited to dinner with the then BBC Radio Head of Sport Leslie Robinson. This kind of occasion was when CMJ would come into his own. Yes, he would be the butt of a few wind-ups and he didn't need much of a shove to fall into even the most lightly-baited traps, but he was also a black belt in leg-pulling himself. And he was wonderful with Fred Trueman.

It was a fine evening chock-full of cricketing anecdotes from in the middle and behind the microphone. Whenever the subject of fast bowling came up, Fred bristled as he always did and in typically terrific form dismissed any rival through history. In addition to being a very fine mimic, Christopher also possessed a great delivery when it came to a wind-up, and the way to get Fred was to tug gently at the ego. With typical deadpan expression, CMJ inquired: 'If you were to write another book right now, Fred, what would be the working title?'

We were all stood around having this conversation and, in all seriousness, with the straightest of faces, Fred replied: 'How about "T'fastest bowler that ever drew breath?"'

'I'm not so sure about that,' CMJ rejoined. 'I do believe that in 1072 Hereward the Wake produced a particularly fine, sustained, hostile spell and the people of the time reckoned his pace would never be beaten.'

'Aye, 'e might 'ave, but I'll tell thee now, whoever he played for, whoever he played against – he warn't as quick as me.'

Even during the mid-1990s, our Fred would inform you he was quicker than Darren Gough 'wiv me coat on'. Spending time with this lot was priceless to me. I recently re-read Chris Waters's biography of Fred and I have to say that I found it spellbinding because I can see Fred on every page. All the stories in there are absolute fact, and reveal something more of the true nature of the man.

You see, Fred was a much nicer bloke than he was depicted at times. He really played up to the persona created for him, and characterised by him, both as a player and later as a nowt-so-good-as-it-was-in-my-day radio summariser.

Fred was my hero. Not particularly from my playing days but certainly from my time post-career, working alongside him and Peter Parfitt at sportsman's dinners. Then in the commentary box he was absolutely sensational because he taught me that not everyone had to be the same. He was curmudgeonly, he didn't suffer fools gladly and he was shy with his praise. But most of it was an act. He absolutely loved being Fred, the public persona.

He was convinced he was a gypsy, coming from a two-up, two-down in Stainton. Times were hard for him in his early life and he typified the down-trodden northern miner type who had done well for himself later in life and wanted to stick two fingers up to everyone else.

The way he acted you would have thought it was him and then the rest. Nobody could come close to him. It's a fabulous line that he gave when he became the first man to 300 Test wickets, a total he reached fittingly in an Ashes contest, when he had Neil Hawke taken at slip by Colin Cowdrey.

Interviewed afterwards, he was quizzed as to whether he believed anyone would ever surpass the landmark tally.

'If anyone does beat it then they'll be bloody tired,' he replied, as if to emphasise the Herculean nature of his own achievement.

The Australians have a saying that a bloke would 'buy tick-ets on himself', as in buy tickets if he was first prize in a raffle, and Fred acted up to this perfectly, but although he was proud of his record, quite honestly he was not as big-headed as he sometimes came across. There was a much more caring side to him, and I can see a hell a lot of me in him, especially in terms of the northern background. He wanted to get away from where he grew up, and wanted to better himself. He did so by becoming the world's premier bowler of that time.

He would come across authority and bristle against it. He would absolutely love that confrontation. Of course, he was one of the best cricketers England has ever produced but he had another great gift. He was a fabulous storyteller and that forthright manner was just a cover, really. It was never really blown because he lived up to it so well.

Not that Fred refrained from occasionally showing an inherent miserliness of spirit from time to time when it came to sharing his wonderful tales with the rest of the crew. I recall once, just after becoming involved with *TMS*, he pulled me outside the back of the commentary box at Lord's. At that time we were committed to quite a few after-dinner engage-ments together. 'Ere,' he told me. 'Don't you be tellin' that Bill Frindall any stories, or at least not any good 'uns, as he'll nick 'em for his af'er dinner stuff.'

It was actually tremendous fun to be in that box, around men like Brian Johnston, Jonathan Agnew and Trevor Bailey. It was awash with tales all revolving around our beautiful game. Aggers and Johnno had their wind-ups down to a tee. 'This bloke looks a helluva player, Fred. How would you go about bowling at him?' All it took was something rather casual to bait the hook, and, of course, Fred didn't need asking twice to have a big bite.

'Awww mmmm, I would love to bowl at this lad, I'll tell thee that. Tries to play everything to the leg-side, he does. I'd bowl him a couple of fast outswingers and I'd follow-up by bowling him neck and crop with yorker.'

He used to possess a default story for occasions when one of us others asked him how he would deal with this bloke or that bloke. Every time he got wound up, he seemed to revert to the time he terrorised the West Indies batsman Easton McMorris.

'Eas'un Muckmorris. Didn't like it up him, he didn't. I sent one bouncer sailing over his head. Next 'un hit him straight in chest. Blood spurting out all over wicket.'

If we dragged up scorecards of the past in which Yorkshire had won the toss and inserted the opposition, who had gone on to stack up in excess of 100 for the first wicket, he would counter with: 'Well, off me they must have scored five or six.'

To be fair, he made me look a bit of a fool in an encounter at Bramall Lane. I kept playing forward, and Fred kept passing my outside edge. The pitch being damp meant the conditions were all in the bowlers' favour, which made Geoff Boycott's pulled six off Brian Statham during that match all the more special, I hate to admit. Brian later said he had slipped and had not meant to dig it in, but Boycs latched onto it a real treat and laced it over the football stand. Yes, over the football stand. It was a magnificent hit, one of the biggest I have ever seen, and he was quite thrilled with it was Geoffrey.

As a player, shower Trueman with praise and he would turn it into a waterfall at your expense. Tell him he'd sent down a good ball at you, and his retort would be a minimal-istic: 'Aye, wasted on thee.'

As part of this wonderful act of his, he used to talk himself up as this fast-bowling Elvis. No-one could touch him, and he made sure the opposition knew what they were up against with his pre-match conversing.

I recall Doug Padgett opening the door and entering our dressing room at Old Trafford one year, throwing in Fred's kitbag and declaring: 'Here's his stuff, he'll be in here more than he'll be in our place.' And he was. Round the room he would go, jabbering on: 'Are you playing? And you? And who exactly are you? Good God, I'm going to get 10-for here.'

It wasn't intimidating because you got the gist of it – it was all an act and one that he played absolutely brilliantly. There was no malice in him whatsoever; this was a way of reinforc-ing a belief in his own ability and to plant seeds of doubt in opponents' minds just in case they were feeling confident of playing him.

I treated Fred as a friend when we worked together. There would be no doubt whatsoever that he would have a critical word about me: 'He's got no idea what he's on about. I don't follow what he says at all.' But I always had my retaliation because, even if I say so myself, I was able to take Fred off pretty well. Impressions of others have been a forte of mine and Fred is one of the best in my repertoire. Since his passing in July 2006, there have been plenty of Fred moments amongst the cricket media and even years later, during social moments, you will find folk having dialogue as Fred. There are not many characters in any sphere that leave such distinct and idiosyn-cratic characteristics from which they can be recognised.

Peter Baxter, the *TMS* producer, to whom I will always remain grateful for my broadcasting chance, used to stock-pile letters in a corner of the commentary box all expressing the same message: 'Get this Trueman off.' Then, when he wasn't on, there would be another sack demanding: 'Where's Fred?'

Fred polarised opinion, and his modern-day equivalent is Bob Willis at Sky Sports, who says it exactly as it is, and couldn't care less about currying favour with anyone. Consequently, there is a massive camp for him and a massive camp against him. There aren't too many left in the middle. But I hope that those on the negative side of the fence realise that he does his job – he is there to say his piece, does so, as he sees it, and will not give you any fancy frills.

Generally there is a great respect for each other inside the commentary boxes in which I have worked. Everyone's either played a bit at the top level or has been there, seen it, and done it when it comes to the broadcasting side of things. But, as in any walk of life and in any workplace, you occasionally get into arguments. A difference of opinion on someone's playing ability or on the current match situation can mean two diametrically opposed views and an unwillingness to back down on either side.

Sir Ian Botham has a rather unique way of settling things when this kind of situation arises, usually meeting his rival squabbler with: 'Well, how many Test wickets have you got?' Funny, I've not heard that old chestnut since Shane Warne joined up with us in 2009.

Tony Greig never changed his outlook on life from the time we were international team-mates to the last few months of 2012 when he was sadly diagnosed with and beaten by lung cancer. He was always very opinionated, and was prepared to put those opinions forward no matter the audience. But his greatest quality was that he would always listen to your side of things, and never drown you out in a conversation. Yes, he would be very forthright with his own view but that didn't mean he was not willing to let you have your own two penn'orth.

He was a wonderful storyteller, and always worth listening to. As recently as September 2012, we were out in Sri Lanka together to commentate on the World Twenty20. As is normal with 20-over tournaments, it was a bloody good competition with all the razzmatazz and music to go alongside the on-field action thrown in. But we couldn't stop chuckling at one aspect of the event.

More often than not these Twenty20 jamborees include the hiring of dancing girls, who tend to get excited every time the ball reaches the boundary or a wicket is taken, shaking themselves this way and that on specially erected podiums (flame throwers positioned behind them optional). These girls have become familiar sights at cricket grounds around the world but this particular troop, not to put too fine a point on it, were a few grades down from the Trini Posse standard we are used to in the Caribbean. Those girls in Trinidad get plenty of attention, and while this lot out in Sri Lanka did too it was for quite another reason.

One day over breakfast in the early days of the tournament, it came to our attention via a report in a local newspaper that the tournament organiser had not been given a very good budget, so, to paraphrase him loosely, he had had to get the ugly ones in. The pretty ones were too expensive, he simply couldn't afford them, he explained. Hysterical!

Tony was born in South Africa, captained England and lived in Australia, yet he was the king of Sri Lanka. He championed their cricket and the Sri Lankan people adored him, even when he downright abused them. To be honest, he seemed to be able to get away with anything when he was over there, and that showed the regard in which he was held. A bit like CMJ, Greigy was always hilarious but rarely knew it.

He was an enormous man, standing 6ft 6in, and when I played with him you would describe him as being tall and thin. He was also debonair and good-looking; larger than life. Post-playing career, however, he was this hulking presence, a real gentle giant who was revered wherever he went around this wonderful Asian island. It was like he was a god to them, or their king. In that really warm, appealing South African voice, he announced to me on the first morning of that trip that he would be driving us to the ground.

'Jaaas, I've got a sponsored Hyundai, a very comfortable car,' he said as if practising a voiceover for an advert.

'Don't tell me you're driving over here!' I protested.

'Jaaas, always drive in Sri Lanka, and the little tea-baggers always get out of the way when I'm on the road.'

I can verify that they did, having being his passenger for a fortnight, and that all other Sri Lankans seem to take care of his every wish too. On that same morning at breakfast, he had come down and sat at his table and demanded that the waiter came over to listen to his order. 'Right, are you in charge heeeere? You'll see me every morning. You can't miss me, I'm a big man. I'll be here every day and every day I want you to bring me the same thing. As soon as you see me walk in here, you start getting my breakfast ready: two eggs, beans, bacon, sausage, mushrooms and a tomato. You do that every time you see me. Do you hear?'

Very abrupt if you ask me but not an ounce of offence was taken by this bloke, and Greigy seemed to get a lot better service than another former England captain. Nasser Hussain had struggled to get any joy at the breakfast table that week. There was a right saga in Kandy at the Victoria Golf and Country Club when he placed his order for two hard-boiled eggs. The waiter toddled off to the kitchen looking Manuelesque, and brought these two eggs back a few minutes later, presenting them beautifully, it has to be said.

Nasser knocks the top off them to find they are runny. 'Excuse me, I asked for two hard-boiled eggs. Now please could you go and get me them?' Nasser barked, in the same kind of tone you could imagine he would use if he had chucked this bloke the new ball and seen him send down a rank half-volley first up.

Anyway, a few minutes later the bloke is back with two new eggs. 'Thank you,' says Nasser through gritted teeth. However, within seconds this bloke is getting the Hussain finger beckoning him back to the table. It was reminiscent of the way he used to signal to his bowlers. 'This is the second lot and they are exactly the same. I asked you for hard-boiled eggs and I would like hard-boiled eggs, please. These are not hard-boiled eggs.'

The waiter is still yet to say a word as he takes them away. Eggs number five and six are then brought. Exasperated,

Nasser knocks the top off them to find this runny yellow yolk once more. 'Right, bring me your manager!' he bellows.

Picture the scene a few minutes later with the manager and the waiter both stood there, tea towels draped over their arms. 'I asked your man here for two hard-boiled eggs,' Nasser informs the more senior of the two. 'I've had six now and every single one of them has been runny.'

'I'm ever so sorry, sir, but he thought you were asking for half-boiled eggs,' came the response. Cue throwing arms in the air, newspaper on the floor as Hussain exited the breakfast room with a chunter.

No such problems for Tony, however, who, true to his word, became my taxi driver for a few weeks. One day, he slammed on the brakes of his sponsored Hyundai rather unexpectedly.

'It was right here!' he exclaimed, as if we had reached the site of some buried treasure.

'What was?' I meekly inquired.

'Last time I was here, there was a pig. Wild boar, right on the road here. Bloody magnificent thing! Would have made a fabulous hog roast. Twelve-bore would have done for it.'

It has been a sad time for commentary boxes around the cricket world losing both CMJ and Greigy over Christmas 2012. But as with all generations, some people go and others come in to take their place. It is only natural to think that CMJ and Greig will be very difficult to replace but they are not irreplaceable. In the past that was said of Alan McGilvray, Brian Johnston and John Arlott. There are some commentators still doing the rounds who are, in my opinion, as good as it gets: Tony Cozier, with his wonderful Caribbean lilt, is one of the greatest ever broadcasters; Jim Maxwell, who has been awarded the order of merit in Australia; and the equally fantastic Brian Waddell, of New Zealand.

Test Match Special has evolved and now includes a new generation of voices including Michael Vaughan and Phil Tufnell. The Corporation have always wanted to move on with the employment of younger blokes and it was that which did for Fred and Trevor Bailey in the end. There was no disputing that they were absolutely terrific, certainly great helps to me, and a great source of humour to everyone who worked with them. But like the game itself the Beeb moves on.

At Sky Sports, we take on a temporary cast depending on the opposition in any given series and I love the Ashes because it means we get Thommo, a man who struggles to live by the rules. When he first came to work for us he did not adhere to the protocols that were put in place. He wasn't a rabble-rouser wanting to cause trouble, he just doesn't dress like the rest of us for any other part of his life, and so our strict dress code that we are sent before each series was a problem.

Those of us who have been around for a while don't need telling twice on this – you are basically instructed to wear this, or that, and it is generally suits and jackets with shirts and ties, so that whenever you are on camera you look smart. However, what our bosses clearly didn't take into consideration was the fact that Thommo never previously wore a tie in his life, and didn't even own one.

Of course, we got round it all okay but if anyone had been able to see below the camera level, once they had dressed him up, they would have noticed that underneath his top half, which was suited, the bottom half was a pair of trousers accompanied by a pair of trainers. A similar situation to the tie here in that he just didn't own a pair of dress shoes. It meant we had to kit him out in all this smart stuff; it wasn't a problem to him, he didn't play up, but put it this way, I think he ripped that tie straight off as soon as the series was over.

Thomson always cracks me up with his stories, and one of his favourites is when he and Allan Border almost saved the 1982–83 Ashes Test in Melbourne. When he went out to join AB in the middle at 218 for nine on the fourth evening, the Aussie lads started packing up and having a beer. After all, they required 74 more runs to win. However, the last-wicket pair gritted it out to an extent that when they returned at the close their team-mates were ratted.

Typical of us superstitious cricketers, I suppose, but next morning, Rod Marsh says: 'Right, resume your positions.' Cans were popped all over the place and they were all drunk again by the time Geoff Miller took the winning catch for England off the bowling of Ian Botham to leave Border stranded on 62 not out with only four more runs needed.

Robin Jackman is another great mate and a fabulous broad-caster and also goes by the name of Inspector Frost, dubbed so after the David Jason television character. Jackers was the opening bowler for Surrey and at one stage England who emigrated to South Africa and subsequently considers himself to be a South African. His past was in England but he has bought into their culture and their country and as far as I am concerned that is just fine.

Good socialisers proliferate in cricket and Jackers is a great one for nattering on over a beer, turning back the clock and recalling bowling in tandem with Geoff Arnold in county cricket. Now when you talk about words being exchanged in England–Australia contests, it's easy to overlook the county scene, because, as far as I was concerned, Jackers was one of the original sledgers. He just didn't draw breath on the field; he would stand there with hands on hips, chuntering away about the state of the pitch, how unlucky he was not to get a wicket and how poor a batsman you were. Every time you played against him, the one recurring feature was that you were a lucky so and so to still be out there listening to him.

In fact, I think the only time I can recall the cat getting his tongue was when he dropped one short at the Oval that Clive Lloyd well and truly got hold of. He connected so well with this pull shot, in fact, did Clive that it sailed out of the ground and hit the wall of Archbishop Tenison's School over the road. Now if you know the dynamics of the ground you will know what a hit that is. It was such a flippin' hammering. No one had ever hit Jackers that far before and no one had rendered him speechless either.

Of course, when you eulogise about commentators you have to mention Bill Lawry. Whilst Fred Trueman was my hero way back when I first wondered into a commentary box, it is fair to say that Bill is my hero now. When you watched him bat, he was the most dour batsman you had ever seen in your life. He would have sent a glass eye to sleep, but he has gone through something of a makeover later in life.

Bill was the Australian Boycott. He was careful, to say the least, when he had a bat in his hand. He is a good age now, into the second half of his 70s, and he seems to have forgotten that he ever played the game the way he did because his enthusiasm knows no bounds. He is constantly getting up out of his seat, and becomes totally carried away with what is unfolding before him, barely able to contain his excitement. When the game is rocking, he just cannot keep still. He describes things in his own way and I think his timing, delivery and vocabulary are absolutely fantastic. Like most really good commentators, it helps that he possesses a distinctive voice and an individualistic way of talking about the game.

He's unbelievably one-eyed, and others like Mark Nicholas can really play on that in rather subtle fashion. To be fair, Bill never tries to hide the fact that he is backing the Baggy Green brigade and it comes through in the passion that he shows. He is very supportive of all Australians but particularly likes to get behind his fellow Victorians. Bill is so pro-Australian that he even sees their pitches as being the best in the world. On occasion he has been known to froth at the mouth when a groundsman has produced a belter. 'Great pitch, we're in for a ripper today, this Australian team could get 3,000 on here,' he'll begin, refusing to budge from his positive attitude even when they're tottering on 78 for six at lunch.

Whenever I get time for a social with him, I like to have a chat with Bill about his pigeons. Pigeon racing's popular around my way and Bill's a keen fancier, having been brought up in a family that have always kept birds. He says he would never be without them, even though he has to 'muck the bastards out at 6 o'clock in the morning' on occasion. In the last Ashes, there was a pigeon race for Glenn McGrath's cancer charity day, when birds representing England and Australia, called Chappelli and Beefy, went head to head. It started as a race but turned into cage fighting halfway home.

Of course, Bill and the great Richie Benaud have been behind the microphone for donkey's years. This always came to mind whenever Greigy used to get onto the subject of commentary. He would talk about Bill, Richie, Chappelli and himself as established hands but he would always pass comment that the jury was still out with some of the younger lads. Younger lads? He was only talking about Mark Taylor and Ian Healy, blokes who had been doing the job for 10 flamin' years! These are two guys closer to retirement than starting their cricket careers, and he still used to talk about them as young whippersnappers.

And what an addition Shane Warne has been to TV coverage all over the globe. Warne was the number one guy when it came to getting into batsmen's heads as a player, because ability-wise he knew he was the best. I am not sure his confidence in himself ever dropped below 100%, and he didn't consider any of the batters to be good enough to even be on the same field. Nor was he shy letting them know, of course, as Adam Hollioake once discovered. In one of his early internationals, Adam walked out to bat to find Warne shadow boxing at the bowler's end. Even when Adam had taken guard, Warnie was still stood at the end of his run going through a sparring routine. A lot had been made of Hollioake's swarthy, tough guy image, but Warne wanted to undermine him. He won't like me for saying this now because he looks a very fit chap these days, but Warnie was a bit portly at that time and he's bobbing up and down saying something like 'this stuff won't help you one little bit'. Physically, there was no comparison but Warne beat opponents up in their heads.

These days his Twitter feed is compelling. I am not interested in his cricket views because I hear enough of those when we are at work together. But his thoughts on poker are unmissable. He can have the worst cards in his hand but he'll make you believe that he's got something like the best. He can have next to nothing good but in these interactive games you half-believe he's got pocket queens.

There was one hand when he was playing and tweeting as he went and you could see what was coming but his enthusiasm and positivity meant that he wouldn't acknowledge it until the turn, and his opponent completed a flush to clean him out. He's always like that, and it made me chuckle to read him saying that he kicked the table and left. He's massively competitive in poker – even wears the glasses, with Liz stood behind him, to ensure he keeps the right playing image.

But his presence amongst us Sky larkers has definitely changed the dynamic. For a start, Beefy has come unstuck. Sir Osis always makes me laugh because he has very strong opinions, and isn't afraid to express them. However, when he is challenged by a really strong argument, and can find no way around the impasse, he resorts to retaliation like the previously mentioned 'How many wickets did you get?' This can prove the case even when the subject is at its most mundane. He could be arguing against the Minister of Transport about a new rail line in Cumbria and he'd want to know how good a bowler he was and what his statistical return was in his career before conceding ground. 'How many wickets did he get?'

Another ex-Ashes captain provides us with a giggle now he has hopped the fence. Although born in Lancashire, Michael

Vaughan likes it to be known that he's a Yorkshireman. And he certainly shows off all the necessary traits. Our Roses rivalry has led to talk over forming the Aye Up Cup, or giving it an alternative title, the Digin Trophy.

We could have one match at Scarborough and the return at Blackpool with a Stanford-style winner takes all. If Fred Boycott ever reveals his true identity he would be the ideal man to present it. One of my favourite Fredisms came in the middle of the Twenty20 World Cup when he asked: 'It's all very well with this reverse sweep lark but can any of them play the reverse block?'

Fred's right. Versatility is the key and Vaughan and I have shown plenty of that in our outings for the PCA Legends. He and I opened in one charity match at Grappenhall, Neil Fairbrother's old club, and put 81 on inside the first six overs.

'I'm sending Mr Flower a text after this match is over,' panted Vaughan as a ripple of applause for the 50 stand died down. 'He should be here.'

To be fair, we were slapping them all over the show at a time when England just couldn't buy two opening batsmen in Twenty20. They seemed to have tried everybody but they hadn't made it to Cheshire for two blokes who had done the job for their country in the distant past. Michael reckoned we'd go down like Hobbs and Sutcliffe in our second lives at the top level. Fearful they were not spreading the net far and wide enough in the search for top talent, I began a text message: 'We are the ones – get us in.' It was sobering up in the bar later on that displaced my courage.

Chapter 6

My wife goes by the name of Diana but in our house she is more affectionately known as Vipers. As in 'my little nest of …'

My job with Sky Sports means that I am away from home for exceedingly long stretches of time – the forthcoming 2013–14 winter Ashes tour will mean I am away for a couple of months – and I am pleased to report that Vipers has lots of different hobbies to keep her occupied while I'm gone. Wouldn't do for her to be idle now, would it?

To give Diana her due, it has to be said that she uses her spare time wisely. Recently, she added to her DIY portfolio, by enrolling for an electrician's course at night school, and I have encouraged her like any good husband should. Growing up in a town like Accrington, I was accustomed to being in a really working-class environment where everyone has a trade, and to her credit, having begun as a bit of an odd-jobs enthusiast, Vipers is intent on adding as many skills as possible.

It has all proved invaluable for the maintenance work that needs doing around the house. I can shuffle off to Manchester Airport for a long-haul flight down under safe in the knowledge that things will be tickety-boo during my absence.

There's always stuff to get stuck into, and extra income from weekend work would be a bonus. You see, I've told her that once she has got her safety certificates, there is no reason why she can't expand and do a bit of plumbing and building as well as a second job in her spare time. If you can do a bit of plastering in the winter, then some slating, even perhaps roofing in the summer, you will not want for work, even in a recession. There was a time when folk would have dismissed it as a man's job but I move with the times. Very modern thinker, me, and if my little *nest of* fancies having a go, I will always encourage her.

In fact, you could say I have played an active part in training her up. About 18 months ago, I tried to get her on a tarmac gang. I had been told by the lads down the pub that there is good money in it, and I reckon a woman joining the group as the knocker would be a masterstroke. Could be some decent commission in a sales job like that. The world's her lobster, really.

Don't get me wrong, Vipers does do ladylike things such as make curtains but the biggest compliment I can pay her is that she really can turn her hand to anything. One of my birthday presents to her last year was an annual subscription to *Builder's Weekly*, and now she is over her fear of heights, she is making good use of the double extending ladders I bought her a few years since. It's very leafy where we live, and we have a real task on our hands to make sure the gutters on the roof don't get blocked. Well, I say we, but strictly speaking I mean she. To tell you the truth, I can't be bothered to go up ladders at my age, with my knees, and my commentators' insurance probably doesn't cover that kind of dangerous activity – it wouldn't do for me to end up like Rod Hull now would it? – so Vipers gets the gig. I must say she has a real talent for guttering. Gets them de-cluttered good and proper every October, and, of course, as I am always thinking ahead of the game, I try to encourage her to use what she collects as mulch in the garden rather than just chuck it away willy-nilly. It was good advice methinks to get her to stop off at the B&Q store next to her place of work and invest in a compost bin.

Now there is another handy purchase I can tell you about from the same store – drain rods. You might own them years and they never get used, but when you do need them you'll be thankful you invested the money. The very best on the market come with a 60-metre run, so there's nothing that you can't reach. Not long after we moved back to Cheadle Hulme in 2011, our drains got blocked, and to her credit, Vipers got these things connected up, and got right to the heart of the problem. I might have had a go myself but it really needs a woman's touch does that job. The fairer sex have got smaller hands, and can manoeuvre the rods no problem, whereas for us blokes it's a little bit more of a struggle.

Gee, she were pleased with them, and how quickly the problem was solved. So much so that another potential change of career direction came up in conversation.

'What's the point in calling Dyna Rod when you've got Diana Rod?' I joked.

It was at that point that a light bulb went off in my head. By my reckoning, Vipers is ready for a change from sitting in an office all day.

'Why don't you get yourself more fresh air and set yourself up, love? I'm sure there'll be plenty of business, especially over in Yorkshire with all those septic tanks.' We've just bought a little holiday home over wrong side of Pennines, you see.

Give Vipers a challenge and seldom does she fail. I must report that she made an excellent job of erecting the shed and the greenhouse while I was off checking out some great golf courses abroad one winter. She even re-roofed it the following year. There are lots of women that like diamonds, perfume, chocolates, that sort of thing, but buying those kind of gifts is fraught with danger because let's face it which bloke really knows what to get, right? Other halves can be a tad fussy, and when things don't fit, are not the right colour or don't smell as they ought, it just encourages arguments. Jewellery is such a personal thing that I find she's better off buying it for herself.

And if you use your nous, you can put a priceless expression on your loved one's face with a gift of difference. What better pressie to unwrap on Christmas Day than a staple gun, eh? For a draper it's a dream. You can't go wrong with one of them. One time when stumped what to buy her for our wedding anniversary, a delightful bib and braces overall set caught my eye. They can look quite nice on a lady, tucked in at the waste. Almost like a fashion statement, they are. There's a nice side pocket for your extending ruler and a tie for your hammer so that you can keep your hands free to get up the steps.

I always ensure I wrap everything up properly, which is easier said than done, of course, when you've plumped for one of those mini cement-mixers. But I managed it, and suffice to say she was thrilled.

She's got plenty of use out of it, anyway. I've always encouraged her to do things for herself, even when it comes to concreting. Let's face it, there's nothing like sand and cement, the old two-and-one mix, rather than heading off to the hardware store and lugging back a load of bags. They can be heavy for lasses, coming in 25kg lots, and I wouldn't want her to injure herself.

When you've built a wall, and you look at it in the knowledge that it is all your own work – that you've mixed it all from scratch and constructed it over many a painstaking hour – how proud are you feeling? 'That wall there is one that I've built, and it's there forever,' you can reflect. At least until somebody leans on it.

She doesn't know this yet and I had hoped to keep it as a surprise for next year but I will share it with you: I've managed to get her on a welding course. Hope she likes her new glasses. Her others kept steaming up something chronic and I'm not actually sure you should wear bifocals when you're doing that kind of thing, so I've invested in some proper welding goggles to be wrapped up with a snazzy new blowtorch.

Vipers is one of the other lot, and whenever we are on her side of the big hills, driving through the country lanes of the Yorkshire Wolds, she gets very excited when we see cows and sheep. She's always been obsessed with farm animals, so my parting gift to her in early November as I head for Australian sunshine will be a fortnight's work experience, coinciding with her annual leave in January 2014.

Because she works in cricket she tends to take her time off in the winter, and allowing her to indulge her fascination with farms at this time of year should be a real thrill for her. It was the least I could do to pull a few strings to get her working on one, and it will certainly be good for personal discipline. It should help her punctuality getting up at five o'clock in the morning to muck out. Getting up at that time never did anyone any harm and it would be good for her to use her days off productively.

I'm always thinking about her well-being and encouraging her in all her activities. On Tuesdays she goes swimming and I always remind her to daub herself in plenty of lard before she dips in. I am presuming that her endgame will be to swim the Channel because there's no point confronting anything half-heartedly. Swim the Channel is what that nice David Walliams did and if you're taking your swimming seriously enough to have lessons, you are obviously wanting to step things up to more extreme levels somewhere along the line. It might only be recreational at the moment but you need to be fully prepared and goose fat is a godsend to serious swimmers. It keeps the body warm in extreme conditions and protects against jellyfish stings – essential if you're swimming down your local authority baths.

Sport plays a big part in our household, as you might expect. Diana loves cricket and like me is football-daft too. She is a big York City fan, and so are all her family. Her brother, nephew and niece go all over the country to watch them, home and away, and she tags along with them on occasion, or ropes me into going to games on others.

This past year has been fun because my heroes Accrington Stanley dwelt in the same division, League Two, and that has meant we've seen a fair bit of the two clubs' fortunes. Sometimes it even led to a difference of opinion on which match we should be heading for. One classic example was when she tried to persuade me to go to York's match at Morecambe on a Tuesday evening in August 2012. The proposal was that we headed off in early afternoon, took the dog for a run on the beach, had a walk on the promenade, took in a fish and chip tea and then strolled on to the match.

My problem was that Stanley were at home against Port Vale the same night, and given my official position at the club I felt obliged to go to there. Of course, when I proposed that she should go to Morecambe and me off to Accrington, and we meet back home and have our fish and chips back later that night, I was met with: 'No, I'd rather go with you. We'll go to Accrington.'

Now from my experience of women, you discuss something thoroughly and then decide that she was right all along with her initial proposal. Naturally, we ended up in Morecambe, and Tags ran amok on the beach. Alas, there was no sea for her to dip into. In fact, it looked like someone had nicked it. It felt like you could see all the way to Alaska but that in turn meant plenty of sand for us to have our stroll on. A fish and chip dinner at the Marine Hotel later and we were ready for the wonderfully named Globe Arena.

Upon arrival, some of the Morecambe club officials spotted me and knowing that I was a board member at Stanley, invited me into their board room. I declined because I was in my civvies and didn't believe wearing jeans was appropriate clobber for such an invitation. They insisted that was nonsense and even refused my cash when I tried to purchase their best tickets. It was very generous of them to allow us the tickets on a complimentary basis but the upshot was that we were sat in the home stand.

Five minutes in, I thought it best to show some interest in the drama (or lack of it) unfolding before us.

'What colour are we?' I asked.

'I don't know,' Diana replied.

'You mean to tell me you don't know which colour your beloved team plays in?'

'No. We're usually in maroon.'

'Well, you are either red or blue tonight, so which one is it?'

Next thing, she gets on the phone to her brother who is situated behind one of the goals.

'We're in blue,' she told me enthusiastically.

'Right, we're supporting the blues then. Oh, just one other thing, though. Which one is Matty Blair?'

'Oh, I'm not sure, I can't see him,' she came back.

'But he's the star man, the leading player, isn't he? When they won the FA Trophy and the Conference play-off final a couple of months ago, he was the one that scored goals in both matches, wasn't he? He must be out there somewhere.'

'He's not on the team sheet, he must be injured. I'll ring my brother.'

'Why is Matty Blair not playing?' I heard her ask.

'Because he's shit!' came the rather matter-of-fact reply.

That's not what the York fans were saying about him when they defeated Newport and Luton in the space of a week in May 2012, I can tell you.

Vipers planned the first of those Wembley outings with an almost military precision. In fact, I heard her organising a very elaborate schedule on the phone the day before, and one way out of touch for the kind of football matches I've been used to.

'We're taking a picnic,' she told me, when I quizzed her on her arrangements.

'What do you mean you're taking a picnic!?'

'For us to eat at half-time, of course.'

'The game only lasts an hour and a half. What on earth are you on about?'

'Well, we'll need something to eat.'

'Get a pie and Bovril like everybody else!'

Could you imagine the security lads at Wembley being confronted with a picnic hamper?

It would be a case of: 'Not today, thanks. Move along now.'

'You'll just have to try to hold out, if you can,' I comforted her. 'If you can fight off the hunger pangs until five o'clock, perhaps you could have some food at the end?'

Posh nosh! At football? I ask you. Don't worry, I brought her back down to earth when I sponsored the match between Accrington and York at the Crown Ground in October 2012. Vipers decided that she would come and have the pre-match meal, a hearty sausage and mash, before fleeing for the stands at kick-off.

This match was a cracker for us as it gave me the chance to take my kids and the grandchildren along, and Diana's brother, nephew and niece came with us too. Being proper football people they opted out of the food offer to sample the atmosphere building on the terraces. Vipers was to join them behind the goal, as I said.

Pre-match all the directors get together and take part in the meet and greet with the opposition hierarchy, so I took the opportunity to introduce the good Mrs Lloyd to Jason McGill, the visiting chairman, and explained that she was a York fan. A bit of a fuss was made of her before she excused herself to go and stand behind one of the goals.

During our conversation, one of my fellow Stanley directors, Murray Dawson, overheard and rather kindly offered to escort her around the ground while I continued with the bits and bobs expected of a match sponsor.

So imagine my surprise at the next sighting of Diana. It was half-time as I was out on the pitch presenting a share certificate to a supporter who had come over from Canada especially for the match. From my position on the halfway line, I could see her approaching out of the corner of my eye.

'Here, what's up?'

'I'm only stood behind the wrong goals!'

'What do you mean you're behind the wrong goals?'

With that she gestured towards the place from whence she came. Right in the thick of the Stanley Ultras, a fearsome group who bang their drums for the cause as if their very lives depend on it.

Of course, to me this was all highly amusing.

'If you don't mind me asking, when exactly did you find out you were in the wrong place?'

'I'm not sure how many minutes had gone,' she began. 'But it was when this chap next to me shouted: "F*** off back to Yorkshire, you bastards!"'

Within seconds I had it sorted that she was marched down the other end by one of the Accrington stewards to take her rightful place, and was able to celebrate a 1–0 victory with the aforementioned Yorkshire bastards courtesy of a late Jason Walker goal.

My only solace that night came via an announcement on the public address system as I parked my bum in the hospitality suite: 'We would like to remind all York City fans that it is ground policy for all away supporters to remain behind for ten minutes while the home supporters disperse.' So while I tucked into a pint, Vipers was penned in.

Although as a Lancastrian I hate losing to Yorkshire at anything, I have to confess to possessing a dirty secret. You see, despite my background and upbringing I really like Yorkshire, and Yorkshire folk. There you are, I've said it.

I am Lancashire through and through but I can't help having a real affection for them too. The only downside since purchasing a place over there was the news that Geoffrey was considering his return from Jersey. House prices dropped 20% overnight, and For Sale signs went up all over the region.

But in all seriousness – what a beautiful place. I am even fond of Yorkshire County Cricket Club. It used to be a soap opera to rival *Emmerdale*, the best in the business in my book, but the lads down there playing for them now are all terrific, and I think Colin Graves, the executive chairman, has done wonders in recent years. Good old Geoffrey is now club president and so that means there's always something going on.

In some ways the Lancashire–Yorkshire rivalry replicates that which exists between England and Australia. It's a real love–hate thing going on. Now I am a part-time resident of the white rose estates I take a lot of guidance on how to conduct myself as a pseudo-Yorkshireman, taking my lead from my mentor Michael Vaughan.

Technically, I shouldn't because he was actually born in Manchester and now lives in Derbyshire but he is keen for everyone to know he's a lad from Sheffield. There were two key phrases for me when getting to know Yorkshire-speak. The first one I mastered was: 'How much?' Said with one corner of the mouth turned down adds to the sense of outrage. The second is simply: 'Hello, I'm from Yorkshire!' It's amazing how many of the local folk feel the need to tell you that – even when you're slap bang in the middle of the county. One of their quirks, I guess.

For further light reading on the spirit of Yorkshire, I suggest an afternoon on Twitter studying the offerings of @fredboycott. He's not one for the faint-hearted, Fred. Nor is he keen on the modern game. Twenty20 is certainly not his bag, preferring the virtues of crease occupation to the crash, bang, wallop of the youth of today. As he points out, though, you have to #digin before you can #crackon (look at us getting down with kids at Hashtag Central).

Joe Root appeared to be from that school of thought when he made his start to life as an England player. In each of his first six international innings, young Joe passed 30, a new record. Our Fred thought that was worth another of those golden post boxes they became so fond of during 2012. Proper batsman that Root, he reckoned; the six hours at the crease compiling scores of 73 and 20 not out on his Test debut in Nagpur the crème de la crème of his performances as far as Fred was concerned. Nothing pleases Yorkies like a give-'em-nowt mentality. Any Fancy Dan can wipe the ball into the stands, according to Fred. But what happened to the leave? Can these boy racers string some maidens together while they're batting? Takes some discipline does that. I am hoping we could see this kind of discipline in our proposed Aye Up Cup. We are well on the way to establishing that, the only sticking point being who is going to pay for the silverware. Michael was adamant his lot wouldn't part with any brass, and so we won't either, on principle.

My beloved sports clubs are not flush with cash right now as it happens. For all the fun they provide me with, I wish others would feel the same about Accrington Stanley. When another local Accrington lad Ilyas Khan bailed the club out at the most critical point in its modern history, footing a £308,000 unpaid tax bill, he was very keen to use me as a bit of a figurehead for the club. In all, I reckon it cost Ilyas nigh-on £1 million to keep it afloat, and when the Save Our Stanley campaign was over he distributed his major shareholding amongst the existing shareholders. What a top man.

People from all over the world have since invested – mainly folk who have left the town for careers elsewhere – but it has remained an almighty financial struggle since raising that initial £50,000 at the start of the share option. Peter Marsden, the new chairman, is in charge of bringing in new money because at a club our size you can never do enough. That includes all of us with an interest in its fortunes, and as a result of Ilyas's persuasion I am on board as a non-executive director.

Intriguingly, that meant me taking the fit-and-proper person test required for people in positions of authority at the 92 Football League clubs in early 2013. Fit? Well I can still hold my own in a gym session, and so I got myself in good shape, expecting a physical challenge. Proper? Well I was confident that I was real, despite some people including my good lady wife having told me I am too good to be true. Turns out that all they really wanted to know was whether I was of the right stock to be a director. From my perspective, all I am doing is publicising the club at any chance I get. I see myself as a bit of an ambassador, really, portraying it in as positive light as possible. That's easy for me because I'm a supporter, a spectator with passion, and it's a real thrill to watch them play. And I am fully behind all the fundraising ventures.

This year, one of the initiatives set up was Run Stanley Run, a race for all standards of competitors all around the town of Accrington. We planned to have proper, serious athletes at the front, followed by fun runners, and dog walkers at the rear. It had to be that way around, I guess, otherwise the serious competitors would have been dodging a steady stream of dog shit up into the hills!

All joking aside, any money we can get, however we can get it, helps. You see, while the results on the pitch have been desperate enough in recent times, our off-field health has been even more precarious. A Football League future is paramount to maintain any kind of financial stability. We are forever banging the drum for support but getting the local community to back the club has proved a lot harder than people from outside could imagine.

Accrington is a town with a population of 35,000 but getting just 2,000 down to the Crown Ground for matches has proved beyond us for a long time now. That is the magical number for us because it is our break-even figure. If you are getting crowds of 1,400 then you are obviously struggling, and the numbers just don't add up for you to survive. It bothers me that we get such a low proportion of the conurbation turning out because I am a strong believer in community, and links between the population and local sports clubs. If you are from the town then that is the club that you support. You might say that you would like to support a Premier League club, and that's fine, but don't forget you've also got a club of your own on your doorstep.

You don't choose your sports team, they choose you, in my book. So, if you're from Southend, you might have a soft spot for West Ham or Arsenal but ultimately you're a Shrimper. If you are from Barrow-in-Furness, same difference, you support Barrow, and it's Conference football for you. If you want to follow Liverpool or Manchester United then that's your choice but remember the team that truly represents you is the one down the road. And I am talking about the high street, not the M6.

One phrase you hear people pedal is that they support their clubs 'through thick and thin' but we really do struggle to get our locals to support us. Probably because what we offer them is the chance to support us through thin and thinner. I'm still like a lot of blokes in that whenever I go abroad I get so excited waiting for news of my team's results. Wherever I go in the world I pack my Stanley shirt, absolutely no question. It was the first thing in my suitcase when we headed to New Zealand earlier this year and will be with me on every future tour I cover no matter where we reside in English football's pyramid.

I grew up watching Accrington in the Third Division North, and from turning out for them in the non-league days that followed it has always remained my team. Whenever I can get across to Accrington these days I do so, and like to keep the ritual of the pre-match pint with my eldest lad Graham in the Peel Park Pub, just over the road from where I went to school. We are a simple, friendly, no-frills lot and that is what we should be in our little Lancashire enclave. It's representative of our people – straightforward and honest.

At our level the only way to get more people in is by bombarding them, reminding them that you are there constantly, and that means lots of leaflet drops, trying to educate them that this is *their* team. It represents them as people from the town. We are not pretending to be Chelsea, we ain't gonna win the European Cup, but we are good fun, our players play with fantastic endeavour and it is committed, honest and down-to-earth football. I drive up there and park outside the offices – which are offices in name only because they are actually nothing grander than a few portakabins – and you see the lads roll out of Fiats, not flash Ferraris, with boots and shin pads tucked under their arms. They give a really decent account of themselves, and I admire that.

The modern Stanley operates mainly on loan players and we make no secret of the fact that we give opportunities for young lads to put themselves in the shop window for clubs higher up the ladder. It's a case of 'you help us and we'll help you'. They might improve us, and we might help them progress to a higher division, so their efforts can be mutually beneficial.

There is passion from the minority that do turn out and wear the colours on the terraces. Have you seen those Stanley Ultras? Well, if you haven't seen them, you must have heard them? They make an incessant racket, and it always puts a smile on my face. There are these two lads that stand in the middle of this hardcore group of fans and hit a pair of drums as hard as you've ever seen. Whenever I take my grandson Josh he always wants to go and stand right next to them. They make for a cracking atmosphere but if I get too close I end up stone deaf the next day so I tend to keep my distance.

There is a history to cherish too. At the time of writing, we are in the process of applying to get a museum installed at the football club, and to get it linked to the tourist information for the area. We believe we've got a wonderfully named football club, a club with great history and tradition, and we want to celebrate its place within the sport. After all, a team from Accrington was one of the 12 founder members of the Football League.

These days the town is quite different to how it was in 1888 but, regardless of the era, community is everything to me and we are representative of such a diverse country that needs to be embraced. Accrington has a massive Asian community because of the mill workers that came over from mainly Pakistan and Bangladesh midway through the 20th century, and you feel the integration around the place.

But from my several decades of experience it has been hard to reflect that in sport. From a cricket perspective, we would like more of the local Asian players to come down and get involved at Accrington. Again, the club is theirs and it is open for them to be a part of. There are other nearby teams they could get involved with too like Enfield and Church, if they would prefer to play their cricket there.

I would like to encourage them all to play, but from experience I have found it is a real slog with these boys. You simply cannot get them to come and commit. They seem to play amongst themselves socially and be a bit nomadic when it comes to joining established league clubs. They never seem to attach to one, preferring to move around as they see fit. This is far from a new problem, and makes me think back to when our Graham was a youth team player at the club. He had a mate at school called Ali, and when they were both 15 Graham was quite keen on getting him to Accrington to play.

'He's a bloody good bowler, dad,' Graham told me. 'We should snap him up.'

With a little gentle persuasion, comparing him favourably to Wasim Akram no doubt, we got him up there, and he turned out for both our Under-15s and Under-18s. He was actually doing okay, until one weekend that is, when we had booked a taxi to go on a family outing. Who should turn up to collect us but Ali. He was driving the bloody cab!

'What on earth are you doing?' I asked him in total shock. 'You are not old enough to drive.'

'Yes, I am. It is true that I am 15 at school,' he said. 'But I am 18 outside school.'

From memory, he didn't turn out for our Under-15s again.

Chapter 7

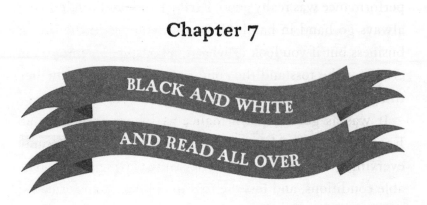

BLACK AND WHITE AND READ ALL OVER

Because my job involves travel, and plenty of it, there tends to be a lot of time spent in hotel rooms with not much to do. So whenever I am away, I scour the local newspapers. I've always loved reading the paper, bar the period when I was in charge of the England team and I got a hammering. I admit that things didn't half get to me when I was on the other side of the fence.

There were times when I just thought: 'That's not fair.' So, during commentary I try to stress that teams are always trying to win but if the opposition, who are doing exactly the same, are better there is going to be an inevitable result. Losing goes with the territory, so what coaches want to concentrate on is performance. Is your team improving? Or is the performance they have put in unacceptable?

You will hear something similar from football managers. If QPR play at Manchester United and get beat, you could not be too critical of Harry Redknapp if he said that the performance was really good. Performance and result do not always go hand in hand. Of course, you are in the results business but if you look at what can conspire against you in cricket – the toss and the conditions for starters – the one thing that is left is how you played.

It was as good a performance as I have seen from an England team in Mumbai in the autumn of 2012 because everything was against them. They were playing in unfavourable conditions, and lost the toss to opponents in form, but their performance was still good enough to dictate the outcome of the match.

Now if you squander a good position inexplicably and perform poorly, that is when your coach gets shitty. But sometimes when teams like Australia were clearly better than us, and we played well, it didn't always surface in reports. That is when I felt miffed, because if I thought performance was poor I would already have let the players know. So I didn't require them being berated for defeat when they had done okay.

In fact, one article I found during my newspaper digging provided a perfect description of how I used to feel about unmerited criticism. It was the reflections of Michael Bogdanov, the artistic director of the English Shakespeare Company, who wrote in the *New Statesman*: 'I am often asked which critic I dislike the most. I am hard-pushed. There are many contenders. There *is* one, though. I'll give you a clue. He is unpredictable, appears to have no criteria, he is whimsical and randomly influenced by who he's with, if he's eaten, where he sits, whether it's raining or he's suffering from a cold. He is a viscous, vituperative, vitriolic, objectionable, abusive, arrogant, excretory, disgruntled, cavilling, small minded, arse lick-ing, toadying, sycophant who should never be let near a theatre again.' If only he had said what he really thought! All joking aside, I knew where Mr Bogdanov was coming from because I had one particular critic – who I have no desire to name in these pages – who I felt attacked me unjustly.

Funny how things turn out in life, I suppose, because these days I would consider a number of journalists to be among my closest friends. And thumbing through the local rags around the world has provided great mirth. I thoroughly recommend it if you are ever travelling, for the absolute gold dust you stumble upon from time to time.

Malcolm Ashton, who was the official England scorer during my tenure in the international coaching role and now a member of the *Test Match Special* team, has always maintained a keen eye for a story too, and so we converse on our findings on a regular basis. If we find a gem, we cut it out and file it away. You have to work harder to find these nuggets in some countries than others, and in Australia it tends to be notices informing you what you are not allowed to do.

Tours to Asia tend to provide gold, and when we last toured Pakistan in 2005–06, we found an intriguing tale about a bloke who had sadly come a cropper on a building site. Unfortunately, according to reports, he had got hold of some electric cable that was live and it threw him 20 feet into the air. There is no coming back from that kind of shock, and he was pronounced dead a matter of minutes later.

His family was informed and a funeral was arranged. However, at the funeral, his coffin was left open and he was dressed in a white shroud so his family and friends could come and pay their respects and say their goodbyes. At the end of the ceremony the entourage walked him down the street to the place where he was to be laid to rest. This was a few days after the incident and so, after laying him down, they got the shock of their lives when he sat up, got out and walked off muttering something or other.

Sometimes, you can pick up a belter on your own doorstep. How about this one, that appeared under the headline BRIDE'S OCH AYE, THE POO! from the *Daily Sport* in May 2011:

A fuming bride DECKED her kilt wearing hubby when he sat on her knee at the reception and left a SKID MARK on her wedding dress!

Like all true Scotsmen, Angus McClure, 26, didn't wear pants under his kilt when he married sweetheart Sarah Grant in Greenock, Renfrewshire.

But his traditionalism led to uproar when he perched his poorly wiped backside on 24-year-old Sarah's pristine frock, leaving an unsightly smear.

After Sarah swiped at Angus, the well refreshed McClure and Grant clans led the reception into bloody mayhem. A police source said: 'I've been a police officer in Greenock for nearly 20 years and so I've seen a lot of wedding parties turn nasty but this was something else.'

In total, seven people were arrested in the grounds of the wedding venue, Greenock Reformed Temperance Hall, and faced public order offences.

It's believed that Angus and Sarah were reconciled when they sobered up, and have no memory whatsoever of the melee.

On the subcontinent, folk tend to get even more explicit regarding their personal details. Take this Dear Deidre style page from the *Times of India*:

1. I am a 22-year-old boy. I travel by bike for around 30 km for work every day. While riding, I feel my testicles rubbing against the petrol tank. I feel uncomfortable for some time after getting off the bike. Can this affect my sex life adversely? What should I do?
Answer: Do not wear tight underwear. Get an extra cushion installed on the bike. After work, dip your testicles in iced water for ten minutes and wear no underwear.

2. We got married last year and my wife has been pregnant for 45 days. What would be the best time to have sex and how long can we engage in the act? Also, what would be the best position for safer sex, and would oral sex or fingering lead to any infection?
Answer: Any time is good time. Strike while the iron is hot should be the motto. The position does not matter as you are using the condom always. It won't matter unless you both don't practise cleanliness.

3. I am 22 years old and my girlfriend is 21. Two days back, she helped me masturbate and I ejaculated on her outer body. I washed my hands after that and then hugged her. Now she is getting vomiting sensations. Is she pregnant?

Answer: What is outer body? If it was anywhere near the vulva (around vagina), then pregnancy is possible. Get a pregnancy test from the chemist and get it checked.

At least those people's problems retained a human element. How about this one:

MAN CHARGED FOR HAVING SEX WITH DONKEY CLAIMS IT WAS A PROSTITUTE

A Zimbabwean man, who was charged for having sex with a donkey, told the court that the animal was actually a prostitute before it transformed into a beast overnight. The police found 28-year-old Sunday Moyo performing a sex act with the donkey, who was lying on the ground tied to a tree.

According to reports, Moyo was arrested in the township of Zvishavane and was charged with bestiality. 'Your worship, I only came to know that I was being intimate with a donkey when I got arrested,' he was quoted as saying. 'I had hired a prostitute and paid $20 for the service at Down Town nightclub, and I don't know how she then became a donkey.' He added that he was in love with the animal and that he thought he was a donkey himself. Unsurprisingly, he was remanded in custody to be examined by psychiatrists.

Animal stories feature heavily in Indian newspapers as it is a country teeming with wildlife. And the way they report certain incidents can provide large dollops of black humour. Take this one, for example, from an incident in New Delhi in 2012:

> Another person, the fifth this year, was killed by a tiger outside the Jim Corbett reserve on Friday, prompting fears that the wrong tiger was shot by forest officials during a recent hunt for the maneater. [eDM]

Again, the madness is not consigned to foreign fields. I love getting down to Soho when I am covering Test matches at Lord's, and this letter in the *Daily Telegraph* painted a great picture of life down there in the Sixties:

CHEERS TO KEITH

When I was running Gerry's Club in the late 1960s, Keith Waterhouse and Willis Hall used to come in a lot, as they had an office across the road and used to stop work about noon. One day near Christmas, Keith was under instruction to return home with a tree. So he wouldn't forget, he went out before lunch and purchased a fine pristine six-foot specimen in its own tub. He brought it down to the club. He ordered a drink for himself and Willis and a gin and tonic for the tree. Keith then said to the tree: 'Your round.' The tree was unable to purchase a drink as he was not a member. A proposer and a seconder were found, forms filled, fees paid and a membership card attached to Mr Tree. A tie was borrowed for the tree and Keith and Mr Tree went to L'Etoile for lunch. During the course of the afternoon the tree became a member of the Kismet Club and the Colony Room. He also visited the French Pub and the Coach and Horses. When he returned to Gerry's in the evening, Mr Tree was drinking champagne and Guinness and in a very sorry state. Keith wasn't much better, but as Mike Molloy pointed out in his excellent obituary, he did cheer us up.

Bunny May, London

I enjoy a tipple or two in those establishments, and they have some pretty strong ales on tap. Nothing, though, to compare to the kick Barrettine Methylated Spirit gives you, according to its fans on Amazon:

'What better way to celebrate yet another restraining order from the ex-wife,' writes Harold Ramp, 'than with a glass or two of this reasonably priced beverage. The initial bouquet can be a little daunting for some but after a glass or two even the uncontrollable defecation that tends to follow can be easily ignored and the words "If you come near me or the kids again, I'm calling the police" sound like a declaration of undying love.'

Not sure I will be following Harold's recommendation but you can't fault his passion.

Chapter 8

SKINFOLDS AT THE READY

Established members of the England cricket team would be the first to admit they endured a mediocre start to their wall-to-wall 2013 Ashes year, but can anyone tell me in any language other than Esperanto what on earth is going on with Australia? When four players were axed at the mid-point of the Test series in India, I almost spat out my Corn Flakes.

Punished for not handing in their homework, eh? Last time I looked it was the management's job to come up with theories and work with the players to apply them. But I guess that's pretty difficult when you've got Pat Howard, a rugby man, in charge of Australian cricket and Kim Littlejohn, a crown green bowls specialist, as the head of New Zealand's selectors.

In my experience, professional elite sportsmen are very suspicious of someone coming in without a basic background in the sport. If you want to take this a step further and reach a logical conclusion, I coached the England cricket team for three years … should I therefore apply for a managerial job at a Premier League club? I think not. However, there was a rumour doing the rounds that Eric Bristow was about to be recruited by the England and Wales Cricket Board to assist Andy Flower in his preparation for this summer, and another one that Monty Panesar was taking on a role as Tom Daley's diving coach.

The process of setting the players written tactical analysis is just alien to me, and I am not sure how the England team I ran would have taken the request to put work in after-hours. Having said that, I do recall Phil Tufnell staying up all night regularly on tours, although I never twigged that he was revising, the swot. I always assumed he was out shagging and partying. As it transpires he was more than likely stat-cramming for a future career on BBC Radio.

To ask players for suggestions on how to improve via text or email is all very well, I suppose, when you are 2–0 down in a four-match series, but to then discipline them for not submitting the answers by a certain deadline confused me. Was Mickey Arthur, the Australia coach, really asking? Or was he telling? Because to me this 'ask' in conjunction with the subsequent punishment for failing to adhere to the instruction leads me to conclude it was actually a command. All I can surmise from this is that the four players in question – Shane Watson, Usman Khawaja, James Pattinson and Mitchell Johnson – did not have any ideas to share.

My interpretation of events – and it is only interpretation because I know no more – is that a lack of respect for coach and captain triggered this whole episode. You would think all of this could have been comfortably handled in-house, and so the conclusion drawn from going public with things is there must have been much more to it. What also came out of Cricket Australia's explanation of the situation was 'lateness and backchat'.

The Australians have always seemed a rootin'-tootin' type of people to me, but now we hear some of their players have lost their intellectual properties and that their skinfolds are excessive! Back in the day, that used to mean you were dool-ally, and a bit fat! I am talking, of course, about another of the demands placed on the players by the management group – the filing of 'wellness reports' while on tour. Sounds like absolute gobbledygook to me.

Imagine filling in one of these forms as an Australian Test player every morning:

Question 1: HOW ARE YOU TRAVELLING AT THIS STAGE?

Answer: Well, I had a great night last night. Went down the Irish bar and had 12 pints of Guinness. Entered the yard of ale comp. Came third. Disappointing as have been as high as second on the field of play recently.

Question 2: HAVE YOU MAINTAINED A BALANCED DIET?

Answer: Well, I got a decent amount of iron from the Guinness, but switched to Jäger Bombs for variation and then climbed into a kebab on the way back to the hotel.

Question 3: HAVE YOU BEEN STIMULATED AWAY FROM CRICKET?

Answer: That was an accident. I inadvertently tuned into the adult channel before throwing up.

Question 4: ARE YOU SLEEPING OKAY?

Answer: Yeah, passed out pretty quickly. Feel like a box of spanners this morning but looking forward to a #digin.

It was while out in New Zealand covering the Test series that news came through of these astonishing developments. It certainly improved my wellness to see the chaos in the Australian camp. For my part, I recorded feeling just chipper after a couple of bottles of red wine, a seafood platter, a rant at some Americans, followed by a late afternoon kip and an attempt to chat up a very attractive 20-year-old.

After studying these recordings, I concluded that I was pretty normal, which is more than could be said about the goings on at Wellington, where I was based for the second Test match between New Zealand and England. The Basin Reserve is a beautiful cricket ground, and one revamped since my previous visit, the improvements including a new irrigation system.

During this work, the groundsman's shed had been demolished, and 600 dead rats were removed from its environs. That's a pretty astonishing number of rodents, although it adds weight to the claim that you are never more than 10 yards away from one of the blessed creatures. But the army of dead rats was certainly not as astonishing as the decision not to replace the shed with a new one after the work was completed.

Come on New Zealand Cricket, a groundsman needs a shed. In fact, every bloke needs a shed, not just a groundsman. Bloke plus shed, is like horse plus carriage to me. They just go together, don't they? Even if you're not in there, it's somewhere to store all your gubbins, isn't it? And cricket ground staff generally have more gubbins than the rest of us.

I know England have had their problems inside their own shed but while the Kevin Pietersen fallout was similar to that which led to Shane Watson quitting the tour of India, I do think that it was handled in a much better way by Andy Flower. There was obviously a problem, he was left out for a while, served his time and came back following a private reconciliation process. Many teams over the years have had internal spats – please don't think that everything is rosy in the dressing room all of the time – and I have been party to some feisty exchanges over the years. But you don't think much of them because that kind of thing goes on in sports teams. If someone is not pulling their weight or pulling in a different direction, it can lead to a flare-up.

Of course, these things are easier to overcome if you are talking about good players, because good players help secure good results, and good results tend to influence the mood around the place. And as far as recent years are concerned England have had the better players of the two.

Actually, if you want some evidence that Australia no longer know who their best players are, then digest this information: between the start of the last Ashes series over here in 2009 and the start of this 2013 international summer they had handed out 23 Test debuts. In the same period England had given 11. And if you want to develop this a stage further, you will see that the problem can be traced back to the disbanding of that awesome team that inflicted the 2006–07 Ashes whitewash. In their 67 matches since then, the Australians have introduced 36 new players. Again, compare that to England, who brought in 21 in 76 matches.

Talk about a role reversal. This is comparable to England in the late 1980s and throughout the 1990s. In 1989, England used a record 29 players across a six-match series against the Aussies. It all adds up to being out-talented by the opposition. The reality is that the golden era has passed, and the days of Glenn McGrath's predictions of 5–0 a distant memory.

When asked on camera while in New Zealand what I thought the combined score would be of the two forthcoming Ashes series, I confidently replied '10–0'. My performance was a bit playful, a bit tongue-in-cheek, and I even thought of proposing we reduce the series to three matches apiece and play four matches against Bangladesh instead. Remember, when Oz were in their pomp, one question went round like a broken record: 'Is this the worst England team ever?' It's nice to be able to give a bit back.

So what of the contemporary Australians? Well, they're not very good. It's as simple as that. They've got one batter, in Michael Clarke, they haven't got a spinner and this lauded pace attack I keep hearing about must be a drastically different one to the one I've witnessed over the last couple of years because it's not much cop. You can roll off a list of two dozen really special players from Australia from the late 1980s to now, a quarter of a century of real talent, but the truth about the current crop is that they ain't up to it.

Put it this way, I am not sure Nathan Lyon, who has been afforded the honour of leader of the Australian team song following the retirement of Mike Hussey, will be needing to exercise his vocal chords this summer. This role of conductor of the Baggy Green Choir has been a tradition passed down some fairly household names. Before, Mr Cricket duties were given to such luminaries as Ricky Ponting, Justin Langer, Allan Border and Rod Marsh.

Hussey obviously thought a lot of Lyon as a bloke – more than the Australian selectors did anyhow. Two Tests later, he was dropped. God only knows what they would have done had they won in Hyderabad. Hussey said he had opted to entrust Lyon with the responsibility because of his 'great character' and the fact he played the game for 'the right reasons'. That's good enough for me, although from past experience it should not be a universal qualification for being allowed to belt out a few notes post-match.

My old opening partner at Lancashire, Barry Wood, always fancied himself as a bit of a crooner. They do say Yorkshiremen are keen on the sound of their own voice, don't they? You know, as in 'I say what I like, and I like what I bloody well say'. Well, Barry backed this theory up perfectly. Trouble was no-one else liked it.

One year we happened to be playing an away match against Glamorgan that coincided with one of their wicketkeeper Eifion Jones's benefit functions. It was at Pontarddulais Working Men's Club and featured members of the world-renowned choir from the town as the evening's entertainment. Eifion, a local, was also a fine vocalist and got up and gave a solo performance. It was fabulous to be present.

Not so when an invite was sent out to the gathered guests to come and give a turn in response. Mr B Wood was not shy (more's the pity) and fancying himself as the new Paul McCartney offered a version of 'Hey Jude'. Well, his own interpretation at any rate. Some of the audience were keener than others, it has to be said, and the management of the Pontarddulais WMC were particular fans. So much so that they were even keen to re-engage his services on Saturday evenings, offering him the slot around closing time. Something to do with helping clear folk out, I believe. Blimey, it was like someone dragging a fender up a back street.

The state of Australian cricket has certainly rattled Shane Warne's cage. To summarise his diatribe, he believes those at the top of the sport down under are the creations of Jim Henson and answer to such names as Kermit, Fozzie and Animal. The nutritionist is a Swedish chef. But all joking aside, I understand his frustration. It goes back to the need for the best people in the strategic positions, and the best people are cricket people.

They certainly don't have to be the best players; in fact the best players rarely are the best when it comes to the decision-making positions, but you need people with top-level cricket experience to administer. Look no further than England's national selector Geoff Miller. He was a bloody good cricketer but he has perhaps been an even better performer since his playing career ended. He certainly has kept everything very settled and calm around the England camp.

Sure, there are other important people around the set-up like the analyst, the psychologist and the physiotherapist. But the backroom staff don't need cricket expertise, just a grasp of their own role. Ideally, you need your support team to be level-headed, easy going and popular figures because it helps the atmosphere around the playing environment, and someone like Mark Saxby, the Volkswagen Campervan-driving masseur, has been a wonderful addition to the set-up. He is good fun and a great social creature.

Warnie will never be short of an opinion, and you will find that all the great players – there is a pattern with the likes of Viv Richards, Clive Lloyd, Barry Richards, Ian Botham, Bob Willis – would always have a strong opinion. There is a school of thought that says that they deserve to have such trenchant views, that they've earned the right to express them because they have been there and done it in their own careers. He felt the need to speak out publicly because he cares so much about Australian cricket. And there is nothing more important to Australian cricketers than the fight for that little urn.

The best comparison for getting ready for an Ashes is probably the preparation an Olympic athlete goes through. An Olympic athlete has four years to prepare and then the time comes, and you get only one shot at doing whatever it is that you do. This is it. The moment is here.

I must confess to being pleased that the Ashes returns to Old Trafford from 2013, and hopefully beyond. It's a proper Test ground and whenever you go there it just smells of cricket. Some places are steeped in tradition and this is one of them. I understand that people were of the opinion that the standard of facilities had dropped over the past couple of decades, that it was looking a tad tired, and they had a general downer on the place, but credit where it is due because the club acted decisively in that regard, and it's looking fabulous these days.

Playing at Old Trafford might provide the chance for England to play two spinners again, just as they did at the start of the previous Ashes in Cardiff. I noted with interest that both sides fielded two in the drawn 'Test' there between England Lions and Australia A in 2012 shortly after the square had been turned.

Monty Panesar showed over the winter in India what a handful he can be in helpful conditions, no matter the quality of the opposition. On his day, he is one of our greatest assets, truly world-class. His biggest problem has been that he has had to contend with Graeme Swann. Because if England play only one spinner then he is the obvious choice if fit – he gives the ball a real rip, offers a threat on all surfaces, scores runs down the order and catches nicely at slip.

Top-quality spin has caused both England and Australia problems over the past couple of years. You need only think back to the start of 2012 when Saeed Ajmal terrorised England in the United Arab Emirates during the Bank Alfalah Mobilink Presents Jazz Cup (nice) – surely the longest and best name for a Test series in history.

England's batsmen were certainly mesmerised by him, and he really played on the mystery aspect of his bowling. One of the biggest mysteries by the way is where he was hiding previously. He didn't establish himself in Pakistan's team until he was into his thirties, and I can't believe he wasn't good enough in his twenties.

Anyway, Saeed played up to all the pre-series talk of him introducing a special delivery – the teesra – into his repertoire in readiness for England. Who was he having on? I understand the doosra, or 'the other one' to give it its translation from Urdu, the ball which instead of turning into the right-handed batsman as an off-break would, goes in the opposite direction. But a teesra, or third one? Surely, it either goes one way or t'other. Which other way could it go?

I was half-expecting a delivery to come out the hand, do the hokey cokey and turn around. What we actually got was what has more commonly been called the straight one – the delivery sent down loaded with backspin from a finger spinner that rushes on rather than going this way or that. The equivalent of a wrist-spinner's slider.

Don't get me wrong, Saeed is a fine bowler, with great skill, and a fine lad to boot. I joked with him before play one day during the first Test in Dubai that if I had been playing he would have been fetching it back from the stands at wide long-on. He was adamant that I would need to play him through the covers.

'No, that's the girl's side,' I told him and, pointing to the Jazz Cup advertising boards, added: 'I would do to you what I did to Murali. You'd be going over there.'

For those of you who haven't seen the footage, I pulverised the great Muttiah Muralitharan in August 2011, launching him for a six that smashed the windscreen of a car parked outside Grappenhall Cricket Club.

With a rare piece of fine timing, Nasser brought me down to earth when he asked me live on TV how many sixes I had managed in my top-level career.

'Er, one!'

Forget the cheap talk, and my gentle joshing, though, because Ajmal and Pakistan turned over a team that was justifiably the number one-ranked Test outfit in the world at the time, a team that had thrashed Australia and India in the previous 12 months. He was the destroyer-in-chief with 10 for 97 in the win that set them on their way to a 3–0 series white-wash. But this was not a scoreline crafted on spitting cobra pitches as you might expect. England were caught out not because of exaggerated turn but almost the complete opposite; it was subtle changes of pace and variety on deliveries homing in on the stumps that proved lethal on a surface that didn't spin.

This series, probably more than any other England series, showed us how the Decision Review System has changed the game, and for the better in my view. Apart from the fact that in the age of DRS sweeping is a suicide note unless the ball is well outside off-stump, it highlighted how many times balls from spinners will go on to hit the wooden pegs. I have all the statistics at my fingertips because I sit on the ICC panel that selects the elite umpires for international cricket, and they are simply overwhelming.

With DRS you get four to five per cent better return on correct decisions, and the top players, featuring in the top series, should want that. I am as pleased that the modern Ashes will feature it as I am baffled that India will not enter-tain it. The use of this technology is effectively the use of the human eye with fallibility removed, whereas when you play India it is just human eye, and of course, that means mistakes. Particularly in India, if you've got 40,000 people screaming in the stands, then the umpires missing the occasional nick is almost inevitable. It's not that the umpires are not up to it, they just can't hear them, and I feel for officials when they have to stand in matches involving India because we go back to an element of guessing.

It remains an absolute mystery to me as to why India do not want to use it. Noise from their camp is that they're uncertain about it because it is not 100 per cent accurate. No, it might not be, but it's five per cent better than what we have when it's not being used. And by the way, it's not far off being 100 per cent.

What we have seen around the world over the past four years is that everyone has got more comfortable with it – that goes for both the umpires themselves and the top players. Teams are much better now at implementing their two challenges, using them far more sensibly than was the case at first. The ICC has taken a lot of stick for not governing on this issue and forcing India to fall into line. But quite simply, the ICC does not have the power to dictate because it is no more than a conglomerate of all the individual boards rather than a separate body, and India, wrongly in my opinion, simply say they are not using it.

It is still a work in progress and I'm sure it will get tinkered with from time to time but critically the umpires accept the principle. Whereas in the past they were very much exposed, and on their own, they now have an aid in the decision-making process. That acceptance is why we are seeing a more relaxed attitude towards it. Rather than make officials look silly as was originally feared, it has probably given them the confidence to judge more definitively when balls are actually going on to hit the stumps for lbws than ever before.

Some will question why we need all this technology to aid decisions. Well, I'll you why. It's because players the world over have gone down the traditional Australian route and forced officials into making the decisions. There is no longer any assistance from the players. Whereas there was a time not so long ago that those that nicked one outside off-stump walked, they are few and far between these days, and batsmen prefer to take their chance.

Because of the increased use of technology I would advocate getting officials equipped with microphones so that their decisions can be relayed to the crowd. If you have 22,000 people crammed into a ground for an Ashes fixture, they should be party to what is going on in the middle. Sometimes things happen so quickly that your average paying spectator just can't tell what is going on. I am not a rugby person but whenever I do watch a match on television, I am relying on the bloke with the whistle to tell me why he has made a certain call. I am dependant on him to understand what's going on.

In cricket, we could replicate that on the decisions that have an influence on the game. Things like leg-before decisions being struck down, for example, and the reason why. It would take little effort to confirm a reversal of a decision because 'it's pitched outside leg-stump' or 'it's going over the top' but it would enhance the experience in the stands. I understand that rugby lasts 80 minutes and cricket is a seven-hour day, but it's not like the umpire would be expected to be chatting every other over.

I am not sure how the old breed of official would have dealt with all this by the way. Men like Frank Chester and Eddie Phillipson, who wore jackets down to their ankles, sported trilbies and bent double over the bails at the bowlers end. For every delivery, they would be at eye level with the stumps.

I have always enjoyed the craic with the men in white coats and became poacher turned gamekeeper in the late Eighties, of course, so I can appreciate how hard the job is. And boy, I have met some characters.

Arthur Jepson was the umpire with the loudest voice you have ever heard. He made Andrew Strauss sound like Whispering Ted Lowe. Arthur just couldn't talk quietly, and it used to get him into some serious scrapes. Maybe never more so than when Neal Radford, then a young bowler with Lancashire, was bowling and I was standing at square-leg.

Radford became a fabulous bowler for Worcestershire but he never really did the business for us. On one of the days it just didn't work for him at Old Trafford, he was running up to bowl – he used to have this shuffling run-up, his feet never got off the ground – when stage whisperer Arthur said: 'Can this bloke bat? Because he can't bowl! He runs up like he wants a shit.'

Unfortunately, this was now booming around every corner of the ground. Norman the postman, one of our most notorious supporters, bellowed back: 'Who wants a shit?'

They can be pretty indiscreet those guys once they've hung up their own boots. For example, I once came on to bowl during a match against Oxford University in The Parks. Arthur was standing, and having received my sweater and cap, turned to me at the end of my economical four-pace run-up and informed me: 'I hope you don't mind me saying this – but you are the worst bowler I have ever seen! Fred Price was a bad 'un but you're worse than him.'

Skinfolds at the Ready

As an up-and-coming player, I experienced an umpire called Tommy Drinkwater who stood in Second XI matches and in the Minor Counties Championship. Tommy only had one arm, and used to love a drink. He used to pop his pot arm on the bar while supping, and on one occasion while having a drink at Old Trafford, he went for a pee, only to find it missing upon his return. It led to several members beginning a hunt high and low, under the tables and behind the bar. They even re-traced his steps back to the gents to no avail. It turned out that Traff, the evil Alsatian that belonged to Burt Fleming, the groundsman, could be found at that very time out in the car park at the ground, worrying the missing limb.

Cricket and bars have always gone together for me. I love chatting about the game over a pint, hearing folk tell their stories from yesteryear. And I can recommend my own ale to the 2013 Australians. It will come in handy for drowning the sorrows.

It's a nutty number called Leave the Car (more appropriate than Start the Car if you are supping) brewed by Thwaites, the brewery that dominates the town of Blackburn. They invited me along to open their new micro-brewery last year, and it was all very interesting to a pub enthusiast like myself. These days you can go on their website and brew your own virtual pint. But I was pleased to be able to go for the practical rather than the theory.

I wanted a flavoursome beer, which means the percentage has to be quite high, and Leave the Car comes in at 4.5 per cent. We produced 29 barrels of the stuff, and I have to say that it's superb. A few of those should help the Australians escape the pain of reality for a while.

Chapter 9

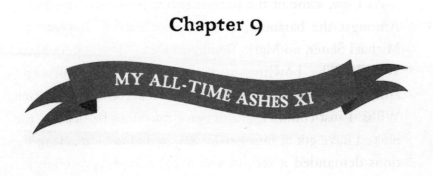

MY ALL-TIME ASHES XI

Of all the players to have graced this wonderful series, if you had to pick an XI of those who have appeared in your own lifetime, who would be in? It's a question I considered when turning my mind back to yesteryear.

So, apologies to all the players who have not made it; those who have not managed to break into this star-studded Bumble XI. You lot will no doubt be wagging a finger at me and saying, 'I would have had him' and 'Why have you picked him?' But stop tutting at me, and go away and pick your own team, and I am sure yours will give mine a hell of a good run for their money.

In terms of selection criteria, this team is not based strictly on facts and figures. I have not simply picked those with the best averages but those whose performance have made the biggest impressions on me, and the ones I believe would give my XI the best chance of winning a Test match in any conditions, against any opposition you would like to name.

As I say, some of the judgements may seem contentious. Amongst the batsmen, there is no Geoffrey Boycott, no Michael Slater, no Mark Taylor, no Ricky Ponting, no Mark Waugh. The bowling attack is more straightforward, although I would have liked to have accommodated Bob Willis. I just couldn't, and when I told him, he insisted the bloke I have got at number 11 simply had to be in. If conditions demanded a second spinner, I might have gone for Graeme Swann but of the great players to have featured in Ashes cricket between 1965, the year of my first-class debut, and now, these are the ones I would be sending out to do my bidding:

1

My team would start with Michael Vaughan. He went quickly from being a rather left-field pick for England on the 1999–2000 tour of South Africa to the heights of being the official best batsman in the world. He reached the pinnacle with three centuries in Australia, and I thought that was a rather special feat for an England player. His batting was simply sublime in that winter of 2002–03, and no opening batsman could hope to play better. I am sure that Michael has reflected on his performances in that series and realised he never bettered that form. He looked so elegant at the crease. People talk about Vaughan's cover drive being his signature stroke but all of his shots seemed classical during that series. Over the course of a month or so, he was invincible, nobody could get him out, everything he did was perfect and it was a pleasure to witness. That Bruno chap and his mate Mad Len would have been standing up to give him a standing ovation and a perfect 10.

2

Okay pop pickers. At number two, Matthew Hayden kept forcing himself into my thoughts but I had to go for a more contemporary batsman still. In the end, it had to be Alastair Cook. He is the nearest thing to a machine that England has ever produced. You just can't get him out. I'd hate to bowl to him. At 28 years of age, he has already shattered the record for England Test hundreds and he is going to get plenty more, I promise you. He is the perfect opening batsman, who blunts the opposition bowling attack and has an insatiable appetite for runs. Technically he is nearly perfect, seeing off the new ball and grinding away. One of the most impressive things about him, though, is the fact that he has expanded his game significantly since he first burst onto the international scene at 21. If you were making a generalisation, you would say that in his early days he just survived, whereas now he scores. To me, this means that he is going to break all the records going in this country. There was a classic moment in the opening Ashes Test of 2010–2011 when, with England nearing their eventual total of 517 for one declared, Ricky Ponting placed a fielder right next to the non-striking batsman. In the commentary box, we couldn't see this guy; for a minute or so it looked to us like Australia were fielding with only 10. Then, a voice boomed from the empty stands: 'Good thinking, Ricky, the last time a catch went to silly mid on was 100 f***ing years ago.' It was a funny moment but an early sign that Australia didn't really know where or how they could get him out.

3

In at first drop I have gone right back to the early Seventies to pick out a truly wonderful player, a most elegant batsman, who was a fabulous straight driver of the ball. One Greg Chappell. He was a tall, slim, lithe guy. All class. For him batting just looked so effortless. He would walk off the field at the end of a day's play and from the sight of him you would think he had just walked on it. A stroke player, easy on the eye, the biggest compliment you could give him as an opponent was that while you always wanted him out you had to concede at the same time that he was great to watch. This place in the order could have been taken by Ricky Ponting, of course, but having witnessed him first hand in 1974 I just felt compelled to go for Chappell.

4

It is the one and only Kevin Pietersen. Kevin. The Kev. KP. That hundred at the Oval in 2005 was truly breathtaking. The way he kept getting down on one knee and pumping Shane Warne to deep midwicket was sensational. To do that in such a pressure situation showed pure class. He was integral to the way that England jockeyed Australia that summer, came hard at their opponents and made it clear there would be no Mr Nice Guy. The bowling was obviously aggressive and in your face, that was pretty obvious, but the same kind of attitude underpinned the batting, and to this end Pietersen was pivotal. He played some unbelievable shots, as only Kevin could, during a series when everybody was on the edge of their seats, biting their nails. He demanded attention when he had the bat in his hand, telling his audience: 'Look at me, I'm a great player.'

5

I didn't have to think long about this position. It is taken by someone who I never really knew as a bloke, other than to say a quick 'hello' to, but someone I really admired. What a phenomenal cricketer Steve Waugh was. This guy was your archetypal nuggety, give-'em-nothing cricketer. During his career people said that he couldn't play the short ball but it didn't often get him out. Bowl it short at him, and he looked good enough to me as he went back and across. Sometimes he would get pinged but he was always willing to take a bruise or two for the cause. In fact, to get him out it sometimes felt like you needed a crowbar. You almost had to prize him from the crease. Think back to the Oval in 2001 when he had a pulled calf muscle and refused to go off, diving into his crease to get to three figures. Waugh was as strong a personality as has featured in Ashes cricket, who gave nothing away with his eyes, a master of facial expression. You would certainly want him in the trenches with you because your enemy would always know they were struggling to win the fight. When there was battle to be done he would not give opponents the steam off his ... well you know the rest. He played as if he hated the English.

6

It's Ian Terence Botham or Sir Osis, as I call him. As in Sir Osis (of the liver). If I mention the year 1981 do I have to say anything else to justify this lad's position in this team? He was a fantastic cricketer for England, one of the finest we have ever produced, and one whose premier quality was arguably his ability to raise his game against the Aussies. In addition to the hundreds that he scored, and the bundles of five-wicket hauls he claimed, he had this wonderful never-say-die attitude, a belief that he was better than the blokes he was being pitted against. The only shame is that he can't remember any game that he played in. There has been a lot of water under the bridge – or more accurately other liquid down the gullet – since then. What wonderful entertainment he would be able to recall. He was as daft as a brush, and always acted completely naturally on the field. Ask him for the secret to fast bowling or aggressive batting and all he could tell you is: 'It sort of clicks.'

7

In at number seven is Andrew Flintoff. The 2005 Flintoff was unbelievably consistent, lifting himself time and time again to put his team into dominant positions with both bat and ball in hand. A buzz went around the ground every time he was thrown the ball and when he went in to bat he showed that he liked to play aggressively. That was when he was at his best. He was a very destructive player in his day but it was his bowling that thrilled me the most. He was relentless. He just kept coming and coming and coming. Ask the Australians and they would have told you that he was simply frightening, the pace he bowled at in 2005. He is one of England's all-time great players in the sense that when he was asked to do some-thing by the captain, seldom did he fail to deliver. Few players have been able to lift themselves in the same way. His stats don't really add up, they don't tell you anything about him as a bloke or his ability to rise to his very best when the competi-tion was at its fiercest. When he came into the attack he rose to his full stature, took a big breath and charged in. He would have been a handful for any batsman in history had they been transported into that series. It is cruel that his appearances in Ashes cricket were cut short by those wonky knees and ankles, but the displays he did provide will live long in the memory for all of those who were fortunate enough to attend those wonderful Test matches.

8

The wicketkeeper's position caused me a load of problems. Who do you pick? You could find reasons to pick Alec Stewart and reasons to pick Alan Knott. Then there's Adam Gilchrist. But I've gone for Rodney Marsh, the belligerent Australian, who fired away at batsmen within earshot from under his Baggy Green. As a batsman, he would walk in and play shots from the off, trying to take the game away from the opposition, but primarily he was a wonderful gloveman. I know that Gilchrist was a fantastic number seven in Test cricket but I'm combining this role of wicketkeeper and batsman and reckon I've got enough runs in my batting line-up. That means I want to see the safest pair of hands behind the stumps and although I could have gone for Knott as he's the best I've ever seen behind the stumps, for the overall package that the specialist gloveman gives you Marsh edges it.

9

So I am down to number nine and I'm not sure I should say too much about this guy. Do you want me to say a thing or two? You will remember him as a chubby lad with bleached blond hair and an earring. Or at least he used to be like that when he played the game. He looks a lot sleeker now he's moved into the commentary box. These days he's slimmed down, looks fit and well, and he's got a Hollywood actress on his arm. And I'm not talking about a tattoo. Rumour has it he's given up on his pizzas and chips but I guess it was going a step too far to ask him to give up on his beloved cigarettes. Shane Warne is the greatest bowler this game has ever seen and a wonderful showman too. It was a great feature of Test cricket when Shane Warne and Muttiah Muralitharan were neck and neck at the top of the wicket-takers' list, but for the combination of control, spin and flight that he had, Warne was the man for me.

10

Dennis Lillee. Just ask any fast bowler: Who would you model yourself on? Who do you think is the greatest fast bowler of the modern era? The answer more often than not would be Dennis Lillee. In fact, if you were picking a Post-War XI from all Test nations he would be in there. He was an artist, with a beautiful action, who possessed the most priceless fast bowler's trait: nastiness. He bowled with a combination of great control and pace and put opposing batsmen under severe examination defensively. He was also a captain's dream in that he would keep going, bowl at any time, at any end and in any situation. What superb stamina. And someone who could get you out in different ways. He could out-skill you and he could do you for speed too.

11

Bringing up the rear, so to speak, is another fella who wouldn't give a door a bang. If you asked Michael Atherton who was the bowler he would least like to face, he would say 'Glenn McGrath'. He still has nightmares about him even now. He was so metronomic, he made you play at every delivery, always asked you questions, and it was that, rather than his pace, that was the problem. The thing about him was that he would only bowl at 80–82 mph but he would kiss the pitch with the ball and it seemed to accelerate off it. He was also such a tall chap that in addition to this he got natural bounce, and managed to get you playing at balls that you maybe could have left. In fact, he was the master of playing on your uncertainty just outside off-stump.